Accounting Essentials for Career Secretaries

FOURTH EDITION

A. B. Carson, PhD, CPA
Professor Emeritus of Accounting
University of California, Los Angeles

Arthur E. Carlson, PhD
Professor of Accounting
School of Business Administration
Washington University in St. Louis

Mary E. Burnet, MBA, CPA
Professor Emeritus of Accounting
Rochester Institute of Technology
Rochester, New York

Published by
SOUTH-WESTERN PUBLISHING CO.

CINCINNATI   WEST CHICAGO, ILL.   DALLAS   PELHAM MANOR, N.Y.   PALO ALTO, CALIF.

Copyright © 1978
by South-Western Publishing Co.
Cincinnati, Ohio

All Rights Reserved

The text of this publication, or any part thereof, may not be reproduced or transmitted in any form or by any means, electronic or mechanical, including photocopying, recording, storage in an information retrieval system, or otherwise, without the prior written permission of the publisher.

ISBN: 0-538-01160-2

Library of Congress Catalog Card Number: 76-46119

4 5 6 7 K 4 3 2 1

Printed in the United States of America

Preface

As the world of business and the professions continually grows larger and more complicated, a knowledge of accounting becomes more and more essential. More opportunities are thus created for those persons who are proficient in secretarial skills and who also have an understanding of the accounting process. *Accounting Essentials for Career Secretaries* presents a system of accounting which can be used in any business office. In addition, special attention is paid to accounting problems and situations encountered by attorneys and physicians and dentists.

The accounting cycle and the income statement and balance sheet are presented early in the course. The remaining chapters in the book are an elaboration of the basic material presented earlier. The student is thus continually building upon and reinforcing his or her knowledge of the underlying structure of accounting. Chapter 3 is devoted to accounting for cash and includes a discussion of banking procedure. Chapter 4 covers payroll accounting. The latter chapters of the book which follow those on accounting for attorneys and physicians and dentists take up the end-of-the-period activities. Because of the widespread use of various data processing procedures, the text material concludes with an appendix, "Computer-Based Accounting Systems — Design and Use."

In order to provide supplementary learning aids, a workbook containing study assignments is available. Accounting problems which may be used for additional work are included in the text following Chapters 4 and 8. In this edition, the glossary of the technical terms used in the text has been expanded.

Two practice sets are available for use with the text. One of the sets covers one month's transactions in the office of an attorney (Wesley R. Baker, Attorney at Law). This set can be effectively started upon the completion of Chapter 5. A second set (Ebersold and Watkins, Physicians and Surgeons) provides practice in recording a month's transactions in a physician's office. This set is designed to be started upon the completion of Chapter 6. For those instructors who wish to emphasize the record keeping of a general business, a third set (John H. Roberts, Management Consultant), designed to correlate with *College Accounting*, is available for use after Chapter 5 or 6. All three sets are designed to give the student a review of the complete accounting cycle.

Tests are available for use following the completion of Chapters 2, 4, 6, and 8.

The authors acknowledge with gratitude the assistance received from the members of the business and professional community whose suggestions contributed to the preparation of this textbook.

A.B. Carson
A.E. Carlson
M.E. Burnet

Contents

Chapter 1	**The Nature of Business Accounting**	1
	The Accounting Process	3
	The Double-Entry Mechanism	11
Chapter 2	**Accounting Procedure**	22
	Journalizing Transactions	22
	Posting to the Ledger; The Trial Balance	33
	The Financial Statements	40
Chapter 3	**Accounting for Cash**	45
	Records of Cash Receipts and Disbursements; Petty Cash	45
	Banking Procedure	53
Chapter 4	**Payroll Accounting**	69
	Earnings and Deductions	69
	Payroll Taxes Imposed on the Employer	91
	Chapters 1-4 Practical Accounting Problems	99
Chapter 5	**Accounting for Personal Service (Attorneys)**	107
Chapter 6	**Accounting for Personal Service (Physicians and Dentists)**	131
Chapter 7	**The Periodic Summary**	157
	End-of-Period Work Sheet	157
	The Financial Statements	163
Chapter 8	**Adjusting and Closing Accounts at End of Accounting Period**	171
	Adjusting Entries	171
	Closing Procedure	174
	Chapters 5-8 Practical Accounting Problems	183
Appendix	**Computer-Based Accounting Systems—Design and Use**	A-1
Glossary		G-1
Index		I-1

1

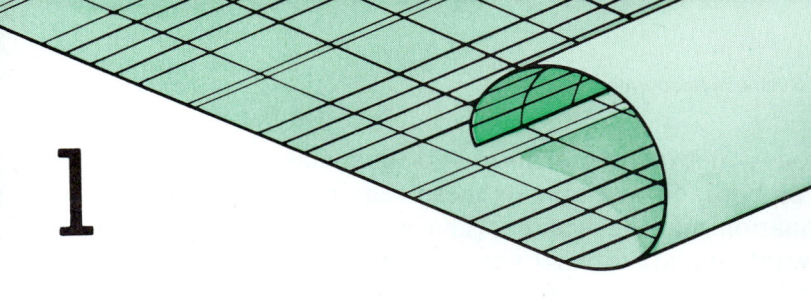

The Nature of Business Accounting

The purpose of business accounting is to provide information about the financial operations and condition of an enterprise to the individuals, agencies, and organizations who have the need and the right to be so informed. These interested parties normally include the following:

- (a) The **owners** of the business — both present and prospective.
- (b) The **managers** of the business. (Often, but not always, the owners and the managers are the same persons.)
- (c) The **creditors** of the business — both present and prospective. (**Creditors** are those who furnish or supply goods and services "on credit" — meaning that payment need not be made immediately. The creditor category also includes banks and individuals who lend money to the business.)
- (d) **Government agencies** — local, state, and national. (For purposes of either regulation or taxation — sometimes both — various governmental agencies must be given certain financial information.)

The preceding four classes of users of information relate to virtually every business enterprise. In connection with many businesses, some or all of the following also make use of relevant information: customers or clients, labor unions, competitors, trade associations, stock exchanges, commodity exchanges, financial analysts, and financial journalists.

The information needed by all of the users is not identical, though most want data regarding either results of operations for a recent period — net income or loss — or financial status as of a recent date, or both. In addition to these requirements, a variety of other information may be wanted. The exact requirement depends upon who wants it and for what purpose. As might be expected, the demand for the greatest quantity and variety of information comes from the managers of the business. They constantly need up-to-the-minute information about many things.

The accountant has the task of accumulating and dispensing needed financial information to users. Since these activities touch upon nearly every phase of business operation and since financial information is communicated in accounting terms, accounting is said to be the "language of business." Anyone intending to engage in any type of business activity is well advised to learn this language.

Since accounting relates to so many phases of business, it is not surprising that there are several fields of specialization in accounting. Some major special fields are tax work, cost accounting, information systems design and installation, and budget preparation. Many accountants have but one employer; whereas others become qualified as public accountants and offer their services as independent contractors or consultants. Some states license individuals as *Public Accountants* or *Registered Accountants*. All states grant the designation *Certified Public Accountant* (CPA) to those who meet various prescribed requirements, including the passing of a uniform examination prepared by the American Institute of Certified Public Accountants. Public accountants perform various functions. One of their major activities is **auditing**. This involves testing and checking the records of an enterprise to be certain that acceptable policies and practices have been consistently followed. In recent years, public accountants have been extending their activities into what is called "management services" — a term that covers a variety of specialized consulting assignments. Specialization is common among members of the accounting profession. Tax work is one important example of specialization. Management services is another.

All of the foregoing comments have related to accounting and accountants in connection with profit-seeking organizations. Since there are thousands of not-for-profit or nonprofit organizations (such as governments, educational institutions, churches, and hospitals) that also need to accumulate information, thousands of accountants are in their employ. These organizations also engage public accountants. While the "rules of the game" are somewhat different for not-for-profit organizations, much of the record keeping is identical with that found in business.

THE ACCOUNTING PROCESS

Business accounting may be defined as the art of analyzing and recording financial transactions and certain business-related economic events in a manner that facilitates classifying and summarizing the information, and reporting and interpreting the results.

Analyzing is the first step. There may be more than one way of looking at something that has happened. The accountant must determine the fundamental significance to the business of each transaction or event in order to record it properly.

Recording traditionally has meant writing something by hand. Much of the record keeping in accounting still is manual, but for years typewriters and many varieties of so-called "bookkeeping machines" (which typically combine the major attributes of typewriters and adding machines or desk calculators) have been in use. Today the recording sometimes takes the form of holes punched in certain places on a card or a paper tape, or of invisible magnetized spots on a special type of tape used to feed information into an electronic computer.

Classifying relates to the process of sorting or grouping like things together rather than merely keeping a simple, diary-like narrative record of numerous and varied transactions and events.

Summarizing is the process of bringing together various items of information to determine or explain a result.

Reporting refers to the process of attempting to communicate the results. In accounting, it is common to use tabular arrangements rather than narrative-type reports. Sometimes a combination of the two is used.

Interpreting refers to the steps taken to direct attention to the significance of various matters and relationships. Percentage analyses and ratios often are used to help explain the meaning of certain related bits of information. Footnotes to financial reports may also be valuable in the interpreting phase of accounting.

Accounting and bookkeeping

Accounting involves forms and records design, policy making, data analysis, report preparation, and report interpretation. A person involved with or responsible for these functions may be referred to as an accountant. Bookkeeping is the recording phase of the accounting process. The person who records the information in the accounting records may be referred to as a bookkeeper. That term goes back to the time when formal accounting records were in the form of books — pages bound together. While this still is sometimes the case, modern practice favors the use of loose-leaf records and cards and, in some instances, computers. When the language catches up with practice, the designation "record keeper" will replace "bookkeeper." Sometimes the accountant also serves as the bookkeeper — an experience that may be very valuable.

Accounting elements

If complete accounting records are to be maintained, all transactions and events that affect the basic accounting elements must be recorded. The basic accounting elements are **assets**, **liabilities**, and **owner's equity**.

Assets. Properties of value that are owned by a business are called assets. Properties such as money, accounts receivable, notes receivable, merchandise, furniture, fixtures, machinery, buildings, and land are common examples of business assets. **Accounts receivable** are unwritten promises by customers to pay at a later date for goods sold to them or for services rendered. **Notes receivable** are formal written promises by debtors to pay specified sums of money at some future time.

It is possible to conduct a business or a professional practice with very few assets. A dentist, for example, may have relatively few assets, such as money, instruments, laboratory equipment, and office equipment. But in many cases, a variety of assets is necessary. A merchant must have merchandise to sell and store equipment on which to display the merchandise, in addition to other assets. A manufacturer must have materials, tools, and various sorts of machinery, in addition to other assets.

Liabilities. An obligation of a business to pay a debt is a business liability. The most common liabilities are accounts payable and notes payable. **Accounts payable** are unwritten promises to pay creditors for property (such as merchandise, supplies, and equipment) purchased on credit or for services rendered. **Notes payable** are formal written promises to pay creditors or lenders specified sums of money at some future time. A business also may have one or more types of *taxes payable*.

Owner's Equity. The amount by which the business assets exceed the business liabilities is termed the owner's equity in the business. The word "equity" used in this sense means "interest in" or "claim of." It would be quite reasonable to call liabilities "creditors' equity," but this is not customary. The terms **proprietorship**, **net worth**, or **capital** are sometimes used as synonyms for owner's equity. If there are no business liabilities, the owner's equity in the business is equal to the total amount of the assets of the business.

In visualizing a business that is owned and operated by one person (traditionally called the proprietor), it is essential to realize that a distinction must be made between that person's *business* assets and liabilities and *nonbusiness* assets and liabilities. The proprietor will certainly have various types of personal property, such as clothing, and will probably have a home, furniture, and a car. Such a person may own a wide variety of other valuable properties quite apart from the business. Likewise, the proprietor may owe money for reasons that do not pertain to the business. Amounts owed to merchants from whom food and clothing have been purchased and amounts owed to doctors and dentists for services received are common examples. Legally there is no distinction between the proprietor's business and nonbusiness assets nor between the business and nonbusiness liabilities; but since it is to be expected that the formal accounting records for the enterprise will relate to the business only, any nonbusiness assets and liabilities should be excluded. While the term "owner's equity" can be used in a very broad sense, its use in accounting is nearly always limited to the meaning: business assets minus business liabilities.

Frequent reference will be made to the owner's acts of investing money or other property in the business, or to the owner's withdrawal of money or other property from the business. All that is involved in either case is that some property is changed from the category of a nonbusiness asset to a business asset or vice versa. It should be apparent that these distinctions are important if the owner is to be able to judge the financial condition and results of the operations of the business apart from his or her nonbusiness affairs.

The accounting equation

The relationship between the three basic accounting elements can be expressed in the form of a simple equation:

ASSETS = LIABILITIES + OWNER'S EQUITY

When the amounts of any two of these elements are known, the third can always be calculated. For example, Donna Musgrave has business assets on December 31 in the sum of $28,400. Her business debts on that date consist of $800 owed for supplies purchased on account and $1,000 owed to a bank on a note. The owner's equity element of her business may be calculated by subtraction ($28,400 − $1,800 = $26,600). These facts about her business can be expressed in equation form as follows:

> ASSETS = LIABILITIES + OWNER'S EQUITY
> $28,400 $1,800 $26,600

In order to increase her equity in the business, Ms. Musgrave must either increase the assets without increasing the liabilities, or decrease the liabilities without decreasing the assets. In order to increase the assets and owner's equity without investing more money or other property in the business, she will have to operate the business at a profit.

For example, if one year later the assets amount to $42,300 and the liabilities to $2,100, the status of the business would be as follows:

> ASSETS = LIABILITIES + OWNER'S EQUITY
> $42,300 $2,100 $40,200

However, the fact that Ms. Musgrave's equity in the business has increased by $13,600 (from $26,600 to $40,200) does not prove that she has made a profit (often called *net income*) equal to the increase. She may have invested additional money or other property in the business. Suppose, for example, that she invested additional money during the year in the amount of $6,000. In that event, the remainder of the increase in her equity ($7,600) would have been due to profit (net income).

Another possibility could be that she had a very profitable year and withdrew assets in an amount less than the amount of profit. For example, her equity might have been increased by $22,000 as a result of profitable operation; and during the year she might have withdrawn a total of $8,400 in cash for personal use. This series of events could account for the $13,600 increase. It is essential that the business records show the extent to which the change in owner's equity is due to the regular operation of the business and the extent to which increases and decreases in owner's equity are due to the owner's acts of investing and withdrawing assets.

Transactions

Any activity of an enterprise which involves the exchange of values is usually referred to as a **transaction**. These values usually are expressed in terms of money. Buying and selling property and services are common transactions. The following typical transactions are analyzed to show that each transaction represents an exchange of values.

Chapter 1 — The Nature of Business Accounting

TYPICAL TRANSACTIONS	ANALYSIS OF TRANSACTIONS
(a) Purchased equipment for cash, $950.	Money was exchanged for equipment.
(b) Received cash in payment of professional fees, $250.	Professional service was rendered in exchange for money.
(c) Paid office rent, $200.	Money was exchanged for the right to use property.
(d) Paid an amount owed to a creditor, $575.	Money was given in settlement of a debt that may have resulted from the purchase of property on account or from services rendered by a creditor.
(e) Paid wages in cash, $125.	Money was exchanged for services rendered.
(f) Borrowed $2,500 at a bank giving an 8 percent interest-bearing note due in 30 days.	A liability known as a note payable was incurred in exchange for money.
(g) Purchased office equipment on account, $400.	A liability known as an account payable was incurred in exchange for office equipment.

Effect of transactions on the accounting equation

Each transaction affects one or more of the three basic accounting elements. For example, the purchase of equipment for cash represents both an increase and a decrease in assets. The assets increased because equipment was acquired; the assets decreased because cash was disbursed. If the equipment had been purchased on account, thereby incurring a liability, the transaction would result in an increase in assets (equipment) with a corresponding increase in liabilities (accounts payable). Neither of these transactions has any effect upon the owner's equity element of the equation.

The effect of any transaction on the basic accounting elements may be indicated by addition and subtraction. To illustrate: Assume that Stanley Jones, an attorney, decided to go into business for himself. During the first month of this venture (June, 1978), the following transactions relating to his business took place:

An Increase in an Asset Offset by an Increase in Owner's Equity

Transaction (a). Mr. Jones opened a bank account with a deposit of $6,000. This transaction caused his new business to receive the asset cash; and since no business liabilities were involved, the owner's equity element was increased by the same amount. As a result of this transaction, the equation for the business would be:

$$\left. \begin{array}{c} \text{ASSETS} \\ \text{Cash} \\ \rightarrow \text{(a) } 6{,}000 \end{array} \right\} = \left\{ \begin{array}{c} \text{LIABILITIES} + \text{OWNER'S EQUITY} \\ \text{Stanley Jones, Capital} \\ 6{,}000 \end{array} \right.$$

An Increase in an Asset Offset by an Increase in a Liability

Transaction (b). Mr. Jones purchased office equipment (desk, chairs, file cabinet, etc.) for $3,500 on 30 days' credit. This transaction caused the asset office equipment to increase by $3,500 and resulted in an equal increase in the liability accounts payable. Updating the foregoing equation by this (b) transaction gives the following result:

```
              ASSETS            ⎫  ⎧ LIABILITIES + OWNER'S EQUITY
        Cash + Office Equipment ⎬ ={  Accounts Payable   Stanley Jones, Capital
Bal.   6,000                    ⎭  ⎩                              6,000
(b)    ___      +3,500                    +3,500                  _____
Bal.   6,000     3,500                     3,500                  6,000
```

An Increase in One Asset Offset by a Decrease in Another Asset

Transaction (c). Mr. Jones purchased office supplies (stationery, carbon paper, pencils, etc.) for cash, $530. This transaction caused a $530 increase in the asset office supplies that exactly offset the $530 decrease in the asset cash. The effect on the equation is as follows:

```
                    ASSETS                  ⎫  ⎧ LIABILITIES + OWNER'S EQUITY
              Office      Office            ⎬ ={  Accounts         Stanley Jones,
       Cash + Equipment + Supplies          ⎭  ⎩  Payable             Capital
Bal.   6,000    3,500                              3,500               6,000
(c)    -530                +530
Bal.   5,470    3,500       530                    3,500               6,000
```

A Decrease in an Asset Offset by a Decrease in a Liability

Transaction (d). Mr. Jones paid $2,000 on account to the company from which the office equipment was purchased. (See Transaction (b).) This payment caused the asset cash and the liability accounts payable both to decrease $2,000. The effect on the equation is as follows:

```
                    ASSETS                  ⎫  ⎧ LIABILITIES + OWNER'S EQUITY
              Office      Office            ⎬ ={  Accounts         Stanley Jones,
       Cash + Equipment + Supplies          ⎭  ⎩  Payable             Capital
Bal.   5,470    3,500       530                    3,500               6,000
(d)   -2,000                                      -2,000
Bal.   3,470    3,500       530                    1,500               6,000
```

An Increase in an Asset Offset by an Increase in Owner's Equity Resulting from Revenue

Transaction (e). Mr. Jones received $1,500 cash from a client for professional services. This transaction caused the asset cash to increase $1,500; and since the liabilities were not affected, the owner's equity increased by the same amount. The effect on the equation is as follows:

	ASSETS			=	LIABILITIES	+ OWNER'S EQUITY
	Cash	+ Office Equipment	+ Office Supplies		Accounts Payable	Stanley Jones, Capital
Bal.	3,470	3,500	530		1,500	6,000
(e)	+1,500					+1,500
Bal.	4,970	3,500	530		1,500	7,500

A Decrease in an Asset Offset by a Decrease in Owner's Equity Resulting from Expense

Transaction (f). Mr. Jones paid $300 for office rent for June. This transaction caused the asset cash to be reduced by $300 with an equal reduction in owner's equity. The effect on the equation is as follows:

	ASSETS			=	LIABILITIES	+ OWNER'S EQUITY
	Cash	+ Office Equipment	+ Office Supplies		Accounts Payable	Stanley Jones, Capital
Bal.	4,970	3,500	530		1,500	7,500
(f)	−300					−300
Bal.	4,670	3,500	530		1,500	7,200

Transaction (g). Mr. Jones paid a bill for telephone service, $35. This transaction, like the previous one, caused a decrease in the asset cash with an equal decrease in the owner's equity. The effect on the equation is as follows:

	ASSETS			=	LIABILITIES	+ OWNER'S EQUITY
	Cash	+ Office Equipment	+ Office Supplies		Accounts Payable	Stanley Jones, Capital
Bal.	4,670	3,500	530		1,500	7,200
(g)	− 35					− 35
Bal.	4,635	3,500	530		1,500	7,165

The financial statements

A set of accounting records is maintained to fill a variety of needs. Foremost is its use as source data in preparing various reports including those referred to as **financial statements**. The two most important of these are the **income statement** and the **balance sheet**.

The Income Statement. The income statement, sometimes called a **profit and loss statement** or **operating statement**, shows the *net income* (*net profit*) or *net loss* for a specified period of time and how it was calculated. A very simple income statement relating to the business of Stanley Jones for the first month's operation, June, 1978, is shown on page 10. The information it contains was obtained by analysis of the changes in the owner's equity element of the business for the month. This element went from zero to $7,165. Part of this increase, $6,000, was due to the investment of Mr. Jones. The remainder of the increase, $1,165, must have been due to net income since Mr. Jones had made no withdrawals. Transaction (e) involved revenue of $1,500; transactions (f) and (g) involved expenses of $300 and $35, respectively. Taken together, these three transactions explain the net income of $1,165.

STANLEY JONES, ATTORNEY
Income Statement
For the Month of June, 1978

Professional fees		$1,500
Expenses:		
Rent expense	$300	
Telephone expense	35	335
Net income for month		$1,165

The Balance Sheet. The balance sheet, sometimes called a **statement of financial condition** or **statement of financial position**, shows the assets, liabilities, and owner's equity of a business at a specified date. A balance sheet for Mr. Jones' business as of June 30, 1978, is shown below. The information it contains was obtained from the accounting equation after the last transaction (g).

STANLEY JONES, ATTORNEY
Balance Sheet
June 30, 1978

Assets		Liabilities	
Cash	$4,635	Accounts payable	$1,500
Office supplies	530		
Office equipment	3,500	Owner's Equity	
		Stanley Jones, capital	7,165
Total assets	$8,665	Total liabilities and owner's equity	$8,665

NOTE: In order to keep the illustrations of transaction analysis, the income statement, and the balance sheet as simple as possible at this point, two expenses were ignored; namely, office supplies used and depreciation of office equipment.

Report No. 1-1

A workbook of study assignments is provided for use with this textbook. Each study assignment is referred to as a report. The work involved in completing Report No. 1-1 requires a knowledge of the principles developed in the preceding textbook discussion. Before proceeding with the following discussion, complete Report No. 1-1 in accordance with the instructions given in the study assignments.

THE DOUBLE-ENTRY MECHANISM

The meanings of the terms asset, liability, and owner's equity were explained in the preceding pages. Examples were given to show how each business transaction causes a change in one or more of the three basic accounting elements. The first transaction (a) shown on page 7 involved an increase in an asset with a corresponding increase in owner's equity. In the second transaction (b), an increase in an asset caused an equal increase in a liability. In the third transaction (c), an increase in one asset was offset by a decrease in another. In each of the transactions illustrated, there was this *dual effect*. This is always true. A change (increase or decrease) in any asset, any liability, or in owner's equity is always accompanied by an offsetting change within the basic accounting elements.

The fact that each transaction has two aspects — a dual effect upon the accounting elements — provides the basis for what is called **double-entry bookkeeping**. This phrase describes a recording system that involves the making of a record of each of the two aspects that are involved in every transaction. Double entry does not mean that a transaction is recorded twice; instead, it means that both of the two aspects of each transaction are recorded.

The technique of double entry is described and illustrated in the following pages. This method of recording transactions is not new. Double entry is known to have been practiced for at least 500 years. This long popularity is easily explained since the method has several virtues. It is orderly, fairly simple, and very flexible. There is no transaction that cannot be recorded in a double-entry manner. Double entry promotes accuracy. Its use makes it impossible for certain types of errors to remain undetected for very long. For example, if one aspect of a transaction is properly recorded but the other part is overlooked, it will soon be found that the records are "out of balance." The bookkeeper then knows that something is wrong and can examine the records to discover the trouble and can make the needed correction.

The account

It has been explained previously that the assets of a business may consist of a number of items, such as money, accounts receivable, notes receivable, merchandise, equipment, buildings, and land. The liabilities may consist of one or more items, such as accounts payable and notes payable. A separate record should be kept of each asset and of each liability. Later it will be shown that a separate record should also be kept of the increases and decreases in owner's equity. The form of record kept for each item is known as an **account**. There are many types of account forms in general use. They may be ruled on sheets of paper and bound in book form or kept in a loose-leaf binder, or they may be ruled on cards and kept in a file of some sort. An illustration is shown below of a **standard form of account** that is widely used.

ACCOUNT							ACCOUNT NO.
DATE	ITEM	POST. REF.	DEBIT	DATE	ITEM	POST. REF.	CREDIT

Standard Form of Account

This account form is designed to facilitate the recording of the essential information regarding each transaction that affects the account. Before any entries are recorded in an account, the title and number of the account should be written on the horizontal line at the top of the form. Each account should be given an appropriate title that will indicate whether it is an asset, a liability, or an owner's equity account. The standard account form is divided into two equal parts or sections which are ruled identically to facilitate recording increases and decreases. The left side is called the debit side, while the right side is called the credit side. The columnar arrangement and headings of the columns on both sides are the same except that the amount column on the left is headed "Debit" while that on the right is headed "Credit." The Date columns are used for recording the dates of transactions. The Item columns may be used for writing a brief description of a transaction when deemed necessary. The Posting Reference columns will be discussed later. The Debit and Credit columns are used for recording the amounts of transactions.

The three major parts of the standard account form are **(1)** the title (and, usually, the account number), **(2)** the debit side, and **(3)** the credit side. To determine the balance of an account at any time, it is necessary only to total the amounts in the Debit and Credit columns and calculate the difference between the two totals. To save time, a "T" form of account is commonly used for instructional purposes. It consists of a two-line drawing resembling the capital letter T and is sometimes referred to as a skeleton form of account.

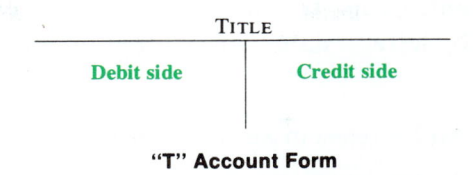

Title
Debit side	Credit side

"T" Account Form

Debits and credits

To debit an account means to record an amount on the left or debit side of the account. To credit an account means to record an amount on the right or credit side of the account. The abbreviation for debit is Dr. and for credit Cr. (based on the Latin terms *debere* and *credere*). Sometimes the word charge is used as a substitute for debit. Increases in assets are recorded on the left side of the accounts; increases in liabilities and in owner's equity are recorded on the right side of the accounts. Decreases in assets are recorded on the right side of the accounts; decreases in liabilities and in owner's equity are recorded on the left side of the accounts. Recording increases and decreases in the accounts in this manner will reflect the basic equality of assets to liabilities plus owner's equity; at the same time it will maintain equality between the total amounts debited to all accounts and the total amounts credited to all accounts. These basic relationships may be illustrated in the following manner:

ASSETS	=	LIABILITIES + OWNER'S EQUITY
DEBITS	=	CREDITS

ALL ASSET ACCOUNTS		ALL LIABILITY ACCOUNTS	
Debit to record increases (+)	Credit to record decreases (−)	Debit to record decreases (−)	Credit to record increases (+)

ALL OWNER'S EQUITY ACCOUNTS	
Debit to record decreases (−)	Credit to record increases (+)

Use of asset, liability, and owner's equity accounts

To illustrate the application of the double-entry process, the transactions discussed on pages 7–9 will be analyzed and their effect on the accounting elements will be indicated by showing the proper entries in "T" accounts. As before, the transactions are identified by letters; dates are omitted intentionally.

An Increase in an Asset Offset by an Increase in Owner's Equity

Transaction (a). Stanley Jones, an attorney, started a business of his own and invested $6,000 in cash.

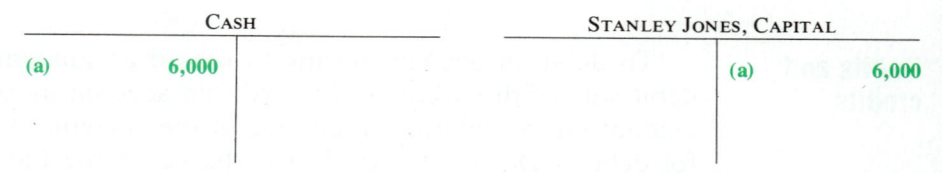

Cash		Stanley Jones, Capital	
(a) 6,000			(a) 6,000

Analysis: As a result of this transaction the business acquired an asset, cash. The amount of money invested by Mr. Jones represents his equity in the business; thus the amount of the asset cash is equal to the owner's equity in the business. Separate accounts are kept for the asset cash and for the owner. To record the transaction properly, the cash account was debited and Stanley Jones' capital account was credited for $6,000.

An Increase in an Asset Offset by an Increase in a Liability

Transaction (b). Purchased office equipment (desk, chairs, file cabinet, etc.) for $3,500 on 30 days' credit.

Office Equipment		Accounts Payable	
(b) *dr* 3,500			(b) *cr* 3,500

Analysis: As a result of this transaction the business acquired a new asset, office equipment. The debt incurred as a result of purchasing the office equipment on 30 days' credit is a liability, accounts payable. Separate accounts are kept for office equipment and for accounts payable. The purchase of office equipment caused an increase in the assets of the business. Therefore, the asset account Office Equipment was debited for $3,500. The purchase also caused an increase in a liability. Therefore, the liability account Accounts Payable was credited for $3,500.

An Increase in One Asset Offset by a Decrease in Another Asset

Transaction (c). Purchased office supplies (stationery, carbon paper, pencils, etc.) for cash, $530.

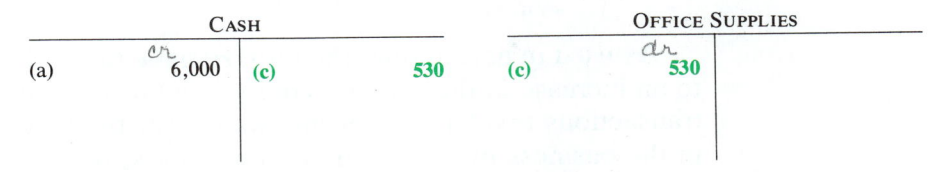

Cash		Office Supplies	
cr		*dr*	
(a) 6,000	(c) 530	(c) 530	

Analysis: As a result of this transaction the business acquired a new asset, office supplies. However, the addition of this asset was offset by a decrease in the asset cash. To record the transaction properly, Office Supplies was debited and Cash was credited for $530. (It will be noted that this is the second entry in the cash account; the account was previously debited for $6,000 when Transaction (a) was recorded.)

It is proper to record office supplies as an asset at time of purchase even though they will become an expense when consumed. (The procedure in accounting for supplies consumed will be discussed later.)

A Decrease in an Asset Offset by a Decrease in a Liability

Transaction (d). Paid $2,000 on account to the company from which the office equipment was purchased. (See Transaction (b).)

Cash		Accounts Payable	
(a) 6,000	(c) 530	(d) 2,000	(b) 3,500
	(d) 2,000		

Analysis: This transaction resulted in a decrease in the liability accounts payable with a corresponding decrease in the asset cash; hence, it was recorded by debiting Accounts Payable and by crediting Cash for $2,000. (It will be noted that this is the second entry in the accounts payable account and the third entry in the cash account.)

Revenue and expense

The owner's equity element of a business or professional enterprise may be increased in two ways as follows:

(a) The owner may invest additional money or other property in the enterprise. Such investments result in an increase both in the assets of the enterprise and in the owner's equity, but they do not further enrich the owner. The owner merely has more property invested in the enterprise and less property outside of the enterprise.

(b) Revenue may be derived from sales of goods or services, or from other sources.

As used in accounting, the term **revenue** in nearly all cases refers to an increase in the owner's equity in a business resulting from any transactions involving asset inflows except the investment of assets in the business by its owner. In most cases, the increase in owner's equity due to revenue results from an addition to the assets without any change in the liabilities. Often it is cash that is increased. However, an increase in cash and other assets can occur in connection with several types of transactions that do not involve revenue. For this reason, revenue is defined in terms of the change in owner's equity rather than the change in assets. Any transaction that causes owner's equity to increase, except investments in the business by its owner, involves revenue.

The owner's equity element of a business or professional enterprise may be decreased in two ways as follows:

(a) The owner may withdraw assets (cash or other property) from the business enterprise.
(b) Expenses may be incurred in operating the enterprise.

As used in accounting, the term **expense** in nearly all cases means a decrease in the owner's equity in a business caused by any transactions involving asset outflows other than a withdrawal by the owner. When an expense is incurred, either the assets are reduced or the liabilities are increased. In either event, owner's equity is reduced. If the transaction causing the reduction is not a withdrawal of assets by the owner, an expense is incurred. Common examples of expense are rent of office or store, salaries of employees, telephone service, supplies consumed, and many types of taxes.

If, during a specified period of time, the total increases in owner's equity resulting from revenue exceed the total decreases resulting from expenses, it may be said that the excess represents the **net income** or net profit for the period. On the other hand, if the expenses of the period exceed the revenue, such excess represents a **net loss** for the period. The time interval used in the measurement of net income or net loss can be chosen by the owner. It may be a month, a quarter (three months), a year, or some other period of time. If the accounting period is a year, it is usually referred to as a **fiscal year**. The fiscal year frequently coincides with the *calendar year*.

Transactions involving revenue and expense always cause a change in the owner's equity element of an enterprise. Such changes could be recorded by debiting the owner's equity account for expenses and crediting it for revenue. If this practice were followed, however, the credit side of the owner's equity account would contain a mixture of increases due to revenue and to the investment of assets in the business by the owner, while the debit side would contain a mixture of decreases due to expenses and to the withdrawal of assets from the business by the owner. In order to calculate the net income or the net loss for each accounting period, a careful analysis of the owner's equity account would be required. It is, therefore, better practice to record revenue and expenses in separate accounts. These are called **temporary owner's equity accounts** because it is customary to close them at the end of each accounting period by transferring their balances to a **summary account**. The balance of this summary account then represents the net income or net loss for the period. The summary account is also a temporary account which is closed by transferring its balance to the owner's equity account.

A separate account should be kept for each type of revenue and for each type of expense. When a transaction produces revenue, the amount of the revenue should be credited to an appropriate revenue account. When a transaction involves expense, the amount of the expense should be debited to an appropriate expense account. The relationship of these temporary accounts to the owner's equity account and the application of the debit and credit theory to the accounts are indicated in the following diagram:

	ALL OWNER'S EQUITY ACCOUNTS
Debit to record decreases (−)	Credit to record increases (+)

ALL EXPENSE ACCOUNTS		ALL REVENUE ACCOUNTS	
Debit to record increases (+)	Credit to record decreases (−)	Debit to record decreases (−)	Credit to record increases (+)

It is important to recognize that the credit side of each revenue account is serving temporarily as a part of the credit side of the owner's equity account. Increases in owner's equity are recorded as credits. Thus, increases in owner's equity resulting from revenue should be credited to revenue accounts. The debit side of each expense account is serving temporarily as a part of the debit side of the owner's equity account. Decreases in owner's equity are recorded as debits. Thus, decreases in owner's equity resulting from expense should be debited to expense accounts.

Use of revenue and expense accounts

To illustrate the application of the double-entry process in recording transactions that affect revenue and expense accounts, the transactions that follow will be analyzed and their effect on the accounting elements will be indicated by showing the proper entries in "T" accounts. These transactions represent a continuation of the transactions completed by Stanley Jones, an attorney, in the conduct of his business. (See pages 14 and 15 for Transactions (a) to (d).)

An Increase in an Asset Offset by an Increase in Owner's Equity Resulting from Revenue

Transaction (e). Received $1,500 in cash from a client for professional services rendered.

CASH				PROFESSIONAL FEES	
(a) 6,000	(c) 530			(e)	1,500
(e) 1,500	(d) 2,000				

Analysis: This transaction resulted in an increase in the asset cash with a corresponding increase in owner's equity because of revenue from professional fees. To record the transaction properly, Cash was debited and an appropriate account for the revenue was credited for $1,500. Accounts should always be given a descriptive title that will aid in classifying them in relation to the accounting elements. In this case the revenue account was given the title Professional Fees. (It will be noted that this is the fourth entry in the cash account and the first entry in the account Professional Fees.)

A Decrease in an Asset Offset by a Decrease in Owner's Equity Resulting from Expense

Transaction (f). Paid $300 for office rent for one month.

CASH				RENT EXPENSE	
(a) 6,000	(c) 530		(f)	300	
(e) 1,500	(d) 2,000				
	(f) 300				

Analysis: This transaction resulted in a decrease in the asset cash with a corresponding decrease in owner's equity because of expense. To record the transaction properly, Rent Expense was debited and Cash was credited for $300. (This is the first entry in the rent expense account and the fifth entry in the cash account.)

Transaction (g). Paid bill for telephone service, $35.

	CASH				TELEPHONE EXPENSE
(a)	6,000	(c)	530	(g)	35
(e)	1,500	(d)	2,000		
		(f)	300		
		(g)	35		

Analysis: This transaction is identical to the previous one except that telephone expense rather than rent expense was the reason for the decrease in owner's equity. To record the transaction properly, Telephone Expense was debited and Cash was credited for $35.

The trial balance

It is a fundamental principle of double-entry bookkeeping that the sum of the assets is always equal to the sum of the liabilities and owner's equity. In order to maintain this equality in recording transactions, the sum of the debit entries must always be equal to the sum of the credit entries. To determine whether this equality has been maintained, it is customary to take a trial balance periodically. A **trial balance** is a list of all of the accounts showing the title and balance of each account. The balance of any account is the amount of difference between the total debits and the total credits to the account. Preliminary to taking a trial balance, the debit and credit amounts in each account should be totaled. This is called **footing** the amount columns. If there is only one item entered in a column, no footing is necessary. To find the balance of an account, it is necessary only to determine the difference between the footings by subtraction. Since asset and expense accounts are debited for increases, these accounts normally have *debit balances*. Since liability, owner's equity, and revenue accounts are credited to record increases, these accounts normally have *credit balances*. The balance of an account should be entered on the side of the account that has the larger total. The footings and balances of accounts should be written in small figures just below the last entry. A pencil is generally used for this purpose. If the footings of an account are equal in amount, the account is said to be *in balance*.

The accounts of Stanley Jones are reproduced below. To show the relationship to the fundamental accounting equation, the accounts are arranged in three columns under the headings of Assets, Liabilities, and Owner's Equity. It will be noted that the cash account has been footed and the balance inserted on the left side. The two debits totaled $7,500; the four credits totaled $2,865. Thus, the debit balance was $4,635. The footings and the balance are printed in italics. It was not necessary to foot any of the other accounts because none of them contained more than one entry on either side. The balance of the accounts payable account is shown on the credit side in italics. It was not necessary to enter the balances of the other accounts because there were entries on only one side of those accounts.

ASSETS	=	LIABILITIES	+	OWNER'S EQUITY

CASH | ACCOUNTS PAYABLE | STANLEY JONES, CAPITAL

(a) 6,000 | (c) 530 | (d) 2,000 | (b) 3,500 | (a) 6,000
(e) 1,500 | (d) 2,000 | | *1,500* |
4,635 | *7,500* | (f) 300 | |
 | (g) 35 | | | PROFESSIONAL FEES
 | *2,865* | | | (e) 1,500

OFFICE SUPPLIES

(c) 530 | | | | RENT EXPENSE
 | | | | (f) 300

OFFICE EQUIPMENT

(b) 3,500 | | | | TELEPHONE EXPENSE
 | | | | (g) 35

A trial balance of Stanley Jones' accounts is shown on page 21. The trial balance was taken on June 30, 1978; therefore, this date is shown in the third line of the heading. The trial balance reveals that the debit and credit totals are equal in amount. This is proof that in recording Transactions (a) to (g) inclusive the total of the debits was equal to the total of the credits.

A trial balance is not a formal statement or report. Normally it is never seen by anyone except the accountant or bookkeeper. It is used to aid in preparing the income statement and the balance sheet. If the trial balance on the following page is studied in conjunction with the income statement and balance sheet shown on page 10, it will be seen that those statements could have been prepared quite easily from the information that this trial balance provides.

Chapter 1 — The Nature of Business Accounting

Stanley Jones, Attorney
Trial Balance
June 30, 1978

Account	Dr. Balance	Cr. Balance
Cash	4635 00	
Office Supplies	530 00	
Office Equipment	3500 00	
Accounts Payable		1500 00
Stanley Jones, Capital		6000 00
Professional Fees		1500 00
Rent Expense	300 00	
Telephone Expense	35 00	
	9000 00	9000 00

Stanley Jones' Trial Balance

Report No. 1-2

Refer to the study assignments and complete Report No. 1-2 in accordance with the instructions given therein. The work involved in completing the assignment requires a knowledge of the principles developed in the preceding discussion. Any difficulty experienced in completing the report will indicate a lack of understanding of these principles. In such event further study should be helpful. After completing the report, you may continue with the textbook discussion in Chapter 2 until the next report is required.

2

Accounting Procedure

The principles of double-entry bookkeeping were explained and illustrated in the preceding chapter. To avoid distraction from the fundamentals, the mechanics of collecting and classifying information about business transactions were ignored. In actual practice the first record of a transaction (sometimes called the "source document") is made in the form of a business paper, such as a check stub, receipt, cash register tape, sales ticket, or purchase invoice. The information supplied by source documents is an aid in analyzing transactions to determine their effect upon the accounts.

JOURNALIZING TRANSACTIONS

The first formal double-entry record of a transaction is usually made in a record called a **journal** (frequently in book form). The act of recording transactions in a journal is called **journalizing**. It is necessary to analyze each transaction before it can be journalized properly. The purpose of the journal entries is to provide a chronological record of all transactions completed showing the date of each transaction, titles of accounts to be debited and credited, and amounts of the debits and credits. The journal then provides all the information needed to record the debits and credits in the proper accounts. The flow of data concerning transactions can be illustrated in the following manner:

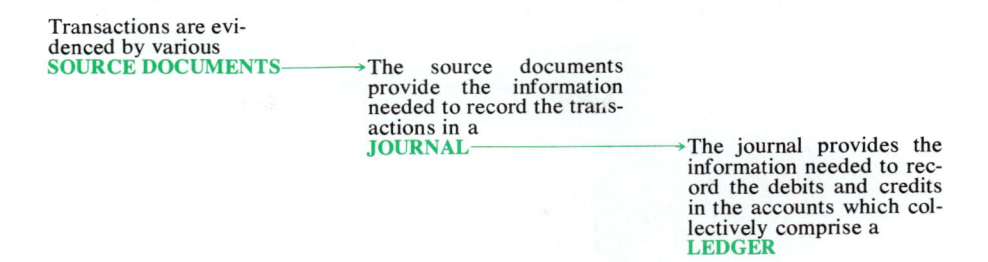

Chapter 2   Accounting Procedure   **23**

Transactions are evidenced by various **SOURCE DOCUMENTS** ⟶ The source documents provide the information needed to record the transactions in a **JOURNAL** ⟶ The journal provides the information needed to record the debits and credits in the accounts which collectively comprise a **LEDGER**

Source documents

The term source document covers a wide variety of forms and papers. Almost any document that provides information about a business transaction can be called a source document.

SOURCE DOCUMENTS

Examples:	Provide information about:
(a) Check stubs or carbon copies of checks	Cash disbursements
(b) Receipt stubs, or carbon copies of receipts, cash register tapes, or memos of cash register totals	Cash receipts
(c) Copies of sales tickets or sales invoices issued to customers or clients	Sales of goods or services
(d) Purchase invoices received from vendors	Purchases of goods or services

The journal

While the original record of a transaction usually is a source document as explained above, the first formal double-entry record of a transaction is made in a journal. For this reason a journal is commonly referred to as a **book of original entry**. The ruling of the pages of a journal varies with the type and size of an enterprise and the nature of its operations. The simplest form of journal is a **two-column journal**. A standard form of such a journal is illustrated on page 24. It is referred to as a two-column journal because it has only two amount columns, one for debit amounts and one for credit amounts. In the illustration the columns have been numbered as a means of identification in connection with the following discussion.

Column No. 1 is a *date* column. The year should be written in small figures at the top of the column immediately below the column heading and need only be repeated at the top of each new page unless an entry for a new year is made farther down on the page. The

Standard Two-Column Journal

date column is a double column, the perpendicular single rule being used to separate the month from the day. Thus in writing June 20, the name of the month should be written to the left of the single line and the number designating the day of the month should be written to the right of this line. The name of the month need only be shown for the first entry on a page unless an entry for a new month is made farther down on the page.

Column No. 2 is generally referred to as a *description* or an *explanation* column. It is used to record the titles of the accounts affected by each transaction, together with a description of the transaction. Two or more accounts are affected by each transaction, and the titles of all accounts affected must be recorded. Normally the titles of the accounts debited are written first and then the titles of the accounts credited. A separate line should be used for each account title. The titles of the accounts to be debited are generally written at the extreme left of the column, while the titles of the accounts to be credited are usually indented about one-half inch (about 1.3 centimeters). The description should be written immediately following the credit entry, and usually is indented an additional one-half inch. Reference to the journal reproduced on pages 31 and 32 will help to visualize the arrangement of the copy in the Description column. An orderly arrangement is desirable.

Column No. 3 is a *posting reference* column — sometimes referred to as a *folio* column. No entries are made in this column at the time of journalizing the transactions; such entries are made only at the time of posting (which is the process of entering the debits and credits in the proper accounts in the ledger). This procedure will be explained in detail later in this chapter.

Column No. 4 is an *amount* column in which the amount that is to be *debited* to any account should be written on the same line on which the title of that account appears. In other words, the name of the account to be debited should be written in the Description column and the amount of the debit entry should be written on the same line in the Debit column.

Column No. 5 is an *amount* column in which the amount that is to be *credited* to any account should be written on the same line on which the title of that account appears. In other words, the name of the account to be credited should be written in the Description column and the amount of the credit entry should be written on the same line in the Credit column.

Journalizing

Journalizing involves recording the significant information concerning each transaction either **(1)** at the time the transaction occurs or **(2)** subsequently, but in the chronological order in which it and the other transactions occurred. For every transaction the entry should record the date, the title of each account affected, the amounts, and a brief description. The only affect a transaction can have on any account is either to increase or to decrease the balance of the account. Before a transaction can be recorded properly, therefore, it must be analyzed in order to determine:

(a) Which accounts are affected by the transaction.
(b) What effect the transaction has upon each of the accounts involved; that is, whether the balance of each affected account is increased or decreased.

The chart of accounts

In analyzing a transaction preparatory to journalizing it, the accountant or bookkeeper must know which accounts are being kept. When an accounting system is being established for a new business, the first step is to decide which accounts are required. The accounts used will depend upon the information needed or desired. Ordinarily it will be found desirable to keep a separate account for each type of asset and each type of liability, since it is certain that information will be desired in regard to what is owned and what is owed. A permanent owner's equity or capital account should be kept in order that information may be available as to the owner's interest or equity in the business. Furthermore, it is advisable to keep separate accounts for each type of revenue and each kind of expense. The revenue and expense accounts are the temporary accounts that are used in recording increases and decreases in owner's equity from asset movements apart from changes caused by the owner's investments and withdrawals. The specific accounts to be kept for recording the increases and the decreases in owner's equity depend upon the nature and the sources of the revenue and the nature of the expenses incurred in earning the revenue.

A professional person or an individual engaged in operating a small enterprise may need to keep relatively few accounts. On the other hand, a large manufacturing enterprise, a public utility, or any large business may need to keep a great many accounts in order that the information required or desired may be available. Regardless of the number of accounts kept, they can be segregated into the three major classes and should be grouped according to these classes in the ledger. The usual custom is to place the asset accounts first, the liability accounts second, and the owner's equity accounts, including the revenue and the expense accounts, last. It is common practice to prepare a list of the accounts that are to be kept. This list, often in the form of an outline, is called a **chart of accounts**. It has become a general practice to give each account a number and to keep the accounts in numerical order. The numbering usually follows a consistent pattern and becomes a *code*. For example, asset accounts may be assigned numbers that always start with "1," liability accounts with "2," owner's equity accounts with "3," revenue accounts with "4," and expense accounts with "5."

To illustrate: Suppose that on December 1, 1978, Laura A. Eason enters the employment agency business under the name of The Eason Employment Agency. She decides to keep her accounts on the calendar-year basis; therefore, her first accounting period will be for one month only, that is, the month of December. It is decided that a two-column journal and a ledger with the standard form of account will be used. Mrs. Eason realizes that she will not need many accounts at present because the business is new. She also realizes that additional accounts may be added as the need arises. Following is a chart of the accounts to be kept at the start:

THE EASON EMPLOYMENT AGENCY
Chart of Accounts

*Assets**
  111 Cash
  112 Office Supplies
  121 Office Equipment

Liabilities
  211 Accounts Payable

Owner's Equity
  311 Laura A. Eason, Capital
  312 Laura A. Eason, Drawing

Revenue
  411 Placement Fees

Expenses
  511 Rent Expense
  512 Salary Expense
  513 Traveling Expense
  514 Telephone Expense
  515 Office Supplies Expense
  516 Miscellaneous Expense

*Words in italics represent headings and not account titles.

Chapter 2　　Accounting Procedure　　**27**

Journalizing procedure illustrated

To illustrate journalizing procedure, the transactions completed by The Eason Employment Agency through December 31, 1978, will be journalized. A *narrative* of the transactions follows. It provides all of the information that is needed in journalizing the transactions. Some of the transactions are analyzed to explain their effect upon the accounts, with the journal entry immediately following the explanation of the entry. The journal of The Eason Employment Agency with all of the entries recorded is reproduced on pages 31 and 32.

THE EASON EMPLOYMENT AGENCY

NARRATIVE OF TRANSACTIONS

Friday, December 1, 1978

Mrs. Eason invested $3,000 cash in a business enterprise to be known as The Eason Employment Agency.

> As a result of this transaction, the business acquired the asset cash in the amount of $3,000. Since neither a decrease in any other asset nor an increase in any liability was involved, the transaction caused an increase of $3,000 in owner's equity. Accordingly, the entry to record the transaction is a debit to Cash and a credit to Laura A. Eason, Capital, for $3,000.

DATE	DESCRIPTION	POST. REF.	DEBIT	CREDIT
1978 Dec. 1	Cash		3000 00	
	Laura A. Eason, Capital			3000 00
	Original investment			
	in employment agency.			

JOURNAL　　PAGE 1

Note that the following steps were involved:

(a) Since this was the first entry on the journal page, the year was written at the top of the Date column.

(b) The month and day were written on the first line in the Date column.

(c) The title of the account to be debited, Cash, was written on the first line at the extreme left of the Description column. The amount of the debit, $3,000, was written on the same line in the Debit column.

(d) The title of the account to be credited, Laura A. Eason, Capital, was written on the second line indented one-half inch from the left side of the Description column. The amount of the credit, $3,000, was written on the same line in the Credit column.

(e) The explanation of the entry was started on the next line indented an additional one-half inch. The second line of the explanation was also indented the same distance as the first.

Monday, December 4

Paid office rent for December, $350.

This transaction resulted in a decrease in owner's equity because of expense, with a corresponding decrease in the asset cash. The transaction is recorded by debiting Rent Expense and by crediting Cash for $350.

5	4 Rent Expense	350 00	5
6	Cash		350 00	6
7	Paid December rent.			7

Note: Mrs. Eason ordered several pieces of office equipment. Since the dealer did not have in stock what Mrs. Eason wanted, the articles were ordered from the factory. Delivery is not expected until the latter part of the month. Pending arrival of the equipment, the dealer loaned Mrs. Eason some used office equipment. No entry is required until the new equipment is received.

Tuesday, December 5

Purchased office supplies from the Adams Supply Co. on account, $261.41.

In this transaction the business acquired a new asset which represented an increase in the total assets. A liability was also incurred because of the purchase on account. The transaction is recorded by debiting Office Supplies and by crediting Accounts Payable for $261.41. As these supplies are consumed, the amount will become an expense of the business.

8	5 Office Supplies	261 41	8
9	Accounts Payable		261 41	9
10	Adams Supply Co.			10

Wednesday, December 6

Paid the Consolidated Telephone Co. $32.50 covering the cost of installing a telephone in the office, together with the first month's service charges payable in advance.

This transaction caused a decrease in owner's equity because of expense and a corresponding decrease in the asset cash. The transaction is recorded by debiting Telephone Expense and by crediting Cash for $32.50.

11	6 Telephone Expense	32 50	11
12	Cash		32 50	12
13	Paid telephone bill.			13

Thursday, December 7

Paid $8 for a subscription to a trade journal.

This transaction resulted in a decrease in owner's equity due to expense and a corresponding decrease in the asset cash. The transaction is recorded by debiting Miscellaneous Expense and by crediting Cash for $8.

14	7 Miscellaneous Expense		8 00		14
15	Cash			8 00	15
16	Trade journal sub.				16

Friday, December 8

Received $450 from James Paynter for placement services rendered.

This transaction resulted in an increase in the asset cash with a corresponding increase in owner's equity because of revenue from placement fees. The transaction is recorded by debiting Cash and by crediting Placement Fees for $450. In keeping her accounts, Mrs. Eason follows the practice of not recording revenue until it is received in cash. This practice is common to professional and personal service enterprises.

17	8 Cash		450 00		17
18	Placement Fees			450 00	18
19	James Paynter.				19

Monday, December 11

Paid the World Travel Service $145.30 for an airplane ticket to be used later in the week for an employment agency convention trip.

20	11 Traveling Expense		145 30		20
21	Cash			145 30	21
22	Airplane fare—convention.				22

Friday, December 15

Paid Carl Hogan $350 covering his salary for the first half of the month.

Mr. Hogan is employed by Mrs. Eason as her assistant at a salary of $700 a month. The transaction resulted in a decrease in owner's equity because of salary expense with a corresponding decrease in the asset cash. The transaction is recorded by debiting Salary Expense and by crediting Cash for $350. (The matter of payroll taxes is purposely ignored at this point. These taxes will be discussed in detail in Chapter 4.)

23	15 Salary Expense		350 00		23
24	Cash			350 00	24
25	Paid assistant's salary.				25

Note: The Posting Reference column has been left blank in the eight preceding journal entry illustrations. This is because the column is not used until the amounts are posted to the accounts in the ledger, a process to be described starting on page 33. Account numbers are shown in the Posting Reference column of the journal illustrated on pages 31 and 32, since the illustration shows how the journal appears *after* the posting has been completed.

The journal entries for the following transactions (as well as for those to this point) are illustrated on pages 31 and 32.

Monday, December 18

Received $500 from Elena Torrez for services rendered.

Wednesday, December 20

Mrs. Eason withdrew $600 for personal use.

> Amounts of cash withdrawn for personal use by the owner of a business enterprise represent a decrease in owner's equity. Although amounts withdrawn might be recorded as debits to the owner's capital account, it is better practice to record withdrawals in a separate account. Doing it in this way makes it a little easier to summarize the decreases in owner's equity caused by the owner's withdrawals. This transaction is recorded in the journal by debiting Laura A. Eason, Drawing, and by crediting Cash for $600.

Thursday, December 21

Received $650 from Susan Taylor for services rendered.

Friday, December 22

Paid $50 membership dues in the American Association of Employment Agencies.

Wednesday, December 27

Received the office equipment ordered December 4. These items were purchased on account from the Walker Office Equipment Co. Cost: $2,948.17. The dealer removed the used equipment that had been loaned to Mrs. Eason.

Thursday, December 28

Paid the Adams Supply Co. $261.41 for the office supplies purchased on December 5.

> This transaction caused a decrease in the liability accounts payable with a corresponding decrease in the asset cash. The transaction was recorded by debiting Accounts Payable and by crediting Cash for $261.41.

Received $500 from Bradford Davis for services rendered.

Friday, December 29

Paid Carl Hogan $350 covering his salary for the second half of the month. (Paid this day as it is the last workday of the month.)

Office supplies used during the month, $45.

> By referring to the transaction of December 5, it will be noted that office supplies amounting to $261.41 were purchased and were recorded as an asset. By taking an inventory, counting the supplies in stock at the end of the month, Mrs. Eason was able to determine that the cost of supplies used during the month amounted to $45. The expenses for the month of December would not be reflected properly in the accounts if the supplies used during the month were not taken into consideration. Therefore, the cost of supplies used was recorded by debiting the expense account, Office Supplies Expense, and by crediting the asset account, Office Supplies, for $45.

JOURNAL
PAGE 1

DATE	DESCRIPTION	POST. REF.	DEBIT	CREDIT
1978 Dec. 1	Cash	111	3000 00	
	Laura A. Eason, Capital	311		3000 00
	Original investment			
	in employment agency.			
4	Rent Expense	511	350 00	
	Cash	111		350 00
	Paid December rent.			
5	Office Supplies	112	261 41	
	Accounts Payable	211		261 41
	Adams Supply Co.			
6	Telephone Expense	514	32 50	
	Cash	111		32 50
	Paid telephone bill.			
7	Miscellaneous Expense	516	8 00	
	Cash	111		8 00
	Trade journal sub.			
8	Cash	111	450 00	
	Placement Fees	411		450 00
	James Paynter.			
11	Traveling Expense	513	145 30	
	Cash	111		145 30
	Airplane fare-convention.			
15	Salary Expense	512	350 00	
	Cash	111		350 00
	Paid assistant's salary.			
18	Cash	111	500 00	
	Placement Fees	411		500 00
	Elena Torrez			
20	Laura A. Eason, Drawing	312	600 00	
	Cash	111		600 00
	Withdrawn for personal use.			
21	Cash	111	650 00	
	Placement Fees	411		650 00
	Susan Taylor.			
22	Miscellaneous Expense	516	50 00	
	Cash	111		50 00
	A.A.E.A. dues.			
27	Office Equipment	121	2948 17	
	Accounts Payable	211		2948 17
	Walker Office Equip. Co.			
			9345 38	9345 38

The Eason Employment Agency Journal
(continued on next page)

	JOURNAL			PAGE 2
DATE	DESCRIPTION	POST. REF.	DEBIT	CREDIT
1978 Dec. 28	Accounts Payable	211	261 41	
	Cash	111		261 41
	Adams Supply Co.			
28	Cash	111	500 00	
	Placement Fees	411		500 00
	Bradford Davis.			
29	Salary Expense	512	350 00	
	Cash	111		350 00
	Paid assistant's salary			
29	Office Supplies Expense	515	45 00	
	Office Supplies	112		45 00
	Cost of supplies used during December.			
			1156 41	1156 41

The Eason Employment Agency Journal (concluded)

Note: Some bookkeepers leave a blank line after the explanation of each entry. This practice is acceptable though not recommended.

Proving the journal

Because a double entry is made for each transaction, the equality of debit and credit entries on each page of the journal may be proved merely by totaling the amount columns. The total of each column is usually entered as a footing immediately under the last entry. When a page of the journal is filled, the footings may be entered just under the last single horizontal ruled line at the bottom of the page as shown in the illustration on page 31. When the page is not filled, the footings should be entered immediately under the last entry as shown in the illustration above.

Report No. 2-1

Refer to the study assignments and complete Report No. 2-1. To complete this assignment correctly, the principles developed in the preceding discussion must be understood. Review the text assignment if necessary. After completing the report, continue with the following textbook discussion until the next report is required.

Chapter 2   Accounting Procedure   **33**

POSTING TO THE LEDGER; THE
TRIAL BALANCE

The purpose of a journal is to provide a chronological record of financial transactions expressed as debits and credits to accounts. These accounts are kept to supply desired information. Collectively the accounts are described as the **general ledger** or, often, simply as "the ledger." The account forms may be on sheets of paper or on cards. When on sheets of paper, the sheets may be bound in book form or they may be kept in a loose-leaf binder. Usually a separate page or card is used for each account. The accounts should be classified properly in the ledger; that is, the asset accounts should be grouped together, the liability accounts together, and the owner's equity accounts together. Proper grouping of the accounts in the ledger is an aid in preparing the various reports desired by the owner. Mrs. Eason decided to keep all of the accounts for The Eason Employment Agency in a loose-leaf ledger. The numbers shown in the agency's chart of accounts on page 26 were used as a guide in arranging the accounts in the ledger. The ledger of The Eason Employment Agency is reproduced on pages 35–37. Note that the accounts are in numerical order.

Since Mrs. Eason makes few purchases on account, she does not keep a separate account for each creditor. When invoices are received for items purchased on account, the invoices are checked and recorded in the journal by debiting the proper accounts and by crediting Accounts Payable. The credit balance of Accounts Payable indicates the total amount owed to creditors. After each invoice is recorded, it is filed in an unpaid invoice file, where it remains until it is paid in full. When an invoice is paid in full, it is removed from the unpaid invoice file and is then filed under the name of the creditor for future reference. The balance of the accounts payable account may be proved at any time by determining the total of the unpaid amounts of the invoices.

Posting

The process of transcribing (often called "entering") information in the ledger from the journal is known as **posting**. All amounts entered in the journal should be posted to the accounts kept in the ledger in order to summarize the results. Such posting may be done daily or at frequent intervals. The ledger is not a reliable source of information until all of the transactions recorded in the journal have been posted.

Since the accounts provide the information needed in preparing financial statements, a posting procedure that insures accuracy in maintaining the accounts must necessarily be followed. Posting from the journal to the ledger involves recording the following information in the accounts:

(a) The date of each transaction.
(b) The amount of each transaction.
(c) The page of the journal from which each transaction is posted.

As each amount in the journal is posted to the proper account in the ledger, the number of that account should be entered in the Posting Reference column in the journal so as to provide a cross-reference between the journal and the ledger. The first entry to be posted from the journal (a segment of which is reproduced below) required a debit to Cash of $3,000. This was accomplished by entering the year, "1978," the month, abbreviated "Dec.," and the day, "1," in the Date column of the cash account (reproduced below); the number "1" in the Posting Reference column (since the posting came from Page 1 of the journal); and the amount, "$3,000.00" in the Debit column. Inasmuch as the number of the cash account is 111, that number was entered in the Posting Reference column of the journal on the same line as the debit of $3,000.00 that was just posted to Cash. The same pattern was followed in posting the credit part of the entry — $3,000 to Laura A. Eason, Capital, Account No. 311 (reproduced below).

Reference to the journal of The Eason Employment Agency (reproduced on pages 31 and 32) and its ledger (reproduced below and on pages 36 and 37) will indicate that a similar procedure was followed in posting every amount from the journal. Note also that in the ledger, the year "1978" was entered only at the top of each Date column, and that the month "Dec." was entered only with the first posting to an account.

ACCOUNT Cash							ACCOUNT NO. 111
DATE	ITEM	POST. REF.	DEBIT	DATE	ITEM	POST. REF.	CREDIT
1978 Dec. 1		1	3000.00	1978 Dec. 4		1	350.00
8		1	450.00	6		1	32.50
18		1	500.00	7		1	8.00
21		1	650.00	11		1	145.30
28		2	500.00	15		1	350.00
	2,952.79		5100.00	20		1	600.00
				22		1	50.00
				28		2	26.41
				29		2	350.00
							2147.21

ACCOUNT Office Supplies							ACCOUNT NO. 112
DATE	ITEM	POST. REF.	DEBIT	DATE	ITEM	POST. REF.	CREDIT
1978 Dec. 5		1	261.41	1978 Dec. 29		2	45.00
	216.41						

ACCOUNT Office Equipment							ACCOUNT NO. 121
DATE	ITEM	POST. REF.	DEBIT	DATE	ITEM	POST. REF.	CREDIT
1978 Dec. 27		1	2948.17				

ACCOUNT Accounts Payable							ACCOUNT NO. 211
DATE	ITEM	POST. REF.	DEBIT	DATE	ITEM	POST. REF.	CREDIT
1978 Dec. 28		2	261.41	1978 Dec. 5		1	261.41
				27		1	2948.17
					2,948.17		3209.58

The Eason Employment Agency Ledger (*continued on next page*)

ACCOUNT: Laura A. Eason, Capital — ACCOUNT NO. 311

DATE	ITEM	POST. REF.	DEBIT	DATE	ITEM	POST. REF.	CREDIT
				1978 Dec. 1		1	3000 00

ACCOUNT: Laura A. Eason, Drawing — ACCOUNT NO. 312

DATE	ITEM	POST. REF.	DEBIT	DATE	ITEM	POST. REF.	CREDIT
1978 Dec. 20		1	600 00				

ACCOUNT: Placement Fees — ACCOUNT NO. 411

DATE	ITEM	POST. REF.	DEBIT	DATE	ITEM	POST. REF.	CREDIT
				1978 Dec. 8		1	450 00
				18		1	500 00
				21		1	650 00
				28		2	500 00
							2100 00

ACCOUNT: Rent Expense — ACCOUNT NO. 511

DATE	ITEM	POST. REF.	DEBIT	DATE	ITEM	POST. REF.	CREDIT
1978 Dec. 4		1	350 00				

ACCOUNT: Salary Expense — ACCOUNT NO. 512

DATE	ITEM	POST. REF.	DEBIT	DATE	ITEM	POST. REF.	CREDIT
1978 Dec. 15		1	350 00				
29		2	350 00				
			700 00				

ACCOUNT: Traveling Expense — ACCOUNT NO. 513

DATE	ITEM	POST. REF.	DEBIT	DATE	ITEM	POST. REF.	CREDIT
1978 Dec. 11		1	145 30				

The Eason Employment Agency Ledger *(continued)*

ACCOUNT	Telephone Expense				ACCOUNT NO. 514	
DATE	ITEM	POST. REF.	DEBIT	DATE ITEM	POST. REF.	CREDIT
1978 Dec. 6		1	32 50			

ACCOUNT	Office Supplies Expense				ACCOUNT NO. 515	
DATE	ITEM	POST. REF.	DEBIT	DATE ITEM	POST. REF.	CREDIT
1978 Dec. 29		2	45 00			

ACCOUNT	Miscellaneous Expense				ACCOUNT NO. 516	
DATE	ITEM	POST. REF.	DEBIT	DATE ITEM	POST. REF.	CREDIT
1978 Dec. 7		1	8 00			
22		1	50 00			
			58 00			

The Eason Employment Agency Ledger *(concluded)*

It will be seen from the preceding discussion that there are four steps involved in posting — three involving information to be recorded in the ledger and one involving information to be recorded in the journal. The date, the amount, and the effect of each transaction are first recorded in the journal. The same information is later posted to the ledger. Posting does not involve an analysis of each transaction to determine its effect upon the accounts. Such an analysis is made at the time of recording the transaction in the journal, and posting is merely transcribing the same information in the ledger. In posting, care should be used to record each debit and each credit entry in the proper columns so that the entries will reflect correctly the effects of the transactions on the accounts.

When the posting is completed, the same information is provided in both the journal and the ledger as to the date, the amount, and the effect of each transaction. A cross-reference from each book to the other book is also provided. This cross-reference makes it possible to trace the entry of December 1 on the debit side of the cash account in the ledger to the journal by referring to the page indicated in the Posting Reference column. The entry of December 1 on the credit side of the account for Laura A. Eason, Capital, may also be traced to the journal by referring to the page indicated in the Posting Reference column. Each entry in the journal may be traced to the

Accounting Procedure

ledger by referring to the account numbers indicated in the Posting Reference column of the journal. By referring to pages 31 and 32, it will be seen that the account numbers were inserted in the Posting Reference column. This was done as the posting was completed.

The trial balance

The purpose of a trial balance is to prove that the totals of the debit and credit balances in the ledger are equal. In double-entry bookkeeping, equality of debit and credit balances in the ledger must be maintained. A trial balance may be taken daily, weekly, monthly, or whenever desired. Before taking a trial balance, all transactions previously completed should be journalized and the posting should be completed in order that the effect of all transactions will be reflected in the ledger accounts.

Footing Accounts. When an account form similar to the one illustrated on page 37 is used, it is necessary to foot or add the amounts recorded in each account preparatory to taking a trial balance. The footings should be recorded immediately below the last item in both the debit and credit amount columns of the account. The footings should be written in small figures close to the preceding line so that they will not interfere with the recording of an item on the next ruled line. At the same time, the balance, the difference between the footings, should be computed and recorded in small figures in the Item column of the account on the side with the larger footing. In other words, if an account has a debit balance, the balance should be written in the Item column on the debit or left side of the account. If the account has a credit balance, the balance should be written in the Item column on the credit or right side of the account. The balance or difference between the footings should be recorded in the Item column just below the line on which the last regular entry appears and in line with the footing.

Reference to the accounts kept in the ledger shown on pages 35–37 will reveal that the accounts have been footed and will show how the footings and the balances are recorded. When only one item has been posted to an account, regardless of whether it is a debit or a credit amount, no footing is necessary.

Care should be used in computing the balances of the accounts. If an error is made in adding the columns or in determining the difference between the footings, the error will be carried to the trial balance; and considerable time may be required to locate the mistake. Most accounting errors result from carelessness. For example, a careless bookkeeper may write an account balance on the wrong side of an account or may enter figures so illegibly that they may be misread later. Neatness in writing the amounts is just as important as accuracy in determining the footings and the balances.

Preparing the Trial Balance. It is important that the following procedure be followed in preparing a trial balance:

(a) Head the trial balance, being certain to show the name of the individual, firm, or organization; the title, "Trial Balance"; and the date. (The date shown is the day of the last transaction that is included in the accounts — usually the last day of a month. Actually, the trial balance might be prepared on January 3; but if the accounts reflected only transactions through December 31, this is the date that should be used.)

(b) List the account titles in order, showing each account number.

(c) Record the account balances in parallel columns, entering debit balances in the left amount column and credit balances in the right amount column.

(d) Add the columns and record the totals, ruling a single line across the amount columns above the totals and a double line below the totals in the manner shown in the illustration below.

A trial balance is usually prepared on ruled paper (though it can be written on plain paper if desired). An illustration of the trial balance, as of December 31, 1978, of the ledger of The Eason Employment Agency is shown below.

Account	Acct. No.	Dr. Balance	Cr. Balance
Cash	111	2952 79	
Office Supplies	112	216 41	
Office Equipment	121	2948 17	
Accounts Payable	211		2948 17
Laura A. Eason, Capital	311		3000 00
Laura A. Eason, Drawing	312	600 00	
Placement Fees	411		2100 00
Rent Expense	511	350 00	
Salary Expense	512	700 00	
Traveling Expense	513	145 30	
Telephone Expense	514	32 50	
Office Supplies Expense	515	45 00	
Miscellaneous Expense	516	58 00	
		8048 17	8048 17

Model Trial Balance

Even though the trial balance indicates that the ledger is in balance, there still may be errors in the ledger. For example, if a journal entry has been made in which the wrong accounts were debited or credited, or if an item has been posted to the wrong account, the ledger will still be in balance. It is important, therefore, that extreme care be used in preparing the journal entries and in posting them to the ledger accounts.

Report No. 2-2

> Refer to the study assignments and complete Report No. 2-2. To complete this assignment correctly, the principles developed in the preceding discussion must be understood. Review the text assignment if necessary. After completing the report, continue with the following textbook discussion until the next report is required.

THE FINANCIAL STATEMENTS

The transactions completed by The Eason Employment Agency during the month of December were recorded in a two-column journal (see pages 31 and 32). The debits and credits were subsequently posted to the proper accounts in a ledger (see pages 35–37). At the end of the month a trial balance was taken as a means of proving that the equality of debits and credits had been maintained throughout the journalizing and posting procedures (see page 39).

Although a trial balance may provide much of the information that the owner of a business may desire, it is primarily a device used by the bookkeeper for the purpose of proving the equality of the debit and credit account balances. Although the trial balance of The Eason Employment Agency taken as of December 31 contains a list of all of the accounts and shows the amounts of their debit and credit balances, it does not clearly present all of the information that Mrs. Eason may need or desire regarding either the results of operations during the month or the status of her business at the end of the month. To meet these needs it is customary to prepare two types of financial statements. One is known as an income statement and the other as a balance sheet or statement of financial position.

The income statement

The purpose of an income statement is to provide information regarding the results of operations *during a specified period of time*. It is an itemized statement of the changes in owner's equity resulting from the revenue and expenses of a specific period (month, quarter, year). Such changes are recorded in temporary owner's equity accounts known as revenue and expense accounts. Changes in owner's equity resulting from investments or withdrawals of assets by the owner are not included in the income statement because they involve neither revenue nor expense.

A model income statement for The Eason Employment Agency showing the results of operations for the month ended December 31, 1978, is reproduced below. The heading of an income statement consists of the following:

(a) The name of the business.
(b) The title of the statement — Income Statement.
(c) The period of time covered by the statement.

```
            The Eason Employment Agency
                  Income Statement
              For the Month Ended December 31, 1978

Revenue:
    Placement fees                                      $2,100.00
Expenses:
    Rent expense                        $350.00
    Salary expense                       700.00
    Traveling expense                    145.30
    Telephone expense                     32.50
    Office supplies expense               45.00
    Miscellaneous expense                 58.00
        Total expenses                                   1,330.80
Net income                                               $769.20
```

Model Income Statement

The body of an income statement consists of (1) an itemized list of the sources and amounts of revenue received during the period and (2) an itemized list of the various expenses incurred during the period. It is said that the "heart" of income measurement is the process of *matching* on a *periodic basis* the revenue and expenses of a business. The income statement carries out this matching concept.

The financial statements usually are prepared first on ruled paper. Such handwritten copies may then be typed so that a number of copies will be available for those who are interested in examining the statements. Since the typewritten copies are not on ruled paper, dollar signs are included in the handwritten copy so that the typist will understand just where they are to be inserted. Note that a dollar sign is placed beside the first amount in each column and the first amount below a ruling in each column. The income statement illustrated on page 41 is shown on two-column ruled paper; however, the columns do not have any debit-credit significance.

In the case of The Eason Employment Agency, the only source of revenue was placement fees that amounted to $2,100. The total expenses for the month amounted to $1,330.80. The revenue exceeded the expenses by $769.20. This represents the amount of the net income for the month. If the total expenses had exceeded the total revenue, the excess would have represented a net loss for the month.

The trial balance supplied the information needed in preparing the income statement. However, it can be seen readily that the income statement provides more information concerning the results of the month's operations than was supplied by the trial balance.

The balance sheet

The purpose of a balance sheet is to provide information regarding the status of the assets, liabilities, and owner's equity of a business enterprise *as of a specified date*. It is an itemized statement of

	The Eason Balance December
Assets	
Cash	$2,952.79
Office supplies	216.41
Office equipment	2,948.17
Total assets	$6,117.37

Model Balance Sheet — Account Form (Left Page)

the respective amounts of these basic accounting elements at the close of business on the date indicated in the heading.

A model balance sheet for The Eason Employment Agency showing the status of the business when it closed on December 31, 1978, is reproduced below and on page 42. The heading of a balance sheet contains the following:

  (a) The name of the business.
  (b) The title of the statement — Balance Sheet.
  (c) The date of the statement (as of the close of business on that day).

The body of a balance sheet consists of an itemized list of the assets, the liabilities, and the owner's equity, the latter being the difference between the total amount of the assets and the total amount of the liabilities. The balance sheet illustrated is arranged in account form. Note the similarity of this form of balance sheet to the standard account form illustrated on page 12. The assets are listed on the left side, and the liabilities and owner's equity are listed on the right side. The information provided by the balance sheet of The Eason Employment Agency may be summarized in equation form as follows:

ASSETS	=	LIABILITIES	+	OWNER'S EQUITY
$6,117.37		$2,948.17		$3,169.20

Model Balance Sheet — Account Form (Right Page)

The trial balance was the source of the information needed in listing the assets and liabilities in the balance sheet. The amount of the owner's equity may be calculated by subtracting the total liabilities from the total assets. Thus, Mrs. Eason's equity as of December 31, 1978, is as follows:

Total assets	$6,117.37
Less total liabilities	2,948.17
Owner's equity	$3,169.20

Proof of the amount of the owner's equity as calculated above may be determined by taking into consideration these factors:

(a) The amount invested in the enterprise by Mrs. Eason on December 1 as shown by her capital account.
(b) The amount of the net income of The Eason Employment Agency for December as shown by the income statement.
(c) The total amount withdrawn for personal use during December as shown by Mrs. Eason's drawing account.

The trial balance on page 39 shows that Mrs. Eason's equity in The Eason Employment Agency on December 1 amounted to $3,000. This is indicated by the credit balance of her capital account. The income statement on page 41 shows that the net income of The Eason Employment Agency for December amounted to $769.20. The trial balance shows that the amount withdrawn by Mrs. Eason for personal use during the month amounted to $600. This is indicated by the debit balance of her drawing account. On the basis of this information, Mrs. Eason's equity in The Eason Employment Agency as of December 31, 1978, is as follows:

Amount of capital December 1		$3,000.00
Net income for December	$769.20	
Less amount withdrawn for personal use during the month	600.00	169.20
Capital at close of business December 31		$3,169.20

Report No. 2-3

Refer to the study assignments and complete Report No. 2-3. This assignment provides a test of your ability to apply the principles developed in Chapters 1 and 2 of this textbook. The textbook and the study assignments go hand in hand, each serving a definite purpose in the learning process. Inability to solve correctly any problem included in the report indicates that you have failed to master the principles developed in the textbook. After completing the report, you may proceed with Chapter 3 until the next report is required.

3

Accounting for Cash

In the preceding chapters the purpose and nature of business accounting, transaction analysis, and the mechanics of double-entry bookkeeping were introduced. Explanations and illustrations were given of **(1)** *journalizing* (recording transactions in a *general journal* — a "book of original entry"), **(2)** *posting* (transcribing the entries to the accounts that, all together, comprise the *general ledger*), **(3)** taking a *trial balance*, and **(4)** using the latter to prepare an *income statement* and a *balance sheet* (two basic and important *financial statements*). This chapter is devoted to a discussion of the handling of and accounting for cash receipts and disbursements, including various considerations that are involved when cash is kept in a commercial bank. (The use of bank "checking accounts" is a near-universal business practice.)

RECORDS OF CASH RECEIPTS AND DISBURSEMENTS; PETTY CASH

The term **cash** has several different, though not totally dissimilar, meanings. In a very narrow sense, cash means currency and coin. In a broader sense, cash includes checks, drafts, and money orders. All of these, as well as currency and coin, are sometimes called "cash items." Usually any reference to the **cash receipts** of a business relates to the receipt of checks, drafts, and money orders payable to the business, as well as to the receipt of currency and coin.

Accounting for Cash

The amount of the balance of the cash account, as well as the amount shown for cash in a balance sheet, normally includes cash and cash items on hand plus the amount on deposit in a bank checking account. In some cases the balance sheet figure for cash includes amounts on deposit in more than one bank. In accounting for cash, it is rather rare to make a distinction between "cash on hand" and "cash in bank," but sometimes this is done.

The cash account

This account is debited when cash is increased and credited when cash is decreased. This means that the cash account has a debit balance unless the business has no cash. In the latter case, the account will be *in balance* — meaning that the account has no balance since the total of the debits is equal to the total of the credits.

Cash Receipts. It is vital that an accurate and timely record be kept of cash receipts. When the volume of the receipts is large in both number and amount, a practice designed to reduce the danger of mistake and embezzlement may be followed. When there are numerous receipts of currency and coin from customers paying in person for goods or services just received, it is customary to use a cash register. Such a machine usually provides a listing of amounts recorded as the money is received. A cash register may have the capability of accumulating subtotals that permit classification of amounts — sales by departments, for example. When money comes in by mail (nearly always checks), it is usual for the one remitting to enclose a presupplied form showing name, address, and the amount on the enclosed check or money order. A good example is the top part of a monthly statement the customer has received. Sometimes a written receipt must be prepared. A carbon copy of the receipt provides the initial record of the cash received.

In any case, a record of each amount received should be prepared by someone other than the bookkeeper. The money received (including checks and money orders) is placed in the custody of whoever handles bank deposits and cash on hand. The bookkeeper gets the records to use in preparing proper journal entries for cash receipts. Under such a plan the bookkeeper does not actually handle any cash; instead the bookkeeper enters cash receipts from records prepared by other persons. The procedure of having transactions involving cash handled by two or more persons reduces the danger of fraud and is one of the important features of a system of internal control.

Cash Disbursements. Disbursements may be made in cash or by bank check. When a disbursement is made in cash, a receipt or a receipted voucher should be obtained as evidence of the payment. When a disbursement is made by bank check, it is not necessary to obtain a receipt since the canceled check that is returned by the bank serves as a receipt.

Recording Cash Receipts and Disbursements. In the preceding chapter, transactions involving the receipt and disbursement of cash were recorded in a two-column general journal along with other transactions. If the number of cash transactions is relatively small, the manner of recording that was illustrated is quite satisfactory. If, however, the number of such transactions is large, the repetition entailed in making numerous debit postings or credit postings to the cash account is time-consuming, tedious, and burdensome. A discussion of a journal with special columns is deferred until Chapter 5.

Proving Cash. The process of determining whether the amount of cash (on hand and in the bank) is the amount that should be there according to the records is called **proving cash**. Cash should be proved at least once a week and, perhaps, more often if the volume of cash transactions is large. The first step is to determine from the records what amount of cash should be on hand. The cash balance should be calculated by adding the total of the receipts to the opening balance and subtracting the total of the payments. The result should be equal to the amount of cash on deposit in the bank plus the total of currency, coins, checks, and money orders on hand. Normally, an up-to-date record of cash in bank is maintained — often by using stubs in a checkbook for this purpose. There is space provided on the stubs to show deposits as well as the record of checks drawn, and the resulting balance after each deposit made or check drawn. (See check stubs illustrated on page 61.) The amount of cash and cash items on hand must be determined by actual count.

Cash Short and Over. If the effort to prove cash is not successful, it means that either **(1)** the records of receipts, disbursements, and cash on deposit contain one or more errors, **(2)** the count of cash and cash items was incorrect, or **(3)** a "shortage" or an "overage" exists. If a verification of the records and the cash count does not uncover any error, it is evident that due to some mistake in handling cash, either not enough or too much cash is on hand.

Finding that cash is slightly short or over is not unusual. If there are numerous cash transactions, it is difficult to avoid occasional errors in making change. (There is always the danger of shortages due to dishonesty, but most discrepancies are the result of mistakes.) Many businesses have a ledger account entitled *Cash Short and Over*. If, in the effort to prove cash, it is found that a shortage exists, its amount is treated as a cash disbursement transaction involving a debit to Cash Short and Over. Any overage discovered is regarded as a cash receipt transaction involving a credit to Cash Short and Over. By the end of the fiscal year it is likely that the cash short and over account will have both debits and credits. If the total of the debits exceeds the total of the credits, the balance represents an expense or loss; if the reverse is the case, the balance represents revenue.

The petty cash fund

A good policy for a business enterprise to adopt is one which requires that all cash and cash items which it receives shall be deposited in a bank. When this is done, its total cash receipts will equal its total deposits in the bank. It is also a good policy to make arrangements with the bank so that all checks and other cash items received by the business from customers or others in the usual course of business will be accepted by the bank for deposit only. This will cause the records of cash receipts and disbursements of the business to agree exactly with the bank's record of deposits and withdrawals.

When all cash and cash items received are deposited in a bank, an office fund or **petty cash fund** may be established for paying small items. ("Petty" means small or little.) Such a fund eliminates the necessity of writing checks for small amounts.

Operating a Petty Cash Fund. To establish a petty cash fund, a check should be drawn for the amount that is to be set aside in the fund. The amount may be $25, $50, $100, or any amount considered necessary. The check may be made payable to "Cash," "Petty Cash," "Office Fund," or to the person who will have custody of the fund. When the check is cashed by the bank, the money is placed in a cash drawer, a cash register, or a safe at the depositor's place of business; and a designated individual in the office is authorized to make payments from the fund. The one who is responsible for the fund should be able to account for the full amount of the fund at any time. Disbursements from the fund should not be made without obtaining a voucher or a receipt. A form of petty cash voucher is shown on page 49. Such a voucher should be used for each expenditure unless a receipt or receipted invoice is obtained.

PETTY CASH VOUCHER

No. 4   Date December 12, 1978
Paid To J. L. Porter
For Red Cross
Amount 10|00
Charge To Donations Expense
Payment Received:
J. L. Porter   Approved By Minia Sarros

Petty Cash Voucher

The check drawn to establish the petty cash fund may be recorded in the journal by debiting Petty Cash Fund and by crediting Cash. When it is necessary to replenish the fund, the petty cashier usually prepares a statement of the expenditures, properly classified. A check is then drawn for the exact amount of the total expenditures. This check is recorded in the journal by debiting the proper accounts indicated in the statement and by crediting Cash.

The petty cash fund is a revolving fund that does not change in amount unless the fund is increased or decreased. The actual amount of cash in the fund plus the total of the petty cash vouchers or receipts should always be equal to the amount originally charged to the petty cash fund.

This method of handling a petty cash fund is sometimes referred to as the **imprest method**. It is the method most commonly used.

Petty Cash Disbursements Record. When a petty cash fund is maintained, it is good practice to keep a formal record of all disbursements from the fund. Various types of records have been designed for this purpose. One of the standard forms is illustrated on pages 50 and 51. The headings of the Distribution columns may vary with each enterprise, depending upon the desired classification of the expenditures. It should be remembered that the headings represent accounts that eventually are to be charged for the expenditures. The desired headings may either be printed on the form or they may be written in. Often the account numbers instead of account titles are used in the headings to indicate the accounts to be charged.

The petty cashier should have a document for each disbursement made from the petty cash fund. Unless a receipt or receipted invoice is obtained, the petty cashier should prepare a voucher. The vouchers should be numbered consecutively.

A model petty cash disbursements record is shown below and on page 51. It is a part of the records of Minia Sarros, an attorney. Since Miss Sarros is out of the office much of the time, she provides a petty cash fund from which her secretary is authorized to make petty cash disbursements not to exceed $20 each. A narrative of the petty cash transactions completed by Dorothy Melvin, Miss Sarros' secretary, during the month of December follows:

MINIA SARROS
Narrative of Petty Cash Transactions

Dec. 1. Issued check for $100 payable to Dorothy Melvin. She cashed the check and placed the proceeds in a petty cash fund.

    This transaction was recorded in the journal by debiting Petty Cash Fund and by crediting Cash. A memorandum entry was also made in the Description column of the petty cash disbursements record reproduced below and on page 51.

During the month of December, the following disbursements were made from the petty cash fund:

6. Gave Miss Sarros $14.60 to reimburse her for the amount spent in having her automobile serviced. Petty Cash Voucher No. 1.

PAGE 1 — PETTY CASH DISBURSEMENTS

DAY	DESCRIPTION	VOU. NO.	TOTAL AMOUNT	Tel. Exp.	Auto. Exp.
	AMOUNTS FORWARDED				
1	Received in fund	✓	100.00		
6	Automobile repairs	1	14 60		14 60
7	Client luncheon	2	10 00		
12	Minia Sarros, personal use	3	20 00		
12	Red Cross	4	10 00		
15	Typewriter repairs	5	7 50		
19	Traveling expense	6	7 80		
20	Washing automobile	7	1 75		1 75
22	Postage expense	8	1 25		
22	Salvation Army	9	5 00		
26	Postage stamps	10	10 00		
27	Long distance call	11	3 20	3 20	
			91 10	3 20	16 35
			91 10	3 20	16 35
29	Balance		8 90		
29	Received in fund		91 10		
	Total		100 00		

auxiliary record

Minia Sarros' Petty Cash Disbursements Record (Left Page)

Chapter 3 Accounting for Cash

7. Gave Miss Sarros $10 to reimburse her for the amount spent in entertaining a client at lunch. Petty Cash Voucher No. 2.
12. Gave Miss Sarros $20, personal use. Petty Cash Voucher No. 3.

   This item was entered in the Amount column provided at the extreme right of the petty cash disbursements record since no special distribution column had been provided for recording amounts withdrawn by the owner for personal use.

12. Gave the Red Cross a $10 donation. Petty Cash Voucher No. 4.
15. Paid $7.50 for typewriter repairs. Petty Cash Voucher No. 5.
19. Gave Miss Sarros $7.80 to reimburse her for traveling expenses. Petty Cash Voucher No. 6.
20. Gave Miss Sarros $1.75 to reimburse her for the amount spent in having her automobile washed. Petty Cash Voucher No. 7.
22. Paid $1.25 for mailing a package. Petty Cash Voucher No. 8.
22. Donated $5 to the Salvation Army. Petty Cash Voucher No. 9.
26. Paid $10 for postage stamps. Petty Cash Voucher No. 10.
27. Gave Miss Sarros $3.20 to reimburse her for a long distance telephone call made from a booth. Petty Cash Voucher No. 11.
29. Issued check for $91.10 payable to Dorothy Melvin to replenish the petty cash fund.

   This transaction was recorded in the journal by debiting the proper accounts and by crediting Cash for the total amount of the expenditures.

FOR MONTH OF December 1978   PAGE 1

DISTRIBUTION OF CHARGES

#	Post. Exp.	Don. Exp.	Travel Exp.	Misc. Exp.	Account	Amount
1						
2						
3						
4				10 00		
5					Minia Sarros, Drawing	20 00
6		10 00				
7				7 50		
8			7 80			
9						
10	1 25					
11		5 00				
12	10 00					
13	11 25	15 00	7 80	17 50		20 00
14	11 25	15 00	7 80	17 50		20 00

Minia Sarros' Petty Cash Disbursements Record (Right Page)

Proving the Petty Cash Disbursements Record. To prove the petty cash disbursements record, it is first necessary to foot all of the amount columns. The sum of the footings of the Distribution columns should equal the footing of the Total Amount column. After proving the footings, the totals should be recorded and the record should be ruled as shown in the illustration. The illustration shows that a total of $91.10 was paid out during December. Since it was desired to replenish the petty cash fund at this time, the following statement of the disbursements for December was prepared:

STATEMENT OF PETTY CASH DISBURSEMENTS FOR DECEMBER

Telephone Expense	$ 3.20
Automobile Expense	16.35
Postage Expense	11.25
Donations Expense	15.00
Traveling Expense	7.80
Miscellaneous Expense	17.50
Minia Sarros, Drawing	20.00
Total disbursements	$91.10

The statement of petty cash disbursements provides the information for the issuance of a check for $91.10 to replenish the petty cash fund. After footing and ruling the petty cash disbursements record, the balance in the fund and the amount received to replenish the fund may be recorded in the Description column below the ruling as shown in the illustration. It is customary to carry the balance forward to the top of a new page before recording any of the transactions for the following month.

The petty cash disbursements record reproduced on pages 50 and 51 is an **auxiliary record** that supplements the regular accounting records. No posting is done from this auxiliary record. The total amount of the expenditures from the petty cash fund is entered in the journal at the time of replenishing the fund by debiting the proper accounts and by crediting Cash. A **compound entry** (one that affects more than two accounts, though the sum of the debits is equal to the sum of the credits) is usually required. The statement of petty cash disbursements provides the information needed in recording the check issued to Dorothy Melvin to replenish the petty cash fund. The entry is posted from the journal.

The method of recording the check issued by Minia Sarros on December 29 to replenish the fund is illustrated at the top of the following page.

Chapter 3 Accounting for Cash 53

	DATE	DESCRIPTION	POST. REF.	DEBIT	CREDIT	
1	1978 Dec. 29	Telephone Expense		3 20		1
2		Automobile Expense		16 35		2
3		Postage Expense		11 25		3
4		Donations Expense		15 00		4
5		Traveling Expense		7 80		5
6		Miscellaneous Expense		17 50		6
7		Minia Sarros, Drawing		20 00		7
8		Cash			91 10	8
9		Reimbursement of				9
10		petty cash fund.				10

JOURNAL   PAGE 15

Minia Sarros' Journal

Report No. 3-1

Refer to the study assignments and complete Report No. 3-1. After completing the report, proceed with the textbook discussion until the next report is required.

BANKING PROCEDURE

A bank is a financial institution that receives deposits, lends money, makes collections, and renders other services, such as providing vaults for the safekeeping of valuables and handling trust funds for its customers. Most banks offer facilities for both checking accounts and savings accounts.

Checking account

It is estimated that 90–95 percent of all money payments in the United States are made by checks. A **check**, a piece of commercial paper, is drawn on a bank and is payable on demand. It involves three original parties: **(1)** the **drawer**, the depositor who orders the bank to pay; **(2)** the **drawee**, the bank in which the drawer has money on deposit in a so-called "commercial" account; and **(3)** the **payee**, the person directed to receive the money. The drawer and payee may be the same person, though the payee named in such case usually is "Cash."

A check is **negotiable** (meaning that the right to receive the money can be transferred to someone else) because it complies with the following requirements: It is in writing, is signed by the drawer, contains an unconditional order to pay a specified amount of money, is payable on demand, and is payable to order or bearer. The payee transfers the right to receive the money by *indorsing* the check. If the payee simply signs the back of the check (customarily near the left end), it is called a **blank indorsement**. (This makes the check payable to bearer.) If, as is very common, there are added such words as "For deposit," "Pay to any bank or banker," or "Pay to J. Doe only," it is called a **restrictive indorsement**. A widely used business practice when indorsing checks for deposit is to use a rubber stamp similar to that illustrated on page 56.

Important factors in connection with a checking account are **(1)** opening the account, **(2)** making deposits, **(3)** making withdrawals, and **(4)** reconciling the bank statement.

Opening a Checking Account. To open a checking account with a bank, it is necessary to obtain the approval of an official of the bank and to make an initial deposit. Money, checks, bank drafts, money orders, and other cash items usually will be accepted for deposit, subject to their verification as to amount and validity.

Signature Card. Banks require a new depositor to sign a card or form as an aid in verifying the depositor's signature on checks that may be issued, on cash items that may be indorsed for deposit, and on other business papers that may be presented to the bank. The form a depositor signs to give the bank a signature sample is called a **signature card**. To aid in identification, the depositor's social security number (if any) may also be shown. If desired, others may be authorized to sign the depositor's checks and other business forms. Each person who is so authorized is required to sign his or her own signature on the depositor's signature card. A signature card is one of the safeguards that a bank uses to protect its own interests as well as the interests of its depositors.

Deposit Ticket. Banks provide depositors with a printed form to use for a detailed listing of items being deposited. This form is called a **deposit ticket**. A model filled-in deposit ticket is reproduced on page 55. This illustration is typical of the type of ticket that most banks provide. Note that the number of the depositor's account is preprinted at the bottom in so-called "MICR" numbers (meaning *magnetic ink character recognition*) that can be "read" by a type of

Chapter 3   Accounting for Cash   **55**

	DOLLARS	CENTS
CURRENCY	514	00
COIN	23	92
CHECKS 13-42	181	50
LIST SINGLY 13-22	700	00
13-3	350	00
TOTAL FROM OTHER SIDE		
TOTAL	1,769	42

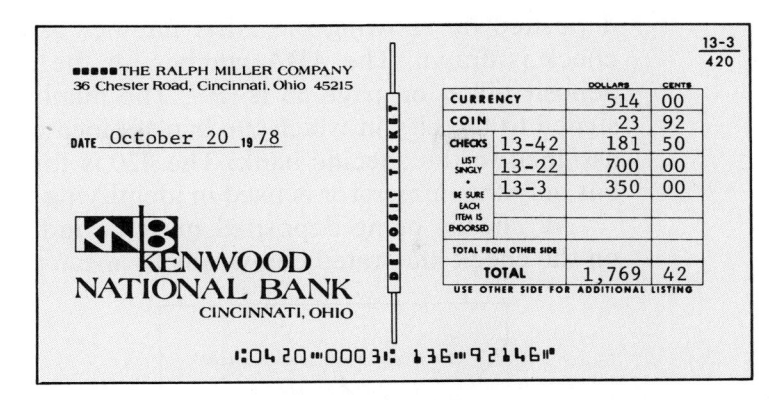

Deposit Ticket

electronic equipment used by banks. This series of digits (which also is preprinted at the bottom of all of the depositor's checks) is actually a code used in sorting and routing deposit slips and checks. In the first set of digits, 0420-0003, the "4" indicates that the bank is in the Fourth Federal Reserve District. The "20" following is what is called a "routing" number. The "3" is a number assigned to the Kenwood National Bank. This numbering method was established by the American Bankers Association (ABA). The second set of digits, 136-92146, is the number assigned by the Kenwood National Bank to the Miller Company's account.

    It is very common practice to prepare deposit tickets in duplicate so that one copy, when receipted by the bank teller, may be retained by the depositor. In preparing a deposit ticket, the date should be written in the space provided. Currency (paper money) should be arranged in the order of the denominations, the smaller denominations being placed on top. The bills should all be faced up and top up. Coins (pennies, nickels, dimes, quarters, and half dollars) that are to be deposited in considerable quantities should be wrapped in coin wrappers, which the bank will provide. The name and account number of the depositor should be written on the outside of each coin wrapper as a means of identification in the event that a mistake has been made in counting the coins. The amounts of cash represented by currency and by coins should be entered in the amount column of the deposit ticket on the lines provided for these items.

    Each additional item to be deposited should be listed on a separate line of the deposit ticket as shown in the illustration above. In listing checks on the deposit ticket, the instructions of the bank should be observed in describing the checks for identification purposes. Banks usually prefer that depositors identify checks being deposited by showing the ABA number of the bank on which the check is drawn. The ABA number for the first check listed on the deposit ticket on page 55 is $\frac{13-42}{420}$. The number 13 is the number assigned to the city in which the bank is located, and the number 42 is assigned to the specific bank. The 420 is the check routing symbol, but only the numerator is used in identifying the deposit.

All checks being deposited must be indorsed. The indorsement on the check illustrated below was by means of a rubber stamp.

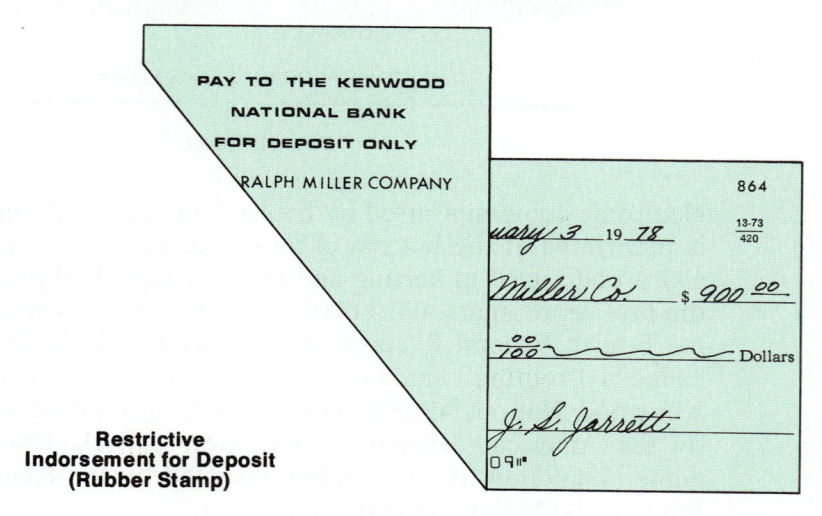

Restrictive Indorsement for Deposit (Rubber Stamp)

The total of the cash and other items deposited should be entered on the deposit tickets. The deposit tickets, prepared in duplicate, together with the cash and the other items to be deposited, should be delivered to the receiving teller of the bank. The teller receipts the duplicate copy and returns it to the depositor.

Instead of preparing deposit slips in duplicate, another practice — very widely followed at one time, and still often used — is for the bank to provide the depositor with a **passbook** in which the bank teller enters the date and amount of each deposit and initials this information. This gives the depositor a receipt for the deposit; a duplicate deposit slip is not needed. Of course, the passbook must be brought in (or sent in) to the bank with each deposit.

Instead of providing the depositor with either duplicate deposit tickets or a passbook, the bank may provide a machine-printed receipt for each deposit. Some banks use **automatic teller machines** in preparing the receipts. The use of such machines saves the time required to make manual entries in a passbook and eliminates the need for making duplicate copies of deposit tickets. Such machines are not only timesaving, but they also promote accuracy in the handling of deposits. The deposits handled by each teller during the day may be accumulated so that at the end of the day the total amount of the deposits received by a teller is automatically recorded by the machine. This amount may be proved by counting the cash and cash items accepted by a teller for deposit during the day.

Dishonored Checks. A check that a bank refuses to pay is described as a **dishonored check**. A depositor guarantees all items that are deposited and is liable to the bank for the amount involved if, for any reason, any item is not honored when presented for payment. When a check or other cash item is deposited with a bank and is not honored upon presentation to the bank upon which it is drawn, the depositor's bank may charge the amount of the dishonored item to the depositor's account or may present it to the depositor for reimbursement. It is not uncommon for checks that have been deposited to be returned to the depositor for various reasons, as indicated on the debit advice below. The most common reason for checks being returned unpaid is "not sufficient funds" (NSF).

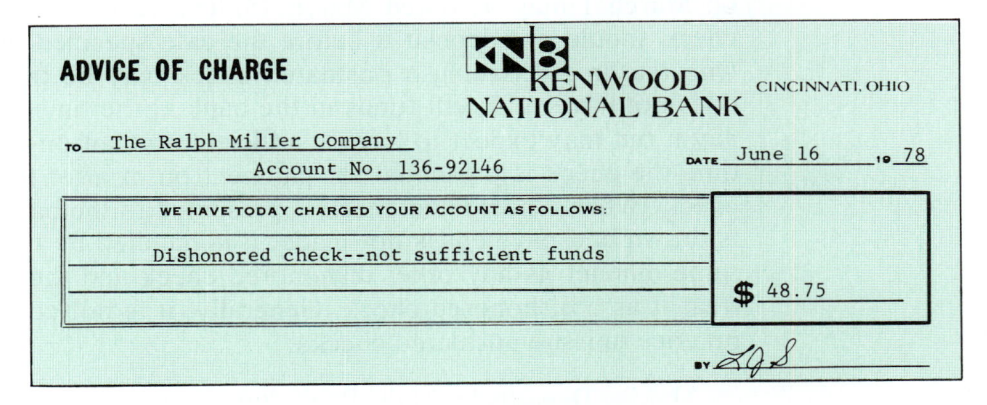

ADVICE OF CHARGE	KNB KENWOOD NATIONAL BANK	CINCINNATI, OHIO
TO The Ralph Miller Company		
Account No. 136-92146	DATE June 16, 19 78	
WE HAVE TODAY CHARGED YOUR ACCOUNT AS FOLLOWS:		
Dishonored check--not sufficient funds		
	$ 48.75	
	BY LJS	

Debit Advice

Under the laws of most states, it is illegal for anyone to issue a check on a bank without having sufficient funds on deposit with that bank to cover the check when it is presented for payment. This action is called an **overdraft**. When a dishonored check is charged to the depositor's account, the depositor should deduct the amount from the balance shown on the checkbook stub.

Most checks that turn out to be "bad" or "rubber" (meaning that they "bounce") are not the result of any dishonest intent on the part of the drawers of such checks. Either the depositor thought that there was enough money in the account when the check was written or expected to get a deposit to the bank in time to "cover" the check before it reached the bank for payment. It is commonly considered to be something of a disgrace to the drawer of a check if the bank will not honor (pay) it. In recent years, many banks have made available (for a fee) plans that guarantee that all checks, within prescribed limits as to amount, will be honored even if the depositor's balance is too low. This amounts to a prearrangement with the bank to make a loan to the depositor. These plans have been given names such as "Ready Reserve Account," "Instant Cash," and others. Sometimes arrangements of this sort are parts of larger plans that involve such things as picture checks, no minimum balance, bank statements that list checks paid in numerical order, "check guarantee cards," travelers checks without fee, safe-deposit boxes, and even bank credit cards. The bank may charge a monthly fee for any or all of these services. Such comprehensive plans are not widely subscribed to by businesses (in contrast to individuals.)

Postdated Checks. Checks dated subsequent to the date of issue are known as **postdated checks**. For example, a check that is issued on March 1 may be dated March 15. The recipient of a postdated check should not deposit it before the date specified on the check. One reason for issuing a postdated check may be that the drawer does not have sufficient funds in the bank at the time of issuance to pay it but may expect to have a sufficient amount on deposit by the time the check is presented for payment on or after the date of the check. When a postdated check is presented to the bank on which it is drawn and payment is not made, it is handled by the bank in the same manner as any other dishonored check and the payee should treat it as a dishonored check. Generally, it is not considered good practice to issue postdated checks.

Making Deposits by Mail. Bank deposits may be made either over the counter or by mail. The over-the counter method of making deposits is generally used. It may not always be convenient, however, for a depositor to make deposits over the counter, especially if the depositor lives at a great distance from the bank. In such a case it may be more convenient to make deposits by mail. When a depositor makes deposits by mail, the bank may provide a special deposit ticket and a form to be self addressed which is subsequently returned to the depositor with a receipt for the deposit.

Night Deposits. Some banks provide night deposit service. While all banks do not handle this in the same way, a common practice is for the bank to have a night safe with an opening on the exterior of the bank building. After the depositor signs a night depository contract, the bank gives the depositor a key to the outside door of the safe, a bag that has an identifying number and in which valuables may be placed, and two keys to the bag itself. Once the depositor places the bag in the night deposit safe, the bag cannot be retrieved because it moves to a vault in the bank that is accessible to bank employees only. Since only the depositor is provided with keys to the bag, the depositor or an authorized representative must go to the bank to unlock the bag. At that time the depositor may or may not deposit in the account in the bank the funds that were previously placed in the night deposit safe.

Night deposit banking service is especially valuable to those individuals and concerns that do not have safe facilities in their own places of business and that accumulate cash and other cash items which they cannot take to the bank during regular banking hours.

Making Withdrawals. The amount deposited in a bank checking account may be withdrawn either by the depositor or by any other person who has been properly authorized to make withdrawals from the depositor's account. Such withdrawals are accomplished by the use of checks signed by the depositor or by others having the authority to sign checks drawn on the account.

Checkbook. Checks used by businesses commonly come bound in the form of a book with two or three blank checks to a page, perforated so that they may be removed singly. To the left of each one is a **check stub** containing space to record all relevant information about the check (check number, date, payee, amount, the purpose of the check and often the account to be charged, along with the bank balance before the check was issued, current deposits, if any, and the resulting balance after the check). The depositor's name and address normally are printed on each check, and the MICR numbers are shown along the bottom edge. Often the checks are prenumbered — commonly in the upper right corner.

Sometimes checks come bound in the form of a pad. There may be a blank page after each check for use in making a carbon copy of the check. (The carbon copy is not a check; it is merely a copy of what was typed or written on the check. However, the essential information is supplied to be entered in the formal records.) Sometimes the depositor is provided with a checkbook that, instead of stubs, is accompanied by a small register in which the relevant information is noted. Checks may be provided by the bank (often for a charge) or purchased directly from firms that specialize in the manufacture of check forms.

Writing a Check. If the check has a stub, the latter should be filled in at the time the check is written. If, instead of a stub, a checkbook register is used, an entry for the check should be made therein. This plan insures that the drawer will retain a record of each check issued.

A depositor may personally obtain cash at the time of making a deposit by indicating on the deposit slip the portion of the total of the items listed to be returned, with the remainder to constitute the deposit. Alternatively, a depositor may draw a check payable to himself or herself or, usually, just to "Cash."

The purpose for which a check is drawn is often noted in some appropriate area of the check itself. Indicating the purpose on the check provides information for the benefit of the payee and provides a specific receipt for the drawer.

The amount of the check is stated on the check in both figures and words. If the amount shown on the check in figures does not agree with the amount shown in words, the bank usually will contact the drawer for the correct amount or will return the check unpaid.

Care must be used in writing the amount on the check in order to avoid any possibility that the payee or a subsequent holder may change the amount. If the instructions given below are followed in the preparation of a check, it will be difficult to change the amount.

(a) The amount shown in figures should be written so that there is no space between the dollar sign and the first digit of the amount.

(b) The amount stated in words should be written beginning at the extreme left on the line provided for this information. The cents should be written in the form of a common fraction; if the check is for an even number of dollars, use two ciphers or the word "no" as the numerator of the fraction. If a vacant space remains, a line should be drawn from the amount stated in words to the word "Dollars" on the same line with it, as illustrated on the next page.

A machine frequently used to write the amount of a check in figures and in words is known as a **checkwriter**. The use of a checkwriter is desirable because it practically eliminates the possibility of a change in the amount of a check.

Each check issued by a depositor will be returned by the bank on which it is drawn after the check has been paid. Canceled checks are returned to the depositor with the bank statement, which is usually rendered each month. Canceled checks will have been indorsed by the payee and any subsequent holders. They constitute receipts that the depositor should retain for future reference. They may be attached to the stubs from which they were removed originally or they may be filed.

Checks and Stubs

Electronic Processing of Checks. It is now nearly universal practice to use checks that can be processed by MICR (magnetic ink character recognition) equipment. The unique characteristic of such checks is that there is imprinted in magnetic ink along the lower margin of the check a series of numbers or digits in the form of a code that indicates **(1)** the identity of the Federal Reserve district in which the bank is located and a routing number, **(2)** the identity of the bank, and **(3)** the account number assigned to the depositor. Sometimes the check number is also shown. In processing checks with electronic equipment, the first bank that handles a check will imprint its amount in magnetic ink characters to further aid in the processing of the check. The amount will be printed directly below the signature line in the lower right-hand corner of the check.

Checks imprinted with the bank's number and the depositor's number can be fed into MICR machines which will "read" the numbers and cause the checks to be sorted in the desired fashion. If the amounts of the checks are printed thereon in magnetic ink, such amounts can be totaled, and each check can be posted electronically to the customer's account. This process can be carried on at extremely high speed with almost no danger of error.

The two checks reproduced on the preceding page illustrate the appearance of the magnetic ink characters that have been printed at the bottom, as well as check stubs properly completed. (For a further discussion of electronic processing of checks, see Appendix, pages A-12 — A-14.)

Recording Bank Transactions. A depositor should keep a record of the transactions that are completed with the bank. The usual plan is to keep this record on the checkbook stubs as shown in the illustration on page 61. It will be noted that the record consists of detailed information concerning each check written and an amount column in which should be recorded (1) the balance brought forward or carried down, (2) the amount of deposits to be added, and (3) the amount of checks to be subtracted. The purpose is to keep a detailed record of deposits made and checks issued and to indicate the balance in the checking account after each check is drawn.

As the amount of each check is recorded in the journal, a check mark may be placed immediately after the account title written on the stub to indicate that it has been recorded. When the canceled check is subsequently received from the bank, the amount shown on the stub may be checked to indicate that the canceled check has been received.

Records Kept by a Bank. The usual transactions completed by a bank with a depositor are:

(a) Accepting deposits made by the depositor.
(b) Paying checks issued by the depositor.
(c) Lending money to the depositor.
(d) Collecting the amounts of various kinds of commercial paper, such as matured bonds, for the account of the depositor.

The bank keeps an account for each depositor. Each transaction affecting a depositor's account is recorded by debiting or crediting the depositor's account, depending upon the effect of the transaction. When a bank accepts a deposit, the account of the depositor is credited for the amount of the deposit. The deposit increases the bank's liability to the depositor.

When the bank pays a check that has been drawn on the bank, it debits the account of the depositor for the amount of the check. If the bank makes a collection for a depositor, the net amount of the collection is credited to the account. At the same time the bank notifies the depositor on a form similar to the one shown below that the collection has been made.

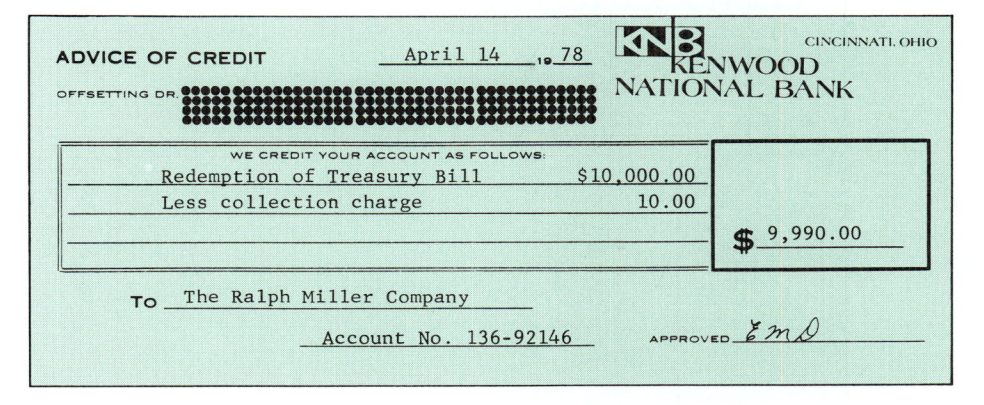

```
ADVICE OF CREDIT          April 14    19 78         KNB      CINCINNATI, OHIO
OFFSETTING DR.                                     KENWOOD
                                                   NATIONAL BANK

            WE CREDIT YOUR ACCOUNT AS FOLLOWS:
            Redemption of Treasury Bill      $10,000.00
            Less collection charge                10.00
                                                              $  9,990.00

        TO   The Ralph Miller Company
                 Account No. 136-92146         APPROVED  EmD
```

Credit Advice

Bank Statement. Once each month a bank renders a statement of account to each depositor. An illustration of a widely used form of bank statement is shown on the next page. It may be mentioned that some banks provide statements that also present information about savings accounts, loan accounts, etc., for those depositors that have such additional accounts. Very commonly, however, a separate statement is furnished for each type of account.

The statement illustrated is for a checking account. It is a report showing **(1)** the balance on deposit at the beginning of the period, **(2)** the amounts of deposits made during the period, **(3)** the amounts of checks honored during the period, **(4)** other items charged to the depositor's account during the period, and **(5)** the balance on deposit at the end of the period. With the bank statement, the depositor also receives all checks paid by the bank during the period, together with any other vouchers representing items charged to the account.

Reconciling the Bank Statement. When a bank statement is received, the depositor should check it immediately with the bank balance record kept on the check stubs. This procedure is known as **reconciling the bank statement**, sometimes called "balancing the statement." The balance shown on the bank statement may not be the same as the amount shown on the check stubs for one or more of the reasons given on pages 64 and 65.

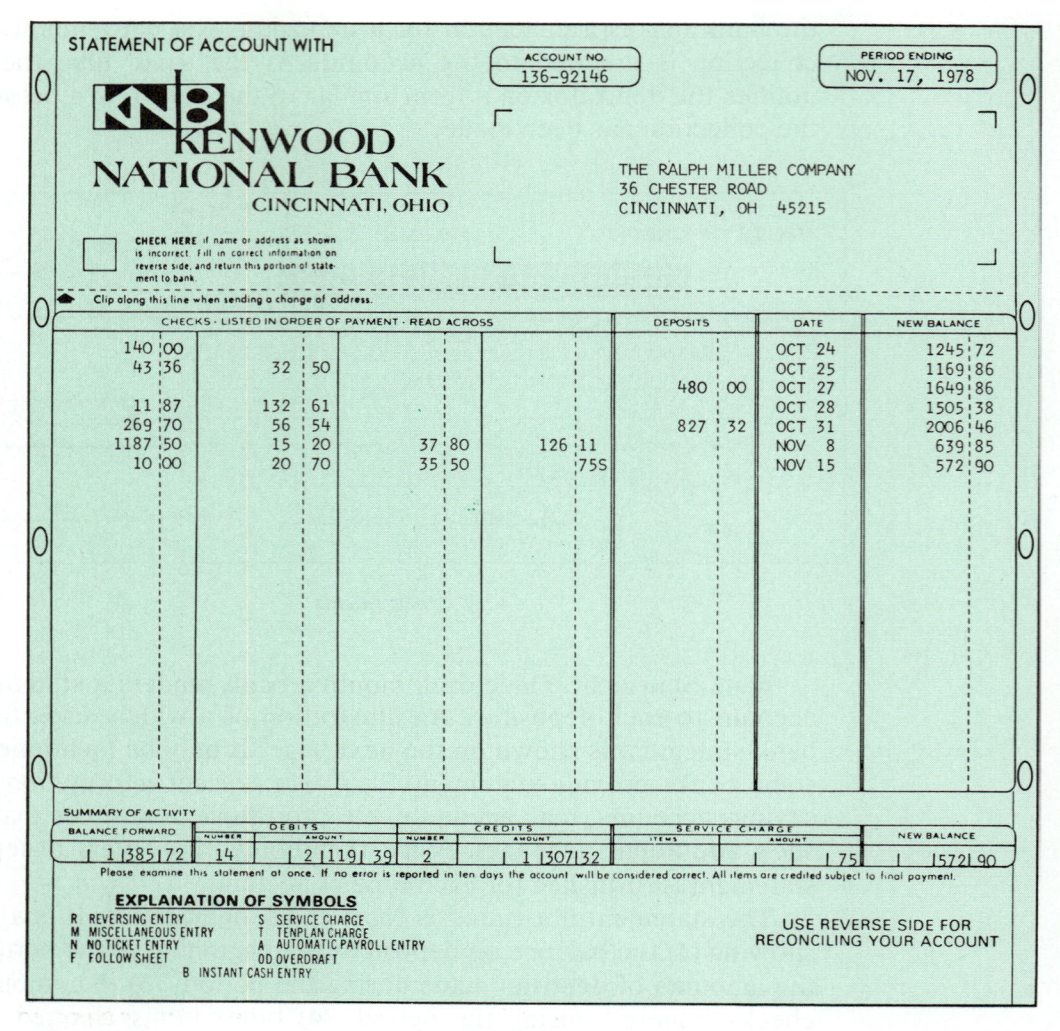

Bank Statement

STATEMENT OF ACCOUNT WITH

KNB KENWOOD NATIONAL BANK
CINCINNATI, OHIO

ACCOUNT NO. 136-92146
PERIOD ENDING NOV. 17, 1978

THE RALPH MILLER COMPANY
36 CHESTER ROAD
CINCINNATI, OH 45215

CHECK HERE if name or address as shown is incorrect. Fill in correct information on reverse side, and return this portion of statement to bank.

Clip along this line when sending a change of address.

CHECKS - LISTED IN ORDER OF PAYMENT - READ ACROSS					DEPOSITS	DATE	NEW BALANCE
140.00						OCT 24	1245.72
43.36	32.50					OCT 25	1169.86
					480.00	OCT 27	1649.86
11.87	132.61					OCT 28	1505.38
269.70	56.54				827.32	OCT 31	2006.46
1187.50	15.20		37.80	126.11		NOV 8	639.85
10.00	20.70		35.50	.75S		NOV 15	572.90

SUMMARY OF ACTIVITY

BALANCE FORWARD	DEBITS NUMBER	AMOUNT	CREDITS NUMBER	AMOUNT	SERVICE CHARGE ITEMS	AMOUNT	NEW BALANCE
1385.72	14	2119.39	2	1307.32	1	.75	1572.90

Please examine this statement at once. If no error is reported in ten days the account will be considered correct. All items are credited subject to final payment.

EXPLANATION OF SYMBOLS
R REVERSING ENTRY   S SERVICE CHARGE
M MISCELLANEOUS ENTRY   T TENPLAN CHARGE
N NO TICKET ENTRY   A AUTOMATIC PAYROLL ENTRY
F FOLLOW SHEET   OD OVERDRAFT
B INSTANT CASH ENTRY

USE REVERSE SIDE FOR RECONCILING YOUR ACCOUNT

Bank Statement

(a) Some of the checks issued during the period may not have been presented to the bank for payment before the statement was prepared. These are known as **outstanding checks**.

(b) Deposits made by mail may have been in transit, or a deposit placed in the night depository may not have been recorded by the bank until the day following the date of the statement.

(c) The bank may have credited the depositor's account for an amount collected, but the depositor may not as yet have noted it on the check stubs — possibly the credit advice had not yet been received.

(d) Service charges or other charges may appear on the bank statement that the depositor has not recorded on the check stubs.

(e) The depositor may have erred in keeping the bank record.
(f) The bank may have erred in keeping its account with the depositor.

If a depositor is unable to reconcile the bank statement, a report on the matter should be made to the bank immediately.

A suggested procedure in reconciling the bank statement is enumerated below:

(a) The amount of each deposit recorded on the bank statement should be checked with the amount recorded on the check stubs.
(b) The amount of each canceled check should be compared both with the amount recorded on the bank statement and with the amount recorded on the depositor's check stubs. When making this comparison, it is a good plan to place a check mark by the amount recorded on each check stub to indicate that the canceled check has been returned by the bank and its amount verified.
(c) The amounts of any items listed on a bank statement that represent credits or charges to a depositor's account which have not been entered on the check stubs should be added to or deducted from the balance on the check stubs and should be recorded in the journal that is being used to record cash disbursements.
(d) A list of the outstanding checks should be prepared. The information needed for this list may be obtained by examining the check stubs and noting the amounts that have not been check marked.

After completing the foregoing steps, the balance shown on the check stubs should equal the balance shown in the bank statement less the total amount of the checks outstanding.

At the top of the next page is a reconciliation of the bank balance shown in the statement reproduced on page 64. In making this reconciliation it was assumed that the depositor's check stub indicated a balance of $757.22 on November 17, that Checks Nos. 416, 419, and 421 had not been presented for payment and thus were not returned with the bank statement, and that a deposit of $456.13 placed in the night depository on November 17 is not shown on the statement. In matching the canceled checks that were returned with the bank statement against the check stubs, an error on the stub for Check No. 394 was discovered. That check was for $11.87. On its stub, the amount was shown as $11.78. This is called a **transposition error**. The "8" and the "7" were transposed (order reversed). On Stub No. 394 and the others that followed, the bank balance shown was 9 cents too large. The correct amount, $11.87, should be shown on Stub No. 394, and the bank balance shown on the stub of the last check used should be reduced $.09. If Check No. 394 was in payment of, say, a telephone bill, an entry should be made debiting Telephone Expense and crediting Cash.

THE RALPH MILLER COMPANY
Reconciliation of Bank Statement
November 17, 1978

Balance, November 17, per bank statement........		$ 572.90
Add: Deposit, November 17		456.13
		$1,029.03
Less checks outstanding, November 17:		
No. 416	$ 85.00	
No. 419	17.40	
No. 421	170.25	272.65
Adjusted bank balance, November 17		$ 756.38
Check stub balance, November 17		$ 757.22
Less: Bank service charge	$ .75	
Error on stub for Check No. 394	.09	.84
Adjusted check stub balance, November 17........		$ 756.38

Service Charges. A service charge may be made by a bank for the handling of checks and other items. The basis and the amount of such charges vary with different banks in different localities. Sometimes a rather elaborate *deposit activity analysis* is involved.

When a bank statement indicates that a service charge has been made, the depositor should record the amount of the service charge by debiting an expense account, such as Miscellaneous Expense, and by crediting Cash. The depositor should also deduct the amount of such charges from the check stub balance.

Keeping a Ledger Account with the Bank. As explained previously, a memorandum account with the bank may be kept on the depositor's checkbook stub. The depositor may also keep a ledger account with the bank if desired. The title of such an account usually is the name of the bank. Sometimes more than one account is kept with a bank, in which case each account should be correctly labeled. Such terms as "commercial," "executive," and "payroll" are used to identify the accounts.

The bank account should be debited for the amount of each deposit and should be credited for the amount of each check written. The account should also be credited for any other items that may be charged to the account by the bank, including service charges.

When both a cash account and a bank account are kept in the ledger, the procedure at the top of the next page should be observed in recording transactions affecting these accounts.

Under this method of accounting for cash and banking transactions, the cash account will be in balance when all cash on hand has been deposited in the bank. To prove the balance of the cash account at any time, it is necessary only to count the cash and cash items on hand and to compare the total with the cash account bal-

Chapter 3   Accounting for Cash   67

CASH		KENWOOD NATIONAL BANK	
Debit	Credit	Debit	Credit
For all receipts of cash and cash items.	(a) For all payments in cash. (b) For all bank deposits.	(a) For all deposits. (b) For collection of amounts for the depositor.	(a) For all checks written. (b) For all service charges. (c) For all other charges, such as for dishonored checks.

ance. To prove the bank account balance, it will be necessary to reconcile the bank balance in the same manner in which it is reconciled when only a memorandum record of bank transactions is kept on the check stubs.

The cash account can be dispensed with when a bank account is kept in the ledger and all cash receipts are deposited in the bank. When this is done, all disbursements (except small expenditures made from a petty cash fund) are made by check. Daily, or at frequent intervals, the receipts are deposited in the bank. If all cash received during the month has been deposited before the books are closed at the end of the month, the total amount of the bank deposits will equal the total cash receipts for the month. If all disbursements during the month are made by check, the total amount of checks issued will be the total disbursements for the month.

Savings account

When a savings account is opened in a bank, a signature card must be signed by the depositor. By signing the signature card, the depositor agrees to abide by the rules and regulations of the bank. These rules and regulations vary with different banks and may be altered from time to time. Deposits to or withdrawals from a savings account may be made at the bank or by mail by the depositor or an authorized agent. Interest is paid by the bank on a savings account. Interest may be computed on a daily, monthly, or quarterly basis. There are special instances in which banks may pay interest on the balances in checking accounts. However, depositors use checking accounts primarily as a convenient means of making payments, while savings accounts are used primarily as a means of accumulating funds with interest.

Savings accounts are not too frequently used by businesses. If the assets of a business include money in a bank savings account, there should be a separate account in the ledger with a title and a number that indicate the nature of the deposit. Sometimes the name of the bank is in the title, as, for example, "Kenwood National

Bank — Savings Account." When the bank credits interest to the account, the depositor should record the interest in the accounts by a debit to the savings account and by a credit to Interest Earned. The interest is revenue whether withdrawn or not (and is taxed to the depositor when earned).

Report No. 3-2

> Refer to the study assignments and complete Report No. 3-2. This assignment provides a test of your ability to apply the principles developed in the first three chapters of the textbook. After completing the report, you may proceed with the textbook discussion in Chapter 4 until the next report is required.

4

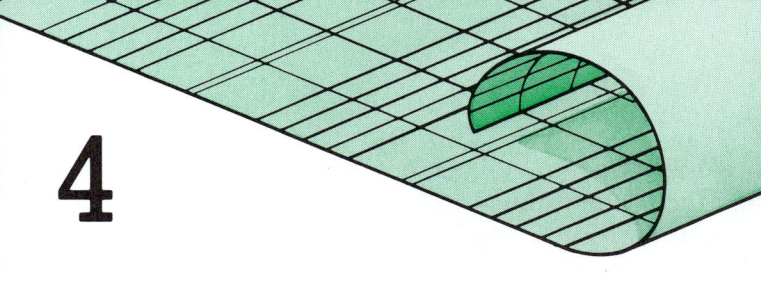

Payroll Accounting

Employers need to maintain detailed and accurate payroll accounting records. Accurate accounting for employees' earnings preserves the legal and moral right of employees to be paid according to their employment contracts and the laws governing such contracts.

Payroll accounting records also provide information useful in the analysis and classification of labor costs. At the same time, payroll accounting information is invaluable in contract discussions with labor unions, in the settlement of company-union grievances, and in other forms of collective bargaining. Clearly, there is virtually no margin for error in payroll accounting.

EARNINGS AND DEDUCTIONS

The first step in determining the amount to be paid to an employee is to calculate the amount of the employee's total or gross earnings for the pay period. The second step is to determine the amounts of any deductions that are required either by law or by agreement. Depending upon a variety of circumstances, either or both of these steps may be relatively simple or quite complicated. An examination of the factors that are involved follows.

Employer-employee relationships

Not every individual who performs services for a business is considered to be an employee. A public accountant, lawyer, or management consultant who sells services to a business does not become its employee. Neither does a plumber nor an electrician who is hired to make specific repairs or installations on business property.

These people are told what to do but not how to do it, and the compensation that they receive for their services is called a **fee**. Any person who agrees to perform a service for a fee and is not subject to the control of those served is called an **independent contractor**.

In contrast, an employee is one who is under the control and direction of the employer with regard to the performance of services. The difference between an independent contractor and an employee is an important legal distinction. The nature and extent of the responsibilities of a contractor and a client to each other and to third parties are quite different from the mutual obligations of an employer and an employee.

Types of compensation

Compensation for managerial or administrative services usually is called **salary**. A salary normally is expressed in terms of a month or a year. Compensation either for skilled or for unskilled labor usually is referred to as **wages**. Wages ordinarily are expressed in terms of hours, weeks, or pieces of accomplishment. The terms salaries and wages often are used interchangeably in practice.

Supplements to basic salaries or wages of employees include bonuses, commissions, cost-of-living adjustments, pensions, and profit-sharing plans. Compensation also may take the form of goods, lodging, meals, or other property, and as such is measured by the fair market value of the property or service given in payment for the employee's efforts.

Determination of total earnings

An employee's earnings commonly are based on the time worked during the payroll period. Sometimes earnings are based on units of output or of sales during the period. Compensation based on time requires a record of the time worked by each employee. Where there are only a few employees, a record of times worked kept in a memorandum book may suffice. Where there are many employees, time clocks commonly are used to record time spent on the job each day. With time clocks, a clock card is provided for each employee and the clock is used to record arrival and departure times. Alternatively, plastic cards or badges with holes punched in them for basic employee data are now being used in computer-based timekeeping systems. Whatever method is used, the total time worked during the payroll period must be computed.

Employees often are entitled to compensation at more than their regular rate of pay for work during certain hours or on certain days. If the employer is engaged in interstate commerce, the Fair Labor

Standards Act (commonly known as the Federal Wage and Hour Law) provides that all employees covered by the Act must be paid one and one-half times the regular rate for all hours worked over 40 per week. Labor-management agreements often require extra pay for certain hours or days. In such cases, hours worked in excess of eight per day or work on Sundays and specified holidays may be paid for at higher rates.

To illustrate, assume that the company which employs Ronald Slone pays time and a half for all hours worked in excess of 40 per week and double time for work on Sunday. Slone's regular rate is $6 per hour; and during the week ended April 16, he worked nine hours each day Monday through Friday, six hours on Saturday, and four on Sunday. Slone's total earnings for the week ended April 16 would be computed as follows:

40 hours @ $6	$240
11 hours @ $9	99
(Slone worked 9 hours each day Monday through Friday and 6 hours on Saturday — a total of 51 hours. Forty hours would be paid for at the regular rate and 11 hours at time and a half.)	
4 hours (on Sunday) @ $12	48
Total earnings for the week	$387

An employee who is paid a regular salary may be entitled to premium pay for any overtime. If this is the case, it is necessary to compute the regular hourly rate of pay before computing the overtime rate. To illustrate, assume that Bessie Smith receives a regular salary of $1,000 a month. Ms. Smith is entitled to overtime pay at the rate of one and one-half times her regular hourly rate for any time worked in excess of 40 hours per week. Her overtime pay may be computed as follows:

$1,000 × 12 months = $12,000 annual pay
$12,000 ÷ 52 weeks = $230.7692 per week
$230.7692 ÷ 40 hours = $5.7692 per regular hour
$5.7692 × 1½ = $8.6538 per overtime hour

NOTE: In computing all overtime rates, hold four places to the right of the decimal point.

Deductions from total earnings

With few exceptions, employers are required to withhold portions of each employee's total earnings both for federal income tax and for social security taxes. Certain states and cities also require income or earnings tax withholding on the part of employers. Besides these deductions, an agreement between the employer and the employee may call for amounts to be withheld for any one or more of the reasons given at the top of page 72.

(a) To purchase United States savings bonds for the employee.
(b) To pay a life, accident, or health insurance premium for the employee.
(c) To pay the employee's union dues.
(d) To add to a pension fund or profit-sharing fund.
(e) To pay to some charitable organization.
(f) To repay a loan from the company or from the company credit union.

Social security and tax account number

Each employee is required to have a social security account and tax account number for payroll accounting purposes. A completed Form SS-5, the official form to be used in applying for an account number, follows:

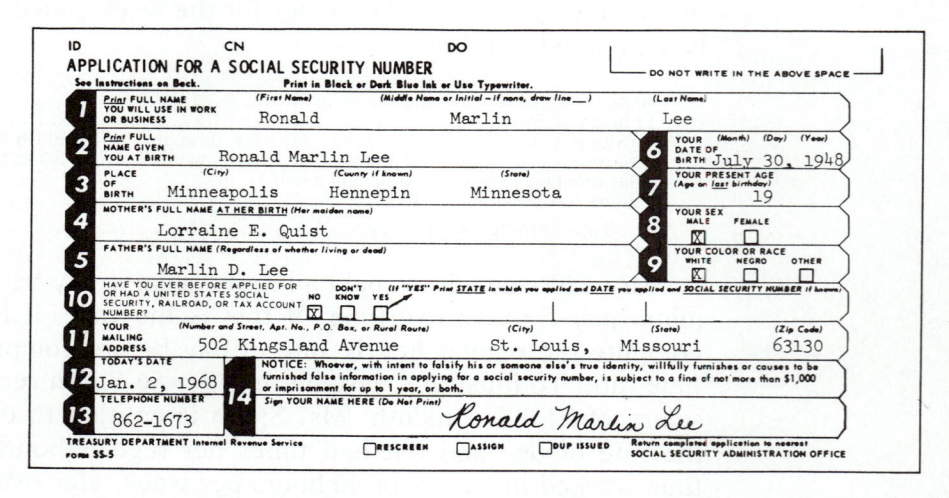

Completed Application for Social Security and Tax Account Number (Form SS-5)

Employees' income tax withheld

Under federal law, employers are required to withhold certain amounts from the total earnings of each employee to be applied toward the payment of the employee's federal income tax. The amount to be withheld is governed by **(1)** the total earnings of the employee, **(2)** the number of **withholding allowances** claimed by the employee, **(3)** the marital status of the employee, and **(4)** the length of the employee's pay period.

Each federal income taxpayer is entitled to one exemption for himself or for herself and one each for certain other qualified relatives whom he or she supports. The law specifies the relationship that must exist, the extent of support required, and the maximum amount the *dependent* may earn and still be claimed as a dependent. As of 1972, each single taxpayer, or each married taxpayer whose spouse is not also employed, has become entitled to one **special withholding allowance**. A taxpayer and spouse each get an extra exemption for age over 65 years and still another exemption for blindness.

An employed taxpayer must furnish the employer with an Employee's Withholding Allowance Certificate, Form W-4, showing the number of allowances, if any, claimed. The allowance certificate completed by Ronald Marlin Lee is shown below.

Form W-4
Department of the Treasury
Internal Revenue Service

Employee's Withholding Allowance Certificate

This certificate is for income tax withholding purposes only. It will remain in effect until you change it. If you claim exemption from withholding, you will have to file a new certificate on or before April 30 of next year.

Type or print your full name	Your social security number
Ronald Marlin Lee	474-52-4829

Home address (number and street or rural route)
502 Kingsland Avenue

City or town, State, and ZIP code
St. Louis, MO 63130

Marital Status:
☐ Single ☒ Married
☐ Married, but withhold at higher Single rate

Note: If married, but legally separated, or spouse is a nonresident alien, check the single block.

1 Total number of allowances you are claiming   4
2 Additional amount, if any, you want deducted from each pay (if your employer agrees) . . . . $ —0—
3 I claim exemption from withholding (see instructions). Enter "Exempt" . . . .

Under the penalties of perjury, I certify that the number of withholding exemptions and allowances claimed on this certificate does not exceed the number to which I am entitled. If claiming exemption from withholding, I certify that I incurred no liability for Federal income tax for last year and that I anticipate that I will incur no liability for Federal income tax for this year.

Signature ▶ Ronald Marlin Lee   Date ▶ January 2, 19 78

Completed Withholding Allowance Certificate (Form W-4)

Employees with large itemized deductions are permitted to claim *additional withholding allowances*. Each additional withholding allowance will give the taxpayer an additional income tax deduction.

Any employee desiring to claim one or more additional withholding allowances must estimate his or her expected total earnings and itemized deductions for the coming year. Generally, the amount of these itemized deductions cannot exceed the amount of itemized deductions (or standard deduction) claimed on the income tax return filed for the preceding year.

The instructions provided for completing Form W-4 include tables from which the taxpayer can determine the number of additional withholding allowances to which he or she may be entitled. As shown on Line 1 of the W-4 illustrated above, Mr. Lee claimed four withholding allowances. This was because his estimated earnings and estimated itemized deductions did not qualify him for any additional withholding allowances. (Mr. Lee is married and has two minor children. However, since his wife is also employed, he would not be entitled to a so-called *special* withholding allowance. A special withholding allowance is *one* additional allowance granted to a single taxpayer with only one job and to a married taxpayer with only one job whose wife or husband does not also work.)

Most employers use the **wage-bracket method** of determining the amount of tax to be withheld. This method involves the use of income tax withholding tables provided by the Internal Revenue Service. Such tables cover monthly, semimonthly, biweekly, weekly, and daily or miscellaneous periods. There are two types of tables: **(1)** single persons and unmarried heads of households and **(2)** married persons. Copies may be obtained from any local Internal Revenue Service office. A portion of a weekly income tax wage-bracket withholding table for married persons is illustrated on page 75. As an example of the use of this table, assume that Ronald M. Lee (who claims 4 allowances) had gross earnings of $380 for the week ending December 15, 1978. On the line showing the tax on wages of "at least $380, but less than $390," in the column headed "4 withholding allowances," $52.40 is given as the amount to be withheld.

Whether the wage-bracket method or some other method is used in computing the amount of tax to be withheld, the employee is given full benefit for all allowances claimed plus a standard deduction of approximately 16 percent. In any event, the sum of the taxes withheld from an employee's wages only approximates the tax on the actual income derived solely from wages. An employee may be liable for a tax larger than the amount withheld. On the other hand, the amount of the taxes withheld by the employer may be greater than the employee's actual tax liability. In such an event, the employee will be entitled to a refund of the excess taxes withheld or may elect to apply the excess to the tax liability for the following year.

Several of the states have adopted state income tax withholding procedures. Some of these states supply employers with withholding allowance certificate forms and income tax withholding tables that are similar in appearance to those used by the federal Internal Revenue Service. Note, however, that each state that has an income tax law uses the specific tax rates and dollar amounts for allowances as required by its law. Some states determine the amount to be withheld merely by applying a fixed percentage to the federal withholding amount.

Employees' FICA tax withheld

Payroll taxes are imposed on almost all employers and employees for old-age, survivors, and disability insurance (OASDI) benefits and health insurance benefits for the aged (HIP) — both under the

WEEKLY Payroll Period — Employee MARRIED

And the wages are-		And the number of withholding allowances claimed is—										
At least	But less than	0	1	2	3	4	5	6	7	8	9	10 or more
		The amount of income tax to be withheld shall be—									
145	150	14.30	11.70	9.10	6.50	4.40	2.20	.10	0	0	0	0
150	160	15.70	13.10	10.50	7.90	5.50	3.30	1.20	0	0	0	0
160	170	17.50	14.90	12.30	9.70	7.10	4.80	2.70	.50	0	0	0
170	180	19.30	16.70	14.10	11.50	8.90	6.30	4.20	2.00	0	0	0
180	190	21.10	18.50	15.90	13.30	10.70	8.10	5.70	3.50	1.40	0	0
190	200	22.90	20.30	17.70	15.10	12.50	9.90	7.30	5.00	2.90	.70	0
200	210	24.70	22.10	19.50	16.90	14.30	11.70	9.10	6.50	4.40	2.20	0
210	220	26.50	23.90	21.30	18.70	16.10	13.50	10.90	8.30	5.90	3.70	1.50
220	230	28.40	25.70	23.10	20.50	17.90	15.30	12.70	10.10	7.50	5.20	3.00
230	240	30.60	27.50	24.90	22.30	19.70	17.10	14.50	11.90	9.30	6.70	4.50
240	250	32.80	29.60	26.70	24.10	21.50	18.90	16.30	13.70	11.10	8.50	6.00
250	260	35.00	31.80	28.60	25.90	23.30	20.70	18.10	15.50	12.90	10.30	7.70
260	270	37.20	34.00	30.80	27.70	25.10	22.50	19.90	17.30	14.70	12.10	9.50
270	280	39.40	36.20	33.00	29.80	26.90	24.30	21.70	19.10	16.50	13.90	11.30
280	290	41.80	38.40	35.20	32.00	28.90	26.10	23.50	20.90	18.30	15.70	13.10
290	300	44.30	40.70	37.40	34.20	31.10	27.90	25.30	22.70	20.10	17.50	14.90
300	310	46.80	43.20	39.60	36.40	33.30	30.10	27.10	24.50	21.90	19.30	16.70
310	320	49.30	45.70	42.10	38.60	35.50	32.30	29.10	26.30	23.70	21.10	18.50
320	330	51.80	48.20	44.60	41.00	37.70	34.50	31.30	28.20	25.50	22.90	20.30
330	340	54.30	50.70	47.10	43.50	39.90	36.70	33.50	30.40	27.30	24.70	22.10
340	350	56.80	53.20	49.60	46.00	42.40	38.90	35.70	32.60	29.40	26.50	23.90
350	360	59.30	55.70	52.10	48.50	44.90	41.30	37.90	34.80	31.60	28.40	25.70
360	370	62.10	58.20	54.60	51.00	47.40	43.80	40.10	37.00	33.80	30.60	27.50
370	380	64.90	60.80	57.10	53.50	49.90	46.30	42.60	39.20	36.00	32.80	29.60
380	390	67.70	63.60	59.60	56.00	52.40	48.80	45.10	41.50	38.20	35.00	31.80
390	400	70.50	66.40	62.40	58.50	54.90	51.30	47.60	44.00	40.40	37.20	34.00
400	410	73.30	69.20	65.20	61.20	57.40	53.80	50.10	46.50	42.90	39.40	36.20
410	420	76.10	72.00	68.00	64.00	59.90	56.30	52.60	49.00	45.40	41.80	38.40
420	430	78.90	74.80	70.80	66.80	62.70	58.80	55.10	51.50	47.90	44.30	40.70
430	440	81.80	77.60	73.60	69.60	65.50	61.50	57.60	54.00	50.40	46.80	43.20

NOTE: As of the date of printing, the above Weekly Federal Income Tax Withholding Table is the most current available.

Portion of Weekly Federal Income Tax Withholding Table for Married Persons

Federal Insurance Contributions Act (FICA). The base of the tax and the tax rate have been changed several times since the law was first enacted and are subject to change by Congress at any time in the future. For purposes of this chapter, the FICA rate is assumed to be 6 percent of the taxable wages paid during the calendar year. It is also assumed that the first $18,000 of the wages paid to each employee in any calendar year is taxable. Any amount of compensation paid in excess of $18,000 is assumed to be exempt from the tax. The employees' portion of the FICA tax must be withheld from their wages by the employer. Although it is true that the base and rate of the tax may be changed at the pleasure of Congress, the accounting principles or methods of recording payroll transactions are not affected.

A few states require employers to withhold a percentage of the employees' wages for unemployment compensation benefits or for disability benefits. In some states and cities, employers are required to withhold a percentage of the employees' wages for other types of payroll taxes. The withholding of income taxes at the state and city level has already been mentioned. Despite the number of withholdings required, each employer must comply with the proper laws in withholding any taxes based on payrolls and in keeping payroll accounting records.

Payroll records

The needs of management and the requirements of various federal and state laws make it necessary for employers to keep records that will provide the following information:

(a) The name, address, and social security number of each employee.
(b) The gross amount of each employee's earnings, the date of payment, and the period of employment covered by each payroll.
(c) The total amount of gross earnings accumulated since the first of the year.
(d) The amount of any taxes or other items withheld from each employee's earnings.

Regardless of the number of employees or type of business, three types of payroll records usually need to be prepared for or by the employer. They are: **(1)** the payroll register or payroll journal; **(2)** the payroll check with earnings statement attached; and **(3)** the earnings record of the individual employee (on a weekly, monthly, quarterly, or annual basis). These records can be prepared either by *manual* or by *automated* methods.

[Auxiliary Record]

[includes this wk's wages]

PAYROLL REGISTER

	NAME	EMPLOYEE NO.	NO. OF ALLOW.	MARITAL STATUS	REGULAR	OVER-TIME	TOTAL	CUMULATIVE TOTAL	UNEMPLOY COMP.	FICA	
1	Akos, Stephen W.	1	2	M	180 00		180 00	9,250 00		180 00	1
2	Brandal, Alma L.	2	3	M	320 00	64 00	384 00	18,500 00			2
3	Cox, Michelle R.	3	1	S	150 00		150 00	7,600 00		150 00	3
4	Lee, Ronald M.	4	4	M	320 00	60 00	380 00	19,734 00			4
5	MacArthur, John D.	5	3	M	240 00	50 00	290 00	13,750 00		290 00	5
6	O'Donnell, James V.	6	3	M	175 00		175 00	9,000 00		175 00	6
7	Paynter, Jane R.	7	2	M	180 00	30 00	210 00	10,000 00		210 00	7
8	Thomas, Wayne D.	8	1	S	160 00		160 00	8,050 00		160 00	8
9					1,725 00	204 00	1,929 00	95,884 00		1,165 00	
					1,725 00	204 00	1,929 00	95,884 00		1,165 00	

Payroll Register — Manually Prepared (Left Page)

Chapter 4   Payroll Accounting   77

Payroll Register. A manually prepared payroll register used by Central States Diversified, Inc., for the payroll period ended December 15, 1978, is illustrated below and on page 76. The usual source of information for preparing a payroll register is a time memorandum book, the batch of time clock cards, or a computer printout. Central States Diversified, Inc., has eight employees, as the illustration shows. Michelle Coxx and Wayne Thomas each claim only one allowance because each has two jobs. Stephen Akos and Jane Paynter each claim only two withholding allowances because their spouses also work. Alma Brandal, John MacArthur and James O'Donnell each get the special withholding allowance, but none as yet has any children. Regular deductions are made from the earnings of employees for FICA tax, federal income tax, and city earnings tax. In addition, for the pay period ending nearest to the middle of the month, deductions are made for life insurance, private hospital insurance, the company credit union, and (if desired) for the purchase of United States savings bonds.

Alma L. Brandal and Ronald M. Lee have each authorized Central States Diversified, Inc., to withhold $15 on the payday nearest to the middle of each month for United States savings bonds. When the amount withheld reaches the sum of $75, a $100 Series E, United States savings bond is purchased at the bank for these employees and delivered to them.

Only the first $18,000 *(change/amend)* of earnings received in any calendar year is subject to FICA tax. Mrs. Brandal's and Mr. Lee's earnings for the week ending December 15 are exempt from the FICA tax because they have already been taxed on earnings totaling $18,000.

FOR PERIOD ENDED December 15 19 78

	FICA TAX *(payable)*	FEDERAL INC. TAX *(payable)*	CITY TAX	LIFE INS.	PRIV. HOSP. INS.	CREDIT UNION	OTHER		TOTAL	NET PAY	CK. NO.
1	10 80	15 90	3 60	6 00		4 00			40 30	139 70	301
2		56 00	7 68			4 00	Sav. Bonds	15 00	82 68	301 32	302
3	9 00	18 60	3 00		4 00				34 60	115 40	303
4		52 40	7 60	7 50	5 00	4 00	Sav. Bonds	15 00	91 50	288 50	304
5	17 40	34 20	5 80	7 50	5 00	4 00			73 90	216 10	305
6	10 50	11 50	3 50	5 00					30 50	144 50	306
7	12 60	21 30	4 20			4 00			42 10	167 90	307
8	9 60	20 60	3 20	5 00	4 00				42 40	117 60	308
	69 90	230 50	38 58	31 00	18 00	20 00		30 00	437 98	1,491 02	
9	69 90	230 50	38 58	31 00	18 00	20 00		30 00	437 98	1,491 02	

Payroll Register — Manually Prepared (Right Page)

After the payroll register has been completed, the amount columns should be footed and the footings proved as follows:

Regular earnings		$1,725.00
Overtime earnings		204.00
Gross earnings		$1,929.00
Deductions:		
FICA tax	$ 69.90	
Federal income tax	230.50	
City earnings tax	38.58	
Life insurance premiums	31.00	
Private hospital insurance premiums	18.00	
Credit union	20.00	
United States savings bonds	30.00	437.98
Net amount of payroll		$1,491.02

After proving the footings, the totals should be entered in ink and the record should be ruled with single and double lines as shown in the illustration. Employees may be paid in cash or by check. Many businesses prepare a check for the net amount of the payroll and deposit it in a special payroll bank account. Individual paychecks are then drawn on that account for the amount due each employee. The employer usually furnishes a statement of payroll deductions to the employee along with each wage payment. Paychecks with detachable stubs, like the one for Ronald M. Lee, illustrated below and on page 79, are widely used. The stub should be detached before the check is cashed, and the stub should be retained by the employee as a permanent record of earnings and payroll deductions.

Employee's Earnings Record. An auxiliary record of each employee's earnings usually is kept in order to provide the information

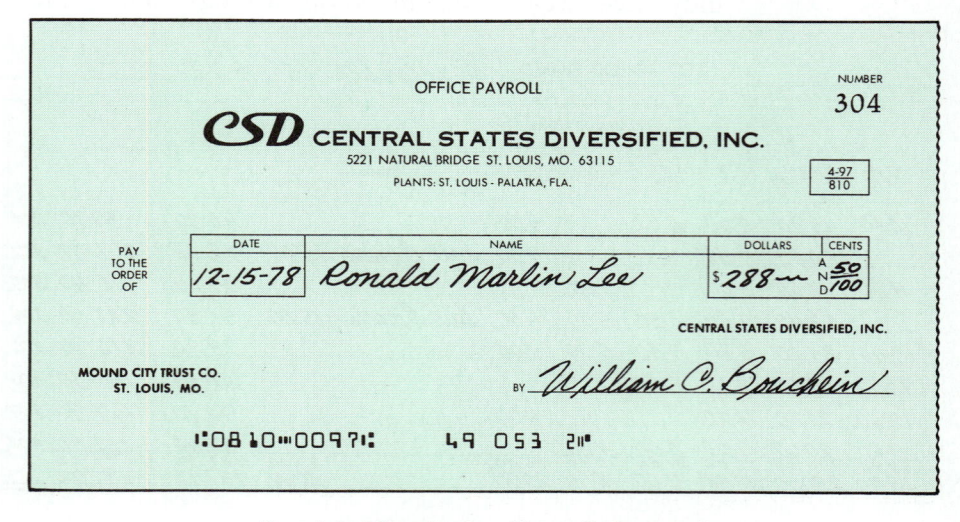

Completed Paycheck — Manually Prepared

needed in preparing the various federal, state, and local reports required of employers. A manually prepared employee's earnings record used by Central States Diversified, Inc., for Ronald M. Lee during the last two quarters of the current calendar year is illustrated on pages 80 and 81. This record may be kept on separate sheets or on cards, which may be filed alphabetically or numerically for ready reference. The information recorded on this form is taken from the payroll register.

Ronald Lee's earnings for the last half of the year up to December 15 are shown on this form. The entry for the pay period ended December 15 is posted from the payroll register illustrated on pages 76 and 77. It can be seen from Mr. Lee's earnings record that his cumulative earnings passed the $18,000 mark during the week ended November 17. Although his total earnings for that week amounted to $374, only $40 of such wages was subject to the FICA tax of 6 percent; hence only $2.40 was withheld from his wages for that week. For the remainder of the current calendar year, his entire earnings will be exempt from further FICA tax withholding.

The payroll register is a summary of the earnings of all employees for each pay period, while the earnings record is a summary of the annual earnings of each employee. The earnings record illustrated on pages 80 and 81 is designed so that a record of the earnings of the employee for the first half of the year may be kept on one side of the form and a record of the earnings for the last half of the year may be kept on the reverse side of the form. Thus, at the end of the year, the form provides a complete record of the earnings of the

CENTRAL STATES DIVERSIFIED, INC.
ST. LOUIS, MO.

STATEMENT OF EARNINGS

MISC.	HOSPITAL	BONDS	INSURANCE	CR. UNION	PARK	CHARITY	CHECK NO.	DATE
	5.00	15.00	7.50	4.00			304	12-15-78
320.00	60.00		52.40		7.60		91.50	288.50
REGULAR	O'TIME	OTHER	WH. TAX	FICA	CITY	STATE	TOTAL DEDUCTIONS	NET PAY
	EARNINGS			TAXES				

NON-NEGOTIABLE

and Deduction Stub

EMPLOYEE'S EARNINGS RECORD

1978 PERIOD ENDING	EARNINGS REGULAR	OVER-TIME	TOTAL	CUMULATIVE TOTAL	TAXABLE EARNINGS UNEMPLOY. COMP.	FICA	DEDUCTIONS FICA TAX	FEDERAL INC. TAX	
1	7/7	320 00		320 00	11,570 00		320 00	19 20	37 70	1
2	7/14	320 00	84 00	404 00	11,974 00		404 00	24 24	57 40	2
3	7/21	320 00		320 00	12,294 00		320 00	19 20	37 70	3
4	7/28	320 00	102 00	422 00	12,716 00		422 00	25 32	62 70	4
5	8/4	320 00		320 00	13,036 00		320 00	19 20	37 70	5
6	8/11	320 00		320 00	13,356 00		320 00	19 20	37 70	6
7	8/18	320 00	72 00	392 00	13,748 00		392 00	23 52	54 90	7
8	8/25	320 00		320 00	14,068 00		320 00	19 20	37 70	8
9	9/1	320 00		320 00	14,388 00		320 00	19 20	37 70	9
10	9/8	320 00	84 00	404 00	14,792 00		404 00	24 24	57 40	10
11	9/15	320 00		320 00	15,112 00		320 00	19 20	37 70	11
12	9/22	320 00	66 00	386 00	15,498 00		386 00	23 16	52 40	12
13	9/29	320 00		320 00	15,818 00		320 00	19 20	37 70	13
	THIRD QUARTER	4,160 00	408 00	4,568 00			4,568 00	274 08	586 40	
1	10/6	320 00		320 00	16,138 00		320 00	19 20	37 70	1
2	10/13	320 00	60 00	380 00	16,518 00		380 00	22 80	52 40	2
3	10/20	320 00	78 00	398 00	16,916 00		398 00	23 88	54 90	3
4	10/27	320 00		320 00	17,236 00		320 00	19 20	37 70	4
5	11/3	320 00		320 00	17,556 00		320 00	19 20	37 70	5
6	11/10	320 00	84 00	404 00	17,960 00		404 00	24 24	57 40	6
7	11/17	320 00	54 00	374 00	18,334 00		40 00	2 40	49 90	7
8	11/24	320 00	60 00	380 00	18,714 00				52 40	8
9	12/1	320 00		320 00	19,034 00				37 70	9
10	12/8	320 00		320 00	19,354 00				37 70	10
11	12/15	320 00	60 00	380 00	19,734 00				52 40	11
12										12
13										13
	FOURTH QUARTER									
	YEARLY TOTAL									

SEX M F	DEPARTMENT Production	OCCUPATION Machinist	SOCIAL SECURITY NO. 474-52-4829	MARITAL STATUS M	ALLOWANCES 4

Employee's Earnings Record — Manually Prepared (Left Page)

employee for the year. It also provides a record of the employee's earnings for each calendar quarter needed by the employer in the preparation of quarterly returns. These returns will be discussed later in this chapter.

Chapter 4 Payroll Accounting 81

FOR PERIOD ENDED December 31, 1978

#	CITY TAX	LIFE INS.	PRIVATE HOSP. INS.	CREDIT UNION	OTHER		TOTAL	NET PAY	CK. NO.	
1	6 40						63 30	256 70	120	1
2	8 08	7 50	5 00	4 00	Sav. Bonds	15 00	121 22	282 78	128	2
3	6 40						63 30	256 70	136	3
4	8 44						96 46	325 54	144	4
5	6 40						63 30	256 70	152	5
6	6 40						63 30	256 70	160	6
7	7 84	7 50	5 00	4 00	Sav. Bonds	15 00	117 76	274 24	168	7
8	6 40						63 30	256 70	176	8
9	6 40						63 30	256 70	184	9
10	8 08						89 72	314 28	192	10
11	6 40	7 50	5 00	4 00	Sav. Bonds	15 00	94 80	225 20	200	11
12	7 72						83 28	302 72	208	12
13	6 40						63 30	256 70	216	13
	91 36	22 50	15 00	12 00		45 00	1,046 34	3,521 66		
1	6 40						63 30	256 70	224	1
2	7 60	7 50	5 00	4 00	Sav. Bonds	15 00	114 30	265 70	232	2
3	7 96						86 74	311 26	240	3
4	6 40						63 30	256 70	248	4
5	6 40						63 30	256 70	256	5
6	8 08						89 72	314 28	264	6
7	7 48	7 50	5 00	4 00	Sav. Bonds	15 00	91 28	282 72	272	7
8	7 60						60 00	320 00	280	8
9	6 40						44 10	275 90	288	9
10	6 40						44 10	275 90	296	10
11	7 60	7 50	5 00	4 00	Sav. Bonds	15 00	91 50	288 50	304	11
12										12
13										13

PAY RATE	DATE OF BIRTH	DATE EMPLOYED	NAME - LAST	FIRST	MIDDLE	EMP. NO.
$320/wk.	7-30-48	1-2-78	Lee,	Ronald	Marlin	4

Employee's Earnings Record — Manually Prepared (Right Page)

Automated payroll systems

Automated payroll systems may involve the use of small-capacity bookkeeping machines, large-capacity (often electronic) bookkeeping machines, or computer equipment. Both bookkeeping machine payroll systems and computerized payroll systems make it possible to prepare a payroll check with deduction stub, an earnings record, and a payroll register simultaneously. This is an application of the **write-it-once principle**, which recognizes that each time the same information is recopied there is another chance for an error.

Automation Companies and Payroll Accounting. The development of automated accounting methods and computer equipment has led to the establishment of a large number of **automation companies**. Automation companies are business organizations engaged in data processing on a contract basis for other businesses of small and medium size. They either are independently operated or are owned and operated by the major business machine manufacturers, banks, or other financial institutions. Their employees are trained in accounting and information systems work and can set up and operate effective payroll systems for customers.

When payroll accounting is done for a business by an automation company, the preliminary work that the business needs to do usually is quite limited. One or more cards are punched for each employee for each payroll period with the aid of a keypunch machine, and these cards contain necessary information such as:

    (a) Employee name
    (b) Employee address
    (c) Employee social security number
    (d) Regular earnings

PAYROLL

NAME	EMPLOYEE NUMBER	NUMBER OF ALLOW.	MARITAL STATUS	REGULAR	OVERTIME	TOTAL	CUMULATIVE TOTAL	UNEMPLOYMENT COMP.	FICA
Akos, Stephen W.	1	2	M	180.00		180.00	9,250.00		180.00
Brandal, Alma L.	2	3	M	320.00	64.00	384.00	18,500.00		
Coxx, Michelle R.	3	1	S	150.00		150.00	7,600.00		150.00
Lee, Ronald Marlin	4	4	M	320.00	60.00	380.00	19,734.00		
MacArthur, John D.	5	3	M	240.00	50.00	290.00	13,750.00		290.00
O'Donnell, James V.	6	3	M	175.00		175.00	9,000.00		175.00
Paynter, Jane R.	7	2	M	180.00	30.00	210.00	10,000.00		210.00
Thomas, Wayne D.	8	1	S	160.00		160.00	8,050.00		160.00
				1,725.00	204.00	1,929.00	95,884.00		1,165.00

Columns under EARNINGS: REGULAR, OVERTIME, TOTAL, CUMULATIVE TOTAL. Columns under TAXABLE EARNINGS: UNEMPLOYMENT COMP., FICA.

Payroll Register — Machine Prepared (Left Page)

Chapter 4   Payroll Accounting

    (e) Overtime earnings
    (f) Federal income tax withheld
    (g) FICA (OASDI and HIP) tax withheld
    (h) Other deductions

These punched cards are picked up by the automation company at regular intervals, and the payroll records desired by the business customer are prepared.

A recent development in payroll accounting is the use of **time sharing**. Several small- to medium-sized businesses may own or rent time on a computer jointly. These businesses contact the computer by telephone over leased lines and carry on their payroll accounting through a typewriter-printer console.

In a manual payroll system, the payroll register normally is prepared first and serves as a journal. The employees' earnings records, checks, and stubs are then prepared from the payroll register information. However, in an automated payroll system, all three records are prepared simultaneously. Because of this, the order of their preparation is not of any concern to the accountant.

Employer-Operated Payroll Systems. A payroll register entry, an earnings record entry, and a payroll check with deduction stub prepared simultaneously on a bookkeeping machine are illustrated below and on the following pages. Assume that these records were

REGISTER

				DEDUCTIONS						
FICA TAX	FEDERAL INC. TAX	CITY TAX	LIFE INS.	PRIVATE HOSP. INS.	CREDIT UNION	U.S. SAVINGS BONDS	TOTAL	DATE	NET PAY	CK. NO.
10.80	15.90	3.60	6.00		4.00		40.30	Dec. 15, '78	139.70	301
	56.00	7.68			4.00	15.00	82.68	Dec. 15, '78	301.32	302
9.00	18.60	3.00		4.00			34.60	Dec. 15, '78	115.40	303
	52.40	7.60	7.50	5.00	4.00	15.00	91.50	Dec. 15, '78	288.50	304
17.40	34.20	5.80	7.50	5.00	4.00		73.90	Dec. 15, '78	216.10	305
10.50	11.50	3.50	5.00				30.50	Dec. 15, '78	144.50	306
12.60	21.30	4.20			4.00		42.10	Dec. 15, '78	167.90	307
9.60	20.60	3.20	5.00	4.00			42.40	Dec. 15, '78	117.60	308
69.90	230.50	38.58	31.00	18.00	20.00	30.00	437.98		1,491.02	

Payroll Register — Machine Prepared (Right Page)

prepared by Central States Diversified, Inc., for its employee, Ronald M. Lee, for the same pay period as the manual records previously illustrated on pages 76 to 81, inclusive. Contrast the two types of payroll systems. The primary advantage of the machine system is the saving of time and labor.

In addition to the *write-it-once* features of modern bookkeeping machines, computer-based payroll systems can also provide speed

EMPLOYEE'S

NAME	RONALD MARLIN LEE	
ADDRESS	502 KINGSLAND AVENUE	
CITY	ST. LOUIS, MISSOURI 63130	
SEX	Male	NUMBER OF ALLOWANCES
MARITAL STATUS	Married	4

EARNINGS				TAXABLE EARNINGS	
REGULAR	OVERTIME	TOTAL	CUMULATIVE TOTAL	UNEMPLOYMENT COMP.	FICA
320.00		320.00	11,570.00		320.00
320.00	84.00	404.00	11,974.00		404.00
320.00		320.00	12,294.00		320.00
320.00	102.00	422.00	12,716.00		422.00
320.00		320.00	13,036.00		320.00
320.00		320.00	13,356.00		320.00
320.00	72.00	392.00	13,748.00		392.00
320.00		320.00	14,068.00		320.00
320.00		320.00	14,388.00		320.00
320.00	84.00	404.00	14,792.00		404.00
320.00		320.00	15,112.00		320.00
320.00	66.00	386.00	15,498.00		386.00
320.00		320.00	15,818.00		320.00
THIRD QUARTER					
4,160.00	408.00	4,568.00			4,568.00
320.00		320.00	16,138.00		320.00
320.00	60.00	380.00	16,518.00		380.00
320.00	78.00	398.00	16,916.00		398.00
320.00		320.00	17,236.00		320.00
320.00		320.00	17,556.00		320.00
320.00	84.00	404.00	17,960.00		404.00
320.00	54.00	374.00	18,334.00		40.00
320.00	60.00	380.00	18,714.00		
320.00		320.00	19,034.00		
320.00		320.00	19,354.00		
320.00	60.00	380.00	19,734.00		
FOURTH QUARTER					
YEARLY TOTAL					

Employee's Earnings Record — Machine Prepared (Left Page)

Chapter 4   Payroll Accounting   85

and storage as well as needed arithmetic ability. Through the use of computerized equipment, adding, subtracting, and multiplying of payrolls can be speeded up; and information such as wage rates and withholding table amounts can be stored inside the equipment. As one would expect, the cost of computerized payroll equipment is noticeably higher than the cost of more conventional bookkeeping machines. The type of computer-based accounting system well

EARNINGS RECORD

DEPARTMENT	Production	SOCIAL SECURITY NUMBER	474-52-4829
OCCUPATION	Machinist	DATE OF BIRTH	July 30, 1948
PAY RATE	$320 Weekly	DATE EMPLOYED	January 2, 1978
EMPLOYEE NO.	4	DATE EMPLOYMENT TERMINATED	

FICA TAX	FEDERAL INC. TAX	CITY TAX	LIFE INS.	PRIVATE HOSP. INS.	CREDIT UNION	U.S. SAVINGS BONDS	TOTAL	DATE	NET PAY	CK. NO.
19.20	37.70	6.40					63.30	July 7, '78	256.70	120
24.24	57.40	8.08	7.50	5.00	4.00	15.00	121.22	July 14, '78	282.78	128
19.20	37.70	6.40					63.30	July 21, '78	256.70	136
25.32	62.70	8.44					96.46	July 28, '78	325.54	144
19.20	37.70	6.40					63.30	Aug. 4, '78	256.70	152
19.20	37.70	6.40					63.30	Aug. 11, '78	256.70	160
23.52	54.90	7.84	7.50	5.00	4.00	15.00	117.76	Aug. 18, '78	274.24	168
19.20	37.70	6.40					63.30	Aug. 25, '78	256.70	176
19.20	37.70	6.40					63.30	Sept. 1, '78	256.70	184
24.24	57.40	8.08					89.72	Sept. 8, '78	314.28	192
19.20	37.70	6.40	7.50	5.00	4.00	15.00	94.80	Sept. 15, '78	225.20	200
23.16	52.40	7.72					83.28	Sept. 22, '78	302.72	208
19.20	37.70	6.40					63.30	Sept. 29, '78	256.70	216
274.08	586.40	91.36	22.50	15.00	12.00	45.00	1,046.34		3,521.66	
19.20	37.70	6.40					63.30	Oct. 6, '78	256.70	224
22.80	52.40	7.60	7.50	5.00	4.00	15.00	114.30	Oct. 13, '78	265.70	232
23.88	54.90	7.96					86.74	Oct. 20, '78	311.26	240
19.20	37.70	6.40					63.30	Oct. 27, '78	256.70	248
19.20	37.70	6.40					63.30	Nov. 3, '78	256.70	256
24.24	57.40	8.08					89.72	Nov. 10, '78	314.28	264
2.40	49.90	7.48	7.50	5.00	4.00	15.00	91.28	Nov. 17, '78	282.72	272
	52.40	7.60					60.00	Nov. 24, '78	320.00	280
	37.70	6.40					44.10	Dec. 1, '78	275.90	288
	37.70	6.40					44.10	Dec. 8, '78	275.90	296
	52.40	7.60	7.50	5.00	4.00	15.00	91.50	Dec. 15, '78	288.50	304

Employee's Earnings Record — Machine Prepared (Right Page)

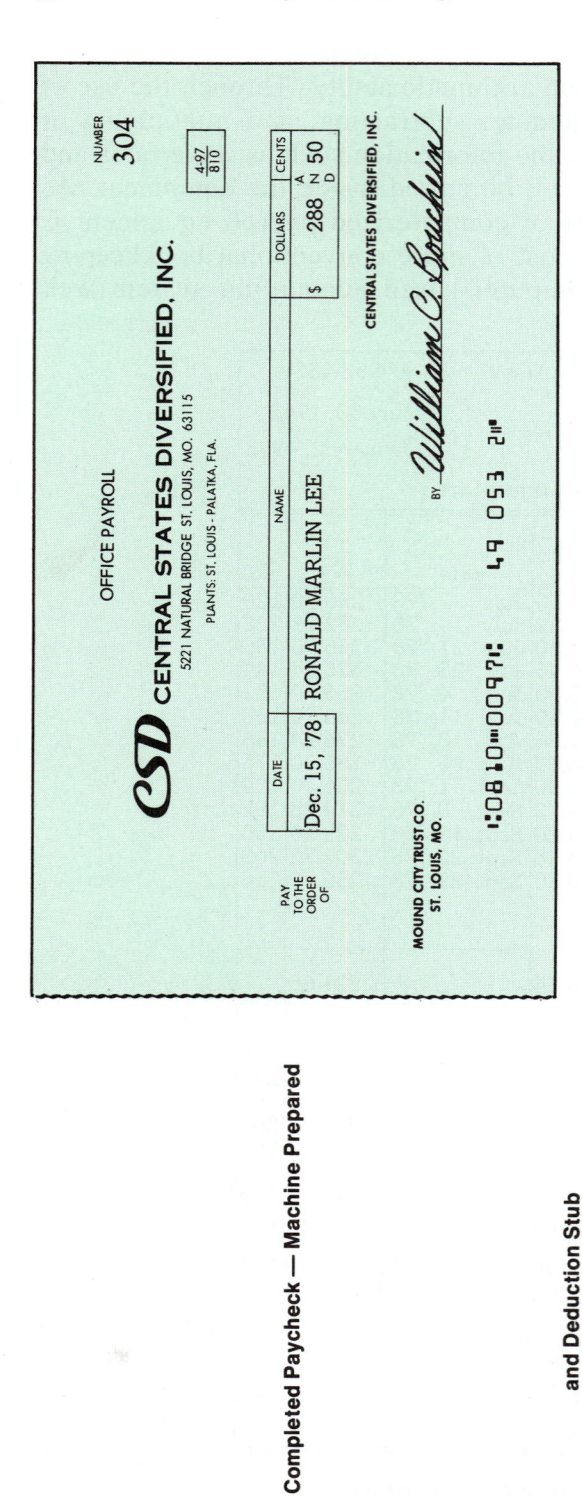

Payroll Accounting

Completed Paycheck — Machine Prepared and Deduction Stub

OFFICE PAYROLL

NUMBER 304

CSD CENTRAL STATES DIVERSIFIED, INC.
5221 NATURAL BRIDGE ST. LOUIS, MO. 63115
PLANTS: ST. LOUIS - PALATKA, FLA.

4-97 / 810

DATE: Dec. 15, '78
NAME: RONALD MARLIN LEE

DOLLARS $ 288   CENTS 50
A N D

PAY TO THE ORDER OF
MOUND CITY TRUST CO.
ST. LOUIS, MO.

CENTRAL STATES DIVERSIFIED, INC.
BY *William C. Bouchein*

⑈0810⑈0097⑈ 49 053 2⑈

CENTRAL STATES DIVERSIFIED, INC.
ST. LOUIS, MO.

STATEMENT OF EARNINGS

EARNINGS					TAXABLE EARNINGS		DEDUCTIONS								
REGULAR	OVERTIME	TOTAL	CUMULATIVE TOTAL		UNEMPLOY- MENT COMP.	FICA	FICA TAX	FEDERAL INC. TAX	CITY TAX	LIFE INS.	PRIVATE HOSP. INS.	CREDIT UNION	U.S. SAVINGS BONDS	TOTAL	DATE	NET PAY	CK. NO.
320.00	60.00	380.00	19,734.00					52.40	7.60	7.50	5.00	4.00	15.00	91.50	Dec. 15, '78	288.50	304

NON-NEGOTIABLE

suited to payroll accounting, among other things, is described and illustrated in the appendix to this textbook.

Much of the work usually required to figure employees' gross earnings, deductions, and net pay may be eliminated if the equipment provides sufficient automation, storage capacity, and electronic calculation capability. When conventional electric bookkeeping machines are used, gross earnings are often computed separately on a calculator, and withholding and other tax amounts are either read from tables or worked out manually.

A computer-based payroll accounting system completes all of the major payroll records at once, just as do modern electronic bookkeeping machines. Also, a computer-based payroll accounting system determines automatically:

(a) The presence of the proper earnings record.
(b) The next available posting line.
(c) Whether overtime earnings are due.
(d) Whether there are other earnings.
(e) Whether the FICA limit has been reached.
(f) What tax deductions should be made.
(g) Whether insurance premiums should be deducted.
(h) Whether there are any other deductions to be made.
(i) Whether there are any delinquent deductions to be made.
(j) Whether there is anything else to be done.

Once this system is properly set up, the operator is relieved of manual figuring and of looking up amounts in tables. The primary job is one of feeding in blank payroll accounting record forms and getting these forms back as completed payroll accounting records. (For a further discussion of computer-based accounting systems and procedures, see Appendix, page A-1.)

Wage and tax statement

Not later than January 31 of each year, the law requires employers to furnish each employee from whom income taxes have been withheld the Wage and Tax Statement, Form W-2, showing the total amount of wages paid and the amount of such tax withheld during the preceding calendar year. This statement should be issued 30 days after the last wage payment to a terminating employee. If the employee's wages were subject to FICA tax as well as federal, state, or local income tax, the employer must report total wages paid and the amounts deducted both for income tax and for FICA tax. Information for this purpose should be provided by the employee's earnings record. A completed Form W-2 is illustrated on page 88.

1 Control number		2 Employer's State number				
	222	21-686001			For Official Use Only	

3 Employer's name, address, and ZIP code	4 Sub-total ☐	Cor-rection ☐	Void ☐	5 Yes ☒ Jan–Mar No ☐	6 Yes ☒ Apr–Jun No ☐
Central States Diversified, Inc. 5221 Natural Bridge St. Louis, MO 63115	7 Employer's identification number 43-0211630			8 Yes ☒ Jul–Sep No ☐	9 Yes ☒ Oct–Dec No ☐

10 Employee's social security number 474-52-4829	11 Federal income tax withheld $2,339.40	12 Wages, tips, other compensation $20,374.00	13 FICA tax withheld $1,080.00	14 Total FICA wages $18,000.00
15 Employee's name (first, middle, last) Ronald Marlin Lee		16 Pension plan coverage? Yes/No Yes	17•	18 FICA tips
502 Kingsland Avenue St. Louis, MO 63130		20 State income tax withheld	21 State wages, tips, etc.	22 Name of State
19 Employee's address and ZIP code		23 Local income tax withheld $407.48	24 Local wages, tips, etc. $20,374.00	25 Name of locality St. Louis

Wage and Tax Statement 1978 COPY A For Social Security Administration

Form W–2   Department of the Treasury—Internal Revenue Service

Completed Wage and Tax Statement (Form W-2)

The number appearing on the Wage and Tax Statement beside the name and address of the employer is an **identification number** assigned to the employer by the Social Security Administration. Every employer of even one person receiving taxable wages must get an identification number within a week of the beginning of such employment. This number must be shown on all reports required of Central States Diversified, Inc., under the Federal Insurance Contributions Act.

Boxes 5, 6, 8, and 9 reflect quarterly FICA information. An X is placed in the Yes square for each calendar quarter that FICA earnings are at least $50. If FICA earnings are less than $50, an X is placed in the No square and the amount of FICA earnings is entered between the Yes and No squares. If there are no FICA earnings, or if the employee did not work for the employer during the quarter, an X is placed in the No square.

Wage and Tax Statements must be prepared in quadruplicate (four copies). Copy A goes to the Social Security Administration. Copies B and C are furnished to the employee, so that he or she can send Copy B in with the federal income tax return as required and keep Copy C as a record. Copy D is kept for the employer's records. In states or cities which have state or city income tax withholding laws, two more copies are furnished. One copy is sent in by the employer to the appropriate state or city tax department, and the other is sent in by the employee with the state or city income tax return.

Chapter 4   Payroll Accounting   **89**

Accounting for wages and wage deductions

In accounting for wages and wage deductions, it is desirable to keep separate accounts for **(1)** wages earned and **(2)** wage deductions. Various account titles are used in recording wages, such as Payroll Expense, Salaries Expense, and Salaries and Commissions Expense. The accounts needed in recording wage deductions depend upon what deductions are involved. A separate account should be kept for recording the liability incurred for each type of deduction, such as FICA tax, employees' income tax, and savings bond deductions.

Payroll Expense. This is an expense account which should be debited for the total amount of the gross earnings of all employees for each pay period. Sometimes separate payroll accounts are kept for the employees of different departments. Thus, separate accounts might be kept for Office Salaries Expense, Sales Salaries Expense, and Factory Payroll Expense.

PAYROLL EXPENSE	
Debit	
to record gross earnings of employees for each pay period.	

FICA Tax Payable. This is a liability account which should be credited for **(1)** the FICA tax withheld from employees' wages and **(2)** the FICA tax imposed on the employer. The account should be debited for amounts paid to apply on such taxes. When all of the FICA taxes have been paid, the account should be in balance.

FICA TAX PAYABLE	
Debit	Credit
to record payment of FICA tax.	to record FICA taxes (a) withheld from employees' wages and (b) imposed on the employer.

Employees Income Tax Payable. This is a liability account which should be credited for the total income tax withheld from employees' wages. The account should be debited for amounts paid to apply on such taxes. When all of the income taxes withheld have been paid, the account will be in balance. A city or state earnings tax payable account is used in a similar manner.

EMPLOYEES INCOME TAX PAYABLE	
Debit	Credit
to record payment of income tax withheld.	to record income tax withheld from employees' wages.

Life Insurance Premiums Payable. This is a liability account which should be credited with amounts withheld from employees' wages for the future payment of life insurance premiums. The

LIFE INSURANCE PREMIUMS PAYABLE	
Debit	Credit
to record the payment of life insurance premiums withheld.	to record amounts withheld for the future payment of life insurance premiums.

account should be debited for the subsequent payment of these premiums to the life insurance company. Accounts for private hospital insurance premiums payable, credit union contributions payable, and savings bond deductions payable are similarly used.

Journalizing Payroll Transactions. The payroll register should provide the information needed in recording wages paid. The payroll register illustrated on pages 82 and 83 provided the information needed in drafting the following general journal entry to record the wages paid on December 15:

	DR	CR
Dec. 15. Payroll Expense	1,929.00	
FICA Tax Payable		69.90
Employees Income Tax Payable		230.50
City Earnings Tax Payable		38.58
Life Insurance Premiums Payable		31.00
Private Hospital Insurance Premiums Payable		18.00
Credit Union Contributions Payable		20.00
Savings Bond Deductions Payable		30.00
Cash		1,491.02
Payroll for week ended December 15.		

It will be noted that the above journal entry involves one debit and eight credits. Regardless of the number of debits and credits needed to record a transaction, the total amount debited must be equal to the total amount credited.

Report No. 4-1

Complete Report No. 4-1 in the study assignments and submit your working papers to the instructor for approval. After completing the report, continue with the following textbook discussion until the next report is required.

PAYROLL TAXES IMPOSED ON THE EMPLOYER

The employer is liable to the government for the taxes which are required by law to be withheld from the wages of employees. These taxes include the federal income tax and the FICA tax which must be withheld from wages paid to employees. Such taxes are not an expense of the employer; nevertheless, the employer is required by law to collect the taxes and is liable for the taxes until payment is made.

Certain taxes are also imposed on the employer for various purposes, such as old-age, survivors, and disability insurance benefits; hospital insurance benefits for the aged; and unemployment, relief, and welfare. Most employers are subject to payroll taxes imposed under the Federal Insurance Contributions Act (FICA) and the Federal Unemployment Tax Act (FUTA). An employer may also be subject to the payroll tax imposed under the unemployment compensation laws of one or more states. These commonly are called "State Unemployment Tax."

Payroll taxes expense

All of the payroll taxes imposed on an employer under federal and state social security laws are an expense of the employer. In accounting for such taxes, at least one expense account should be maintained. This account may be entitled Payroll Taxes Expense. It is an expense account which should be debited for all taxes imposed on the employer under federal and state social security laws. Sometimes separate expense accounts are kept for (1) FICA Tax Expense, (2) FUTA Tax Expense, and (3) State Unemployment Tax Expense. In small business enterprises, it is usually considered satisfactory to keep a single expense account for all federal and state social security taxes imposed on the employer.

PAYROLL TAXES EXPENSE
Debit
to record FICA, FUTA, and State Unemployment Taxes imposed on the employer.

Employer's FICA tax

The taxes imposed under the Federal Insurance Contributions Act apply equally to employers and to employees. As explained on page 75, both the rate and base of the tax may be changed by Congress at any time. In this discussion it is assumed that the combined rate is 6 percent which applies both to the employer and to the employee (a total of 12 percent) with respect to taxable wages. It is also assumed that only the first $18,000 of the wages paid to each employee in any calendar year constitutes taxable wages. Any amount of wages paid to an employee during a year in excess of $18,000 is exempt from FICA tax. While the employer is liable to the government both for the tax withheld from the employees' wages and for the tax imposed on the business, only the latter constitutes an expense of the business.

FICA tax payable

It is customary to keep only one liability account entitled FICA Tax Payable for contributions made by the employer and the employees under the Federal Insurance Contributions Act.

FICA Tax Payable	
Debit	Credit
to record payment of FICA tax.	to record FICA taxes (a) withheld from employees' wages and (b) imposed on the employer.

Employer's FUTA tax

Under the Federal Unemployment Tax Act, a payroll tax is levied on employers for the purpose of implementing more uniform administration of the various state unemployment compensation laws. Employers who employ one or more individuals for at least 20 calendar weeks in the calendar year, *or* who pay wages of $1,500 or more in any calendar quarter, are subject to this tax. The federal law imposes a specific rate of tax but allows a substantial credit against this levy if the state in which the employer is located has an unemployment compensation law that meets certain requirements. Since all states have such laws, the rate actually paid by most employers is much less than the maximum legal rate. As in the case of the FICA tax, Congress can and does change the rate from time to time. For the purpose of this discussion, a rate of 3.4 percent with a credit of 2.7 percent available to most employers is used. The difference of 0.7 percent (3.4 — 2.7) is, then, the effective rate. This is applied to the first $6,000 of compensation paid to each employee during the calendar year. It is important to note this limitation in contrast to the $18,000 limit in the case of the FICA tax. It is also important to note that all of the payroll taxes relate to gross wages paid — not to wages earned. Sometimes wages are earned in one quarter or year but not paid until the following period.

FUTA tax payable

In recording the federal unemployment tax, it is customary to keep a separate liability account entitled FUTA Tax Payable. This is a liability account which should be credited for the tax imposed on employers under the Federal Un-

FUTA Tax Payable	
Debit	Credit
to record payment of FUTA tax.	to record FUTA tax imposed on the employer with respect to wages paid.

employment Tax Act. (As previously mentioned, assume that the federal unemployment tax rate is 0.7 percent of the first $6,000 of wages paid each employee each year.) The account should be debited for amounts paid to apply on such taxes. When all of the FUTA taxes have been paid, the account should be in balance.

State unemployment tax

All of the states and the District of Columbia have enacted unemployment compensation laws providing for the payment of benefits to qualified unemployed workers. The cost of administering the state unemployment compensation laws is borne by the federal government. Under the federal law an appropriation is made for each year by Congress from which grants are made to the states to meet the proper administrative costs of their unemployment compensation laws. As a result of this provision, the entire amount paid into the state funds may be used for the payment of benefits to qualified workers. While in general there is considerable uniformity in the provisions of the state laws, there are many variations in coverage, rates of tax imposed, and benefits payable to qualified workers. The date of payment of unemployment taxes into the state fund also varies from state to state, and a penalty generally is imposed on employers for late payment. Not all employers covered by the Federal Unemployment Tax Act are covered by the unemployment compensation laws of the states in which they have employees. But most employers of one or more individuals are covered by the federal law.

The minimum number of employees specified under state laws varies from 1 to 4. However, in many of the states employers who are covered by the federal law and have one or more individuals employed within the state are also covered by the state law. Furthermore, under the laws of most states employers who are covered by the federal law may elect voluntary coverage in states where they have one or more employees, even though they may have less than the number of employees specified by the law in that particular state. In any event, it is necessary for employers to be familiar with the unemployment compensation laws of all the states in which they have one or more employees; and if such employees are covered, the employers must keep such records and pay such taxes for unemployment compensation purposes as are prescribed by those laws.

In most states the unemployment benefit plan is financed entirely by taxes imposed on employers. However, in a few states employees are also required to contribute, and the amount of the tax imposed on the employees must be withheld from their wages.

In most states the maximum tax imposed upon employers is 2.7 percent of the first $6,000 of wages paid to each employee in any calendar year. However, under the laws of most states there is a **merit-rating** system which provides a tax-saving incentive to employers to stabilize employment. Under this system employers' rates may be considerably less than the maximum rate if they provide steady work for their employees.

There are frequent changes in the state laws with respect to coverage, rates of contributions required, eligibility to receive benefits, and amounts of benefits payable. In this discussion, it is assumed that the state tax rate is 2.7 percent of the first $6,000 of wages paid each employee each year.

State unemployment tax payable

In recording the tax imposed under state unemployment compensation laws, it is customary to keep a separate liability account entitled State Unemployment Tax Payable. This is a liability account

STATE UNEMPLOYMENT TAX PAYABLE

Debit	Credit
to record state unemployment tax paid.	to record liability for state unemployment tax required of employers.

which should be credited for the tax imposed on employers under the state unemployment compensation laws. The account should be debited for the amount paid to apply on such taxes. When all of the state taxes have been paid, the account should be in balance. Some employers who are subject to taxes imposed under the laws of several states keep a separate liability account for the tax imposed by each state.

Journalizing employer's payroll taxes

The payroll taxes imposed on employers may be recorded periodically, such as monthly or quarterly. It is more common to record such taxes at the time that wages are paid so that the employer's liability for such taxes and related expenses may be recorded in the same period as the wages on which the taxes are based. The payroll register illustrated on pages 82 and 83 provides the information needed in recording the FICA tax imposed on Central States Diversified, Inc., with respect to wages paid on December 15. The FICA taxable earnings for the pay period involved amounted to $1,165. Assuming that the combined rate of the tax imposed on the employer was 6 percent, which is the same as the rate of the tax imposed on the employees, the tax would amount to $69.90. (This amount will not necessarily be the same as that calculated by multiplying the tax rate times total taxable earnings due to the rounding up of amounts in calculating the tax deduction for each employee.) If $875 of the earnings for the period had been subject to unemployment taxes (none actually were), the federal and state taxes would have been computed as follows:

State unemployment tax, 2.7% of $875	$23.63
FUTA tax, 0.7% of $875	6.13
Total unemployment taxes	$29.76

The following general journal entry would have been made to record the payroll taxes imposed on the employer with respect to the wages paid on December 15:

	DR	CR
Dec. 15. Payroll Taxes Expense	99.66	
FICA Tax Payable		69.90
FUTA Tax Payable		6.13
State Unemployment Tax Payable		23.63
Payroll taxes imposed on employer with respect to wages paid December 15.		

Filing returns and paying the payroll taxes

When the cumulative amount withheld from employees' wages for income tax and FICA tax purposes plus the amount of the FICA tax imposed on the employer during the first or second month of any quarter is $200 or more, the total must be deposited at a District Federal Reserve Bank or some other United States depositary by the 15th of the following month. If at the end of a quarter the total amount of undeposited taxes is $200 or more, the total amount must be deposited in a federal depositary or Federal Reserve bank on or before the last day of the first month after the end of the quarter. If at the end of a quarter the total amount of undeposited taxes is less than $200, a deposit is not necessary. The taxes may either be paid directly to the Internal Revenue Service along with Form 941 — Employer's Quarterly Federal Tax Return — or a deposit may be made. Form 941 (not illustrated) shows the quarterly total of the wages, tips, and other compensation paid, deposits made, income tax withheld, and FICA taxes.

When the cumulative amount of income and FICA tax is $200 or more but under $2,000, the total is required to be deposited by the 15th day of the next month. If this $200–$2,000 limitation is reached in the third month of any quarter, no deposit need be made until the last day of the month following the quarter.

When the cumulative amount is $2,000 or more by the 7th, 15th, 22nd, or last day of any month, a deposit must be made within three banking days after that quarter-monthly period.

A completed copy of the Federal Tax Deposit, Form 501 — Withheld Income and FICA Taxes, is shown below. The stub is detached by the bank on payment of the taxes due and is the employer's record of the deposit.

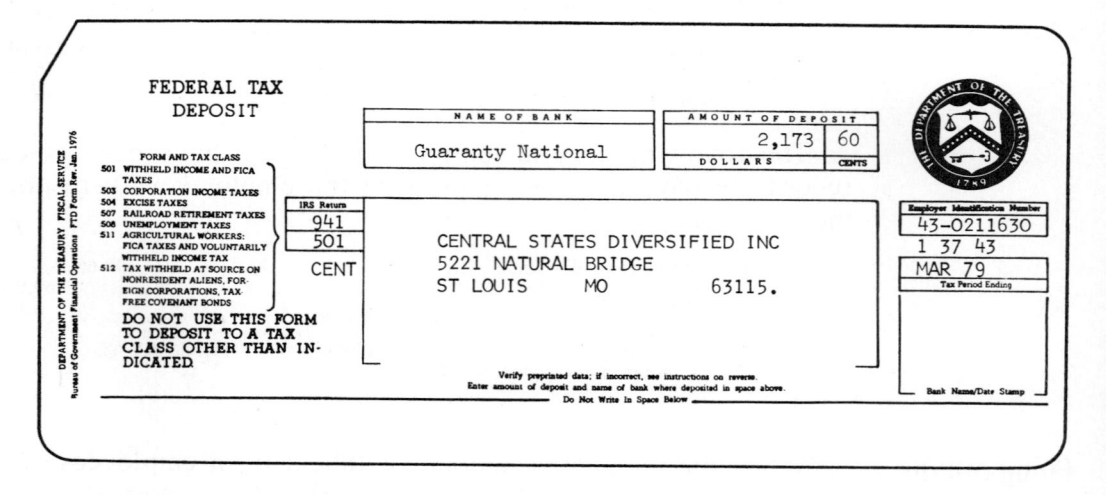

Completed Federal Tax Deposit Form (Form 501)

To illustrate the accounting procedure in recording the payment of employees' income tax and FICA tax withheld, it will be assumed that on February 5 Central States Diversified, Inc., issued a check in payment of the following taxes imposed with respect to wages paid during the month of January:

Employees' income tax withheld from wages		$1,274.40
FICA tax:		
Withheld from employees' wages	$449.60	
Imposed on employer	449.60	899.20
Amount of check		$2,173.60

A check for this amount accompanied by the Federal Tax Deposit form, Form 501, was sent to a bank that is qualified as a depositary for federal taxes. (All national banks are qualified.) This transaction may be recorded as indicated by the following general journal entry:

Feb. 5. FICA Tax Payable	899.20	
Employees Income Tax Payable	1,274.40	
Cash		2,173.60
Remitted $2,173.60 in payment of taxes.		

The amount of the tax imposed on employers under the state unemployment compensation laws must be remitted to the proper state office during the month following the close of the calendar quarter. Each state provides an official form to be used in making a return of the taxes due. Assuming that a check for $494.91 was issued on April 30 in payment of state unemployment compensation tax on wages paid during the preceding quarter ended March 31, the transaction may be recorded as indicated by the following journal entry:

Apr. 30. State Unemployment Tax Payable	494.91	
Cash		494.91
Paid state unemployment tax.		

Federal unemployment tax must be computed on a quarterly basis. If the amount of the employer's liability under the Federal Unemployment Tax Act during any quarter is more than $100, the total must be paid to the District Federal Reserve Bank or some other United States depositary on or before the last day of the first month following the close of the quarter. If the amount is $100 or less, no deposit is necessary, but this amount must be added to the amount subject to deposit for the next quarter.

When paying FUTA tax, it is necessary to complete the Federal Tax Deposit Form, Form 508, and to send or take it to the bank with the remittance. This form is not illustrated here, but it is similar in nature to Form 501, previously illustrated on page 96.

If the amount of the FUTA tax is less than $100 for the entire year, the tax must be paid to the District Director of Internal Revenue by the end of the month following the close of the calendar year. An official form (Form 940) is provided to the employer for use in making a report of the taxes due. This form is not illustrated here.

Assuming that a check for $96.10 was issued on January 31 in payment of the tax imposed under the Federal Unemployment Tax

Act with respect to wages paid during the preceding year ended December 31, the transaction may be recorded as indicated by the following journal entry:

```
Jan. 31.  FUTA Tax Payable ........................................... 96.10
             Cash ...................................................          96.10
            Paid federal unemployment tax.
```

Report No. 4-2

> Complete Report No. 4-2 in the study assignments and submit your working papers to the instructor for approval. After completing the report, you may continue with the textbook discussion in Chapter 5 until the next report is required.

1-4

Practical Accounting Problems

The following problems supplement those in Reports 1-1 through 4-2 of the study assignments. These problems are numbered to indicate the chapter of the textbook with which they correlate. For example, Problem 1-A and Problem 1-B correlate with Chapter 1. Loose-leaf stationery should be used in solving these problems. The paper required includes plain ruled paper, two-column journal paper, two-column and three-column statement paper, and ledger paper.

Problem 1-A

T. B. Murray is a practicing attorney. As of December 31 she owned the following property that related to her business: Cash, $961; office equipment, $1,500; and an automobile, $3,560. At the same time she owed business creditors $860.

REQUIRED: **(1)** On the basis of the above information, compute the amounts of the accounting elements and show them in equation form. **(2)** Assume that during the following year there is an increase in Miss Murray's business assets of $2,200 and a decrease in her business liabilities of $43. Indicate the changes in the accounting elements by showing them in equation form after the changes have occurred.

Problem 1-B

H. L. Scholl, a CPA who has been employed by a large national firm of certified public accountants, decides to go into business for himself. His business transactions for the first month of operations were as follows:

(a) Mr. Scholl invested $10,000 cash in the business.
(b) Paid office rent for one month, $400.
(c) Purchased office equipment from the Von Brocken Office Equipment Co. (a supplier), $1,840 on account.

(d) Paid telephone bill, $53.
(e) Received $500 for services rendered to Public Finance Co.
(f) Paid $600 to the Von Brocken Office Equipment Co., on account.
(g) Received $325 for services rendered to the Kribs Garage.
(h) Paid $500 salary to office secretary.

REQUIRED: **(1)** On a plain sheet of paper, rule eight "T" accounts and enter the following titles: Cash; Office Equipment; Accounts Payable; H. L. Scholl, Capital; Professional Fees; Rent Expense; Telephone Expense; and Salary Expense. **(2)** Record the foregoing transactions directly in the accounts. **(3)** Foot the accounts and enter the balances where necessary. **(4)** Prepare a trial balance of the accounts, using a sheet of two-column journal paper.

Problem 2-A

Following is a narrative of the transactions completed by Ms. C. T. Marks, management consultant, during the first month of her business operations:

Oct. 1. Ms. Marks invested $15,000 cash in the business.
    1. Paid office rent, $425.
    3. Purchased office furniture for $975 cash.
    3. Paid $67.90 for installation of telephone and for one month's service.
    4. Received $225 from The Premier Linen Service for consulting services rendered.
    5. Purchased stationery and supplies on account from W. K. Woods Stationery Co., $189.64.
    6. Paid $6 for subscription to a professional management magazine. (Debit Miscellaneous Expense.)
    8. Paid $35 to Dr. Javier Banvelos, a dentist, for dental service performed for Ms. Marks.
       (Note: This is equivalent to a withdrawal of $35 by Ms. Marks for personal use. Debit her drawing account.)
    9. Received $80 from Tropicana Pools, Inc., for professional services rendered.
   12. Paid $98.63 for an airplane ticket for a business trip.
   14. Paid other traveling expenses, $140.50.
   19. Paid account of W. K. Woods Stationery Co. in full, $189.64.
   20. Received $265 from Wagner Electric Co. for professional services rendered.
   31. Paid $560 monthly salary to secretary.

REQUIRED: Journalize the foregoing transactions, using a sheet of two-column journal paper. Number the pages and use both sides of the sheet if necessary. Select the account titles from the chart of accounts on page 101.

CHART OF ACCOUNTS

Assets
111 Cash
112 Stationery and Supplies
121 Office Furniture

Liabilities
211 Accounts Payable

Owner's Equity
311 C. T. Marks, Capital
312 C. T. Marks, Drawing

Revenue
411 Professional Fees

Expenses
511 Rent Expense
512 Telephone Expense
513 Traveling Expense
514 Salary Expense
515 Miscellaneous Expense

After journalizing the transactions, prove the equality of the debits and credits by footing the amount columns. Enter the footings in pencil immediately under the line on which the last entry appears.

Problem 2-B

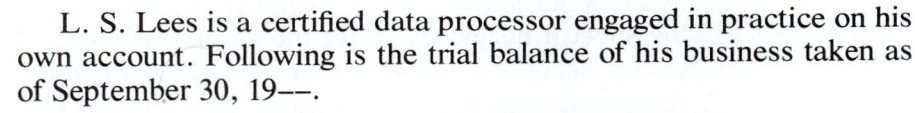

L. S. Lees is a certified data processor engaged in practice on his own account. Following is the trial balance of his business taken as of September 30, 19--.

L. S. LEES, CERTIFIED DATA PROCESSOR
Trial Balance
September 30, 19--

Cash	111	4,526.56	
Office Equipment	121	2,525.00	
Automobile	122	5,200.00	
Accounts Payable	211		312.36
L. S. Lees, Capital	311		12,512.00
L. S. Lees, Drawing	312	11,200.00	
Professional Fees	411		24,000.00
Rent Expense	511	2,550.00	
Telephone Expense	512	338.70	
Salary Expense	513	9,450.00	
Automobile Expense	514	792.70	
Charitable Contributions Expense	515	160.00	
Miscellaneous Expense	516	81.40	
		36,824.36	36,824.36

A narrative of the transactions completed by Mr. Lees during the month of October follows below and on page 102. He has two employees.

NARRATIVE OF TRANSACTIONS FOR OCTOBER

Oct. 1. Paid one month's rent, $425.
2. Paid telephone bill, $53.30.
2. Gave the Salvation Army $10.
5. Received $1,325 from Associated Grocers for services rendered.
7. Paid a garage bill, $27.60.
9. Received $1,100 from the Breckenridge Hotels for services rendered.

Oct. 12. Paid Venture Department Store, $32.40. (Debit Mr. Lees' drawing account.)
  15. Mr. Lees withdrew $975 for personal use.
  16. Paid IBM, Inc., $90 on account.
  19. Received $1,220 from IGA Food Stores for services rendered.
  23. Gave the American Cancer Society $15.
  26. Paid the Data Processing Management Association $150 for annual membership dues and fees.
  29. Received $650 from Barford Motor Sales Co. for professional services.
  31. Mr. Lees withdrew $900 for personal use.
  31. Paid October salaries, $1,575.

REQUIRED: (1) Journalize the October transactions, using a sheet of two-column journal paper. Number the pages and use both sides of the sheet if necessary. Foot the amount columns. (2) Open the necessary accounts, using the standard account form of ledger paper. Allow one page for each account. Record the October 1 balances as shown in the September 30 trial balance and post the journal entries for October. (3) Foot the ledger accounts, enter the balances, and prove the balances by taking a trial balance as of October 31. Use a sheet of two-column journal paper for the trial balance.

Problem 2-C

THE R. E. BURLEW AGENCY
Trial Balance
January 31, 19--

Account	No.	Debit	Credit
Cash	111	2,896.41	
Stationery and Supplies	112	562.76	
Office Furniture	121	1,842.00	
Notes Payable	211		900.00
Accounts Payable	212		643.29
R. E. Burlew, Capital	311		3,516.88
R. E. Burlew, Drawing	312	630.40	
Professional Fees	411		2,147.20
Rent Expense	511	400.00	
Telephone Expense	512	31.60	
Salary Expense	513	480.00	
Traveling Expense	514	316.52	
Stationery and Supplies Expense	515	18.43	
Miscellaneous Expense	516	29.25	
		7,207.37	7,207.37

REQUIRED: (1) Prepare an income statement for The R. E. Burlew Agency showing the results of the first month of operations, January. (2) Prepare a balance sheet in account form showing the financial condition of the agency as of January 31. Use a sheet of two-column statement paper for the income statement. Two sheets of two-column statement paper may be used for the balance sheet. List the assets on one sheet and the liabilities and owner's equity on the other sheet.

Problem 3-A   Mary Ryan is an interior designer. The only book of original entry for her business is a two-column journal. She uses the standard form of account in the general ledger. Following is the trial balance of her business taken as of November 30:

MARY RYAN, INTERIOR DESIGNER
Trial Balance
November 30, 19--

Cash	111	3,634.28	
Office Equipment	112	800.00	
Accounts Payable	211		191.45
Mary Ryan, Capital	311		7,371.93
Mary Ryan, Drawing	312	5,500.00	
Professional Fees	411		11,990.00
Rent Expense	511	2,200.00	
Telephone Expense	512	225.60	
Electric Expense	513	143.70	
Salary Expense	514	6,600.00	
Charitable Contributions Expense	515	325.00	
Miscellaneous Expense	516	124.80	
		19,553.38	19,553.38

NARRATIVE OF TRANSACTIONS FOR DECEMBER

Dec. 1. Paid December office rent, $200.
    1. Paid electric bill, $12.67.
    2. Paid telephone bill, $16.85.
    2. Received a check from Wagner Electric Co. for $500 for services rendered.
    6. Received $400 from Wetterau Grocery Co. for services rendered.
    7. Donated $25 to the Heart Association.
    7. Paid $7.25 for cleaning office.
    8. Received check for $400 from Nooter Corporation for consulting services.
    12. Miss Ryan withdrew $350 for personal use.
    15. Paid secretary's salary for the half month, $300.
    16. Purchased office furniture on credit from Union Furniture Co., $600.
    19. Paid $5 for having the office windows washed.
    20. Received $200 from Associated General Contractors for services rendered.
    22. Paid traveling expenses while on business, $32.25.
    23. Donated $30 to the United Fund.
    26. Paid Union Furniture Co. $200 on account.

Dec. 28. Miss Ryan withdrew $150 for personal use.
   30. Paid secretary's salary for the half month, $300.

REQUIRED: (1) Journalize the December transactions. For the journal, use two sheets of two-column journal paper and number the pages. (2) Open the necessary ledger accounts. Allow one page for each account and number the accounts. Record the December 1 balances and post the journal entries. Foot the ledger accounts and enter the balances. (3) Take a trial balance.

Problem 3-B

Orvinne Sutter, a plumber, completed the following transactions with the Delmar Bank during the month of October:

Oct. 1. Balance in bank per record kept on check stubs.....	$2,500.00	
1. Deposit..........	1,500.00	
1. Check No. 108	288.20	
4. Check No. 109	30.00	
4. Check No. 110	475.00	
4. Check No. 111	110.00	
5. Check No. 112	125.00	
6. Check No. 113	90.00	
7. Check No. 114	155.60	
7. Check No. 115	50.00	
7. Check No. 116	46.00	
7. Deposit..........	268.45	
8. Check No. 117	454.32	
Oct. 12. Check No. 118	$ 80.00	
12. Check No. 119	45.90	
13. Check No. 120	447.75	
14. Check No. 121	41.80	
14. Check No. 122	247.32	
14. Deposit..........	381.43	
18. Check No. 123	125.00	
18. Check No. 124	265.01	
21. Check No. 125	97.45	
21. Deposit..........	971.00	
25. Check No. 126	131.42	
25. Check No. 127	108.38	
27. Check No. 128	277.97	
28. Check No. 129	83.00	
29. Check No. 130	547.63	
29. Deposit..........	825.14	

REQUIRED: (1) A record of the bank account as it would appear on the check stubs. (2) A reconciliation of the bank statement for October which indicated a balance of $2,930.87 on October 29, with Checks Nos. 116, 126, 129, and 130 outstanding, and a service charge of 45 cents.

Problem 3-C

Alex Karlos, a general contractor, had a balance of $100 in his petty cash fund as of June 1. During June the following petty cash transactions were completed:

June 2. Paid $7.50 for typewriter repairs. Petty Cash Voucher No. 22.
   4. Gave Mr. Karlos $3.25 to reimburse him for a long distance telephone call made from a booth. Petty Cash Voucher No. 23.
   8. Gave $10 to the United Fund. Petty Cash Voucher No. 24.
   9. Paid garage for washing car, $1.75. Petty Cash Voucher No. 25.
   11. Gave Mr. Karlos' son $3. (Debit Alex Karlos, Drawing.) Petty Cash Voucher No. 26.
   14. Paid for postage stamps, $13. Petty Cash Voucher No. 27.

June 18. Paid for newspaper for month, $4.75. Petty Cash Voucher No. 28.
    22. Paid for window washing, $2.50. Petty Cash Voucher No. 29.
    28. Paid $10 to the Parent-Teachers Association for dues. (Debit Alex Karlos, Drawing.) Petty Cash Voucher No. 30.
    28. Paid for car lubrication, $4.50. Petty Cash Voucher No. 31.
    29. Donated $15 to the American Red Cross. Petty Cash Voucher No. 32.
    30. Rendered report of petty cash expenditures for month and received the amount needed to replenish the petty cash fund.

REQUIRED: **(1)** Record the foregoing transactions in a petty cash disbursements record, distributing the expenditures as follows:

    Alex Karlos, Drawing   Charitable Contributions Expense
    Automobile Expense   Miscellaneous Expense
    Telephone Expense

(2) Prove the petty cash disbursements record by footing the amount columns and proving the totals. Enter the totals and rule the amount columns with single and double lines. **(3)** Prepare a statement of the petty cash disbursements for June. **(4)** Bring down the balance in the petty cash fund below the ruling in the Description column. Enter the amount received to replenish the fund and record the total.

Problem 4-A   Following is a summary of the hours worked, rates of pay, and other relevant information concerning the employees of The Winston Machine Tool Co., R. J. Winston, owner, for the week ended Saturday, November 6. Employees are paid at the rate of time and one half for all hours worked in excess of 8 in any day or 40 in any week.

No.	Name	Allowances Claimed	M	T	W	T	F	S	Regular Hourly Rate	Cumulative Earnings Jan. 1–Oct. 30
1	Blake, Allen H.	3	8	8	8	8	8	6	$5.00	$10,679
2	Harter, Janet R.	4	8	9	8	8	8	4	9.00	18,810
3	Markland, Marilyn E.	3	8	8	8	8	8	0	5.50	12,740
4	Reardon, John H.	1	8	8	8	9	8	4	4.35	6,434
5	Stevens, Carolyn R.	2	8	8	8	8	0	4	5.40	8,480
6	Willey, James L.	1	8	8	8	8	0	0	6.00	9,922

Blake and Reardon each have $3 withheld this payday for group life insurance. Harter and Willey each have $20 withheld this payday for private hospital insurance. Stevens has $5 withheld this payday as a contribution to the United Fund.

REQUIRED: **(1)** Using plain ruled paper size 8½" by 11", rule a payroll register form similar to that reproduced on pages 76 and 77 and insert the necessary columnar headings. Enter on this form the payroll for the week ended Saturday, November 6. Refer to the Weekly Income Tax Table on page 75 to determine the amounts to be withheld from the wages of each worker for income tax purposes. All of Winston's employees are married. Six percent of the taxable wages of all of the employees except Harter should be withheld for FICA tax. Checks Nos. 511 through 516 were issued to the employees. Complete the payroll record by footing the amount columns, proving the footings, entering the totals, and ruling. (2) Assuming that the wages were paid on November 9, record the payment on a sheet of two-column journal paper.

Problem 4-B   The Clayton Store employs 12 people. They are paid by checks on the 15th and last day of each month. The entry to record each payroll includes the liabilities for the amounts withheld. The expense and liabilities arising from the employer's payroll taxes are recorded on each payday.

Following is a narrative of the transactions completed during the month of January that relate to payrolls and payroll taxes:

Jan. 15. Payroll for first half of month:
    Total salaries $4,480.00
    Less amounts withheld:
      FICA tax $268.80
      Employees' income tax 450.10   718.90
    Net amount paid $3,761.10

15. Social security taxes imposed on employer:
    FICA tax, 6%
    State unemployment tax, 2%
    FUTA tax, 0.7%

28. Paid $1,501.27 for December's payroll taxes:
    FICA tax, $590.47.
    Employees' income tax withheld, $910.80.

28. Paid state unemployment tax for quarter ended December 31, $137.60.

28. Paid FUTA tax for quarter ended December 31, $138.28.

31. Payroll for last half of month:
    Total salaries $4,720.00
    Less amounts withheld:
      FICA tax $283.20
      Employees' income tax 417.20   700.40
    Net amount paid $4,019.60

31. Social security taxes imposed on employer:
    All salaries taxable; rates same as on January 15.

REQUIRED: (1) Journalize the foregoing transactions, using two-column journal paper. (2) Foot the debit and credit amount columns as a means of proof.

5

Accounting for Personal Service (Attorneys)

In contrast to a manufacturing enterprise which manufactures and sells merchandise or a mercantile enterprise which buys merchandise for resale, a personal service enterprise is one in which service is rendered to a company or a person. There are two types of personal service enterprises:

(a) Professional enterprises
(b) Business enterprises

Professional enterprises include public accountants, attorneys, physicians, dentists, engineers, architects, artists, educators, and other professionals whose income is earned chiefly by performing personal services.

Business enterprises of the personal service type include insurance, brokerage, advertising, real estate, entertainment, storage, transportation, and dry cleaning.

In a personal service firm such as that conducted by attorneys, the most valuable asset the attorney has is time. The significance of time to a professional firm cannot be overemphasized. Adequate time records must be maintained by each attorney, including the sole practitioner. Many legal firms believe that it is desirable for each attorney to account for a working day by analyzing the activities that cannot be charged to clients. An analysis of nonchargeable time will disclose the amount of time the firm is devoting to community affairs, research, and other desirable activities.

Time records may be kept in various ways; some attorneys maintain a daily diary, and the chargeable time is posted daily to the client's record. In a large law firm, weekly reports of work for each client may be used to reduce paperwork. A third method of time reporting is to use a consolidated weekly report of all attorney time. Thus, a secretary posts the billable time to the client's record on a weekly rather than a daily basis.

The cash basis of accounting for a personal service enterprise

Most law firms use the cash basis of accounting which means that revenue is not recognized until cash is received and expenses are not recorded until paid. Thus, services may be performed in one month, and the revenue may be accounted for the following month or several months later. The cash basis of accounting violates the **matching principle** which holds that revenues earned and expenses incurred during a period should be matched against each other in order to arrive at as accurate a figure of net income or net loss for the period as possible. In many cases, however, expenses such as rent or telephone bills may be approximately the same each month, so that only a slight distortion is caused by paying and recording an expense in November which actually was incurred in October. The cash basis of accounting is acceptable for federal and state income tax purposes.

It should be noted that accounting cannot be based completely on cash transactions. Property or service accepted in lieu of cash must be recorded as revenue at the fair market value of the property or service at the time it is received. Also, if revenue such as interest on a savings account is available for withdrawal by the owner of the account, the revenue is said to be *constructively received* and must be reported as revenue even though no cash is withdrawn from the account.

Another exception to the cash basis of accounting is made when depreciation is recorded. Assets which provide benefits for several years, such as automobiles or office equipment, will wear out or *depreciate* with the passage of time. When such assets are purchased, they must be debited to asset accounts. As the asset is used, expense is incurred which should be allocated over the estimated life of the asset. The purpose of depreciation is to charge the expense to the period in which it is actually incurred, in accordance with the matching principle explained above. The portion of cost assigned to each period is called **depreciation expense**.

For example, an automobile, possibly the largest item in the balance sheet of a legal firm, must be debited to the asset account Automobile. Depreciation of the automobile is based on the cost, less any residual or scrap value, and the estimated life of the automobile. Since the residual value and the expected useful life are estimates, the amount charged to depreciation expense each period is not entirely accurate; but an allocation of cost over the expected useful life of an asset results in a more equitable profit or loss measurement than charging such an asset to expense in the period it is purchased.

When an entry is made at the end of the period debiting Depreciation Expense, the credit is usually to an account called *Accumulated Depreciation*, such as Accumulated Depreciation — Automobile. Accumulated depreciation accounts are **contra accounts** (meaning "opposite" or "offsetting" accounts) and should be deducted from the related asset accounts in the balance sheet. The difference between the asset account and the accumulated depreciation account is known as the **book value** of the asset. Adjustments for depreciation will be explained further in Chapter 7.

Chart of accounts

To illustrate the cash basis of accounting for an attorney, a chart of accounts for Donald L. Cameron, Attorney at Law, is reproduced below. Note that all asset accounts have account numbers beginning with 1; liability accounts begin with 2; owner's equity accounts begin with 3; revenue accounts begin with 4; expense accounts begin with 5; and contra accounts begin with 0. New accounts may be added as needed without disturbing the numerical order of the existing accounts.

DONALD L. CAMERON, ATTORNEY AT LAW
CHART OF ACCOUNTS

Assets*
  111 First National Bank
  112 Petty Cash Fund
  131 Advances on Behalf of Clients
  141 Law Library
  014 Accumulated Depreciation — Law Library
  151 Office Equipment
  015 Accumulated Depreciation — Office Equipment
  161 Automobile
  016 Accumulated Depreciation — Automobile

Liabilities
  211 Accounts Payable
  221 Employees Income Tax Payable
  231 FICA Tax Payable
  241 FUTA Tax Payable
  251 State Unemployment Tax Payable

Owner's Equity
  311 Donald L. Cameron, Capital
  031 Donald L. Cameron, Drawing
  321 Expense and Revenue Summary

Revenue
  411 Legal Fees Revenue
  412 Collection Fees Revenue

Expenses
  511 Salary Expense
  512 Payroll Taxes Expense
  513 Rent Expense
  514 Telephone Expense
  515 Office Supplies Expense
  516 Automobile Expense
  517 Depreciation Expense
  518 Charitable Contributions Expense
  519 Miscellaneous Expense

*Words in italics represent headings and not account titles.

Many of the accounts in the preceding list have been explained and their uses illustrated in the previous chapters. Accounts appearing for the first time in this chapter will be discussed before the records of Mr. Cameron are presented.

Advances on Behalf of Clients, Account No. 131. Payments for items such as court filing fees, fees charged by accountants for making audits, and the cost of obtaining depositions are sometimes made for clients. Absorption of these expenses by the attorney would be equivalent to lowering fees for certain clients. To avoid unethical "fee cutting," payments made for clients are debited to the account Advances on Behalf of Clients and then billed to the clients on a monthly or quarterly basis. A record of the payments made and remittances received is also made in the client's account on an office docket (an auxiliary record which provides a complete record of each legal case). A minimum amount, usually 50 cents to $1, can be established below which the firm will absorb the expense to save clerical work.

Expense and Revenue Summary, Account No. 321. The expense and revenue summary account is a clearing account which is used only when the books are closed at the end of the accounting period. Use of this account will be explained further in Chapter 8.

Legal Fees Revenue, Account No. 411. Legal Fees Revenue is a revenue account that is credited for cash received from clients in payment of legal work performed. When the accounts are kept on the cash basis, revenue is not recorded in the account until cash is received or until a note or other property is accepted in lieu of cash.

Since legal fees are usually not collected until they are billed, billing is very important. The more frequent the billing, the more frequent the collection. If bills are collected frequently, the firm can operate with a smaller cash investment, and in some cases may collect a larger total fee without impairing the client relationship than would be possible if the entire amount were billed at one time. Many clients of a law firm prefer to be billed on a monthly or quarterly basis even though the legal work is not completed, rather than to receive one large bill at the end of the engagement.

Collection Fees Revenue, Account No. 412. Fees charged for collecting accounts for clients from their customers, clients, or patients are revenue to the attorney making the collections. The account Collection Fees Revenue is credited for the commissions or fees received for collections made on behalf of clients. When a collection is made in partial or in full settlement of an account, the First National Bank account should be debited for the amount received. If the attorney receives much revenue from making collections for clients, an accounts payable account should be credited for the amount received less the amount of the fee. Collection Fees Revenue is credited for the amount of the fee. If Donald Cameron undertakes to collect an account amounting to $120 for the City Department Store on a commission basis of 33⅓%, the following entry should be made when cash is received in payment of the account:

April 14. First National Bank..	120	
Accounts Payable		80
Collection Fees Revenue		40
Collected an account in the amount of $120 on behalf of the City Department Store and recorded fee of $40.		

When the amount owed to the City Department Store ($80) is paid, an entry should be made as follows:

April 17. Accounts Payable	80	
First National Bank		80
Payment to City Department Store of collection made for them.		

If many collections are made for clients, it probably would be advisable to maintain a special account at the bank in which all cash, checks, and other cash items received in settlement of collection cases may be deposited. Maintaining this special account would separate funds collected for clients from funds belonging to the firm. Checks drawn payable to clients should be credited to the special account instead of to the regular disbursement account.

Books of account

Mr. Cameron uses the following books of account:

(a) General books
  (1) Combined cash journal
  (2) General ledger
(b) Auxiliary records
  (1) Petty cash disbursements record
  (2) Lawyer's office docket
  (3) Lawyer's collection docket
  (4) Employee's earnings record

Combined Cash Journal. Mr. Cameron uses only one book of original entry — a combined cash journal. Instead of the two amount columns in the journals illustrated in Chapter 2, Mr. Cameron's combined cash journal, reproduced on pages 122–125, contains eight amount columns, two on the left of the Description column and six on the right. The columnar arrangement follows:

- (a) First National Bank
  - (1) Deposits 111 Dr.
  - (2) Checks 111 Cr.
- (b) General
  - (1) Debit
  - (2) Credit
- (c) Revenue
  - (1) Legal Fees Revenue 411 Cr.
  - (2) Collection Fees Revenue 412 Cr.
- (d) Wage Deductions
  - (1) Employees Income Tax Payable 221 Cr.
  - (2) FICA Tax Payable 231 Cr.

The account numbers in the headings are an aid in completing the summary posting at the end of the month. The combined cash journal contains a Check Number column to the right of the Checks 111 Cr. column and four special columns to the right of the pair of General columns. Such a journal is sometimes called a special column journal because there are special columns for specific items. Special columns for accounts in which frequent entries are made will save time and labor in the bookkeeping process.

A narrative of transactions completed by Mr. Cameron during the month of December is given on pages 116–125. These transactions are recorded in the combined cash journal on pages 122–125. Note that before any transactions were recorded in this journal, the bank balance at the start of the month, $9,100.27, was entered in the Description column just above the words "Amounts Forwarded."

General Ledger. Mr. Cameron uses an account form, called a **balance-column account form**, which has four amount columns: a debit column, a credit column, and two balance columns — one for debit and one for credit. Although the standard two-column account form illustrated to this point is still favored by some, the four-column form of balance-column account has the advantage of providing a place to record the balance of the account. The balance may be determined and recorded after each transaction or only at the end of the month.

The ledger is reproduced on pages 126–130. In each case, the balance as of December 1 has been entered. The accounts in the general ledger are arranged in the order given in the chart of accounts shown on page 109. All posting to the general ledger accounts is from the combined cash journal. A trial balance is taken at the end of each month to prove the equality of the general ledger account balances. The trial balance as of December 31 appears on page 130.

Auxiliary Records. Auxiliary records are used to record information not recorded in the regular accounting records. Mr. Cameron uses a petty cash disbursements record, an office docket, and a collection docket as auxiliary records. An employee's earnings record, similar to the one illustrated in Chapter 4 on pages 80 and 81, is maintained for each employee.

Petty Cash Disbursements Record. Mr. Cameron maintains a petty cash fund in the amount of $50. The petty cash disbursements record is similar to that illustrated on pages 50 and 51.

Lawyer's Office Docket. An **office docket** is a form used to maintain a memorandum record of each legal case with a client. A model filled-in office docket (reproduced on page 114) shows the history of the case of Quality Manufacturing Corporation, plaintiff, vs. Rita Dennison, defendant. The legal information that may be needed in handling the case is recorded on the upper part of the form, and a memorandum account of the charges and credits to the account of the client is kept on the lower part of the form.

When an attorney's accounts are kept on the cash basis, there is no general ledger account for the client, but the information must be kept on the office docket. The client's account, as recorded on the office docket, should be charged for:

    (a) Fees for services rendered.
    (b) Disbursements on behalf of the client, such as filing fees and other expenses paid for the client.

The client's account should be credited for:

    (a) Payments received for services.
    (b) Reimbursements for advances made on behalf of the client.

In the illustration on page 114, the client, Quality Manufacturing Corporation, is charged for the following:

    November 24. Amount of the fee agreed upon at the time the case was taken, $425.
    November 29. Amount advanced in payment of suit fee, $5.

The account is credited for the following:

    December 1. Amount received as a retainer, $200.
    December 27. Amount received in payment of balance due on account, $230.

Lawyer's Office Docket

CLIENT Quality Manufacturing Corporation   **ADDRESS** 220 Market St., City   **NO.** 157

IN RE: Quality Manufacturing Corporation
vs. Rita Dennison

COURT	Common Pleas, Stone County
COURT FILE NO.	15743 19 78
CALENDAR NO.	785 ATTORNEY FOR Plaintiff
OTHER ATTORNEYS	
NATURE OF MATTER	Lawsuit
REMARKS	

DATE	SERVICES RENDERED	FEES AND DISBURSEMENTS		MONEYS RECEIVED PURPOSE	AMOUNT
Nov. 24	Fee for preparing case	425	00		
29	Suit fee	5	00		
Dec. 1				Retainer	200 00
27				Balance due	230 00
	CARRIED FORWARD				

Lawyer's Collection Docket. Lawyers who collect accounts for clients may use a form known as a **collection docket** to keep a record of the necessary information pertaining to collections. A model filled-in copy of a collection docket is shown below.

DEBTOR	James H. Moore			DATE CLAIM REC'D	12-5 1978	NO. 19	
ADDRESS	2236 Lebanon Road, City			DATE DISPOSED OF	1-31-79		
BUSINESS				TOTAL AMOUNT	$ 150.00		
CREDITOR	Jackson Department Store			AMOUNT COLLECTED	$ 150.		
ADDRESS	Main and Sims St., City			FEES	$ 50.00		
REC'D CLAIM FROM				EXPENSE	$		
ATTORNEY FOR DEBTOR				AMOUNT REMITTED	$ 100.		
CALLS ON DEBTOR				CHECK NO.	367 & 390		

		RECEIVED FROM CREDITOR	
	DATE	FOR	AMOUNT
CORRESPONDENCE	12-21	Com.	30 00
	1-15	Com.	20 00

RECEIVED FROM DEBTOR				PAID TO CREDITOR			
DATE	AMOUNT	DATE	AMOUNT	CHECK NO.	AMOUNT	CHECK NO.	AMOUNT
12 21	90 00			367	60 00		
1 15	60 00			390	40 00		

REMARKS: Statement of account. Collection fee 33 1/3%.
No suit without further instructions.

Lawyer's Collection Docket

The docket provides a record of the case of the Jackson Department Store, creditor, vs. James H. Moore, debtor. It also furnishes a record of the amounts collected from the debtor and the amounts paid to the creditor.

Attorneys usually take most collection cases on a percentage basis. Any expenses incurred in making collections should be charged to the expense accounts of the attorney and not to the client. If, however, a client has agreed to pay any expenses incident to a lawsuit, such as court costs, the amounts paid by the attorney should be charged to the client's account just the same as payments made for clients in handling other legal cases.

In the illustration, the following transactions were recorded on the collection docket for the Jackson Department Store:

December 21. Collected $90 from James H. Moore, debtor.
December 28. Paid $60 to the Jackson Department Store.
January 15. Collected $60 from James H. Moore, debtor.
January 31. Paid $40 to the Jackson Department Store.

The amount of the commission of 33⅓% is deducted from the amounts collected from the debtor and is entered on the collection docket as follows:

December 21. $30.
January 15. $20.

Employee's Earnings Record. The employee's earnings record was discussed in Chapter 4.

Following is a narrative of transactions completed by Donald L. Cameron during the month of December. These transactions are recorded in the combined cash journal on pages 122–125.

DONALD L. CAMERON, ATTORNEY AT LAW

Narrative of Transactions

Friday, December 1

Issued Check No. 351 for $450, payable to David Ramos, for the December office rent.

Received $200 from Quality Manufacturing Corporation as a retainer in the lawsuit of Quality Manufacturing Corporation against Rita Dennison. Case No. 157.

The amount received as a retainer constitutes revenue realized on the cash basis. Office Docket No. 157 is reproduced on page 114. This docket is an auxiliary record designed to supplement the information recorded in the regular accounting records and to facilitate the handling of the case.

The transaction was recorded in the combined cash journal by debiting First National Bank, Account No. 111, and by crediting Legal Fees Revenue, Account No. 411. Since this entry was recorded in special columns, individual posting is not required, and a check mark was placed in the Posting Reference column.

Monday, December 4

Issued Check No. 352 for $25.25 to the Columbia Electric Co. for electricity consumed during November. Debit Miscellaneous Expense, Account No. 519.

Received $175 from Miss Marian Gardner for services rendered in preparation of a trust agreement.

Tuesday, December 5

Issued Check No. 353 for $43.18 to the Bell Telephone Co. for November service.

Received a check for $150 from W. C. Macomber in payment of the balance due on Case No. 149.

Received for collection from the Jackson Department Store, Main and Sims Street, City, a statement of its account with James H. Moore, 2236 Lebanon Road, City, for $150. This account is over 18 months past due. Collection fee, 33⅓%; no suit without further instructions. Collection No. 19.

Inasmuch as Mr. Cameron's books are kept on the cash basis, no entry in the regular accounting records is required for this transaction. Collection Docket No. 19 is reproduced on page 115. This docket is an auxiliary record of information designed to supplement the information recorded in the regular accounting records and to facilitate handling the account.

Wednesday, December 6

Received a check for $510 from the Adams Manufacturing Company in full payment of Case No. 152.

Issued Check No. 354 for $89.74 to the Johnson Service Station in payment of the December 1 statement for gasoline, oil, and services rendered during November.

Thursday, December 7

Received a check for $250 from Woods and Meyer, certified public accountants, for drafting a partnership agreement.

Friday, December 8

Mr. Cameron has been engaged to represent the Mildred Cohen Advertising Agency, Inc., in the purchase of a building owned by Albert Snowden at a minimum fee of $825. Case No. 158. Received a check for $150 as a retainer.

Received an invoice of $45.70 from Sanders Stationery Company, 1011 Fifth Avenue, City, for stationery and supplies.

> Since Mr. Cameron's books are kept on the cash basis, invoices for expenses are not recorded until they are paid. When expense invoices are received, they are filed in an invoice file until they are paid. When payment is made, the proper entry is made in the combined cash journal.

Proved the footings of the combined cash journal. Deposits of cash receipts have been made in the First National Bank on the day of receipt. Compared the cash balance in the combined cash journal with the balance in the checkbook ($9,927.10). Completed the individual postings from the General Debit and Credit columns of the combined cash journal to the ledger accounts. As each item was posted, the account number was entered in the Posting Reference column of the combined cash journal and the page number of the combined cash journal was entered in the Posting Reference column of the account.

Monday, December 11

Received a check for $327.18 from Robert J. Wayne in payment of the amount due on Collection No. 17.

> The collection docket shows that Mr. Cameron had agreed to handle this collection on a 33⅓% commission basis. The transaction was entered in the combined cash journal by debiting First National Bank, Account No. 111, for $327.18, by crediting Accounts Payable, Account No. 211, for the amount due to the Nina Rogers Co., $218.12, and by crediting Collection Fees Revenue, Account No. 412, for the commission earned, $109.06. A memorandum entry was also made in the collection docket for the amount received from the debtor.

Tuesday, December 12

Issued Check No. 355 for $886.34 to the Modern Law Book Company for law books.

Wednesday, December 13

Issued Check No. 356 for $25 to the Christmas Bureau Fund.

> The check is recorded in the combined cash journal by debiting Charitable Contributions Expense, Account No. 518, and crediting First National Bank, Account No. 111.

Received $75 from the Toland and Harrison Plumbing Co. for preparing and filing a mechanic's lien on the property of H. R. Ruf.

Thursday, December 14

Issued Check No. 357 for $70 to the State Bar Association for annual dues.

> The amount of this check was debited to Miscellaneous Expense, Account No. 519, since a separate expense account is not maintained for dues.

Received $50 from Mrs. Marsha Wong for preparing a lease on office space in a building owned by Mrs. Wong.

Issued Check No. 358 for $327.60 to the First National Bank in payment of the following payroll taxes based on wages paid during the month of November:

Employees' income tax withheld from wages		$177.60
FICA tax:		
Withheld from employees' wages	$75.00	
Imposed on employer	75.00	150.00
Amount of check		$327.60

A Federal Tax Deposit, Form 501, was filled out and sent with the check. Mr. Cameron will not be required to pay the balance in the FUTA tax payable account until January.

Mr. Cameron telephoned the First National Bank and learned that the check for $327.18 received from Robert J. Wayne had cleared. Issued Check No. 359 to the Nina Rogers Co. in the net amount of $218.12, which represents the full amount of Collection No. 17, $327.18, less a 33⅓% collection fee, $109.06.

> This transaction was recorded in the combined cash journal by debiting Accounts Payable, Account No. 211, and by crediting the bank for the amount of the check. The collection fee had been recorded at the time the remittance was received from the debtor. A memorandum entry, however, was made in the collection docket to record the amount paid to the creditor. Since the claim was settled in full, the following information was entered in the upper right-hand corner of the collection docket: (a) the date the case was disposed of, (b) the total amount collected, (c) the total amount of the attorney's fees, (d) the amount sent to the client, and (e) the check number.

Friday, December 15

Mr. Cameron withdrew $865 for personal use. Check No. 360.

> The check was recorded in the combined cash journal by debiting Donald L. Cameron, Drawing, Account No. 031, and by crediting the First National Bank.

Issued the following checks in payment of salaries for the first half of the month:

No. 361 for $258.80 to Joan Larsen, part-time law clerk, in payment of her salary in the amount of $325, less $19.50 withheld for FICA tax and $46.70 withheld for income tax.

No. 362 for $239.90 to Henrietta Duncan, the office secretary, in payment of her salary in the amount of $300, less $18 withheld for FICA tax and $42.10 withheld for income tax.

Received a check for $725 from R. E. Olds Company, 225 Lake Avenue, City, in full payment of Case No. 151. This remittance is in payment of the balance due for legal fees, $500, and $225 for payment of an audit fee paid by Mr. Cameron on November 10 and debited to Advances on Behalf of Clients.

> The check was recorded in the combined cash journal by debiting First National Bank, Account No. 111, for $725, by crediting Advances on Behalf of Clients, Account No. 131, for $225, and by crediting Legal Fees Revenue, Account No. 411, for $500.

Proved the footings of the combined cash journal. Compared the cash balance in the combined cash journal with the balance in the checkbook ($8,213.52). Completed the individual postings from the General Debit and Credit columns of the combined cash journal to the ledger accounts.

Monday, December 18

Issued Check No. 363 for $45.70 to the Sanders Stationery Company in payment of the invoice received on December 8. Office Supplies Expense is debited.

Mr. Cameron completed the work he had been doing on the settlement of the estate of Albert O. Foster, deceased, and received a check for $8,500 in payment of his services. Case No. 143.

Tuesday, December 19

Received $75 from Ms. Ruth Hamilton for drawing a will.

Wednesday, December 20

Received $100 as a retainer from Melvin Robertson, 1401 Broadway, City, in the case of Williams vs. Robertson. Minimum fee, $500 and costs. Case No. 159.

Issued Check No. 364 for $620.18 to the City Typewriter Co. in payment for a new electric typewriter.

> This transaction was recorded in the combined cash journal by debiting Office Equipment, Account No. 151, and crediting First National Bank, Account No. 111.

Thursday, December 21

Received a check for $90 from James H. Moore to apply on his account with the Jackson Department Store. Collection No. 19.

Received a check for $675 from the Mildred Cohen Advertising Agency, Inc., in payment of the balance due for legal work done in connection with the purchase of a building. Case No. 158.

Friday, December 22

Miss Carolyn Hill, 2705 Seneca Avenue, City, has engaged Mr. Cameron to handle the incorporation of an insurance agency. Minimum fee, $650. A check for $100 was received as a retainer. Case No. 160.

Received an invoice for $84.70 from the Legal Supply Co., 70 Church Street, New York City, for legal forms.

Legal forms used by an attorney are an expense, and invoices for expenses are recorded only when paid in cash.

Proved the footings of the combined cash journal. Compared the cash balance in the combined cash journal with the balance in the checkbook ($17,087.64). Completed the individual postings from the General Debit and Credit columns of the combined cash journal to the ledger accounts.

Wednesday, December 27

Received a check for $230 from the Quality Manufacturing Corporation in payment of the balance due on account. Case No. 157.

The check was recorded in the combined cash journal by debiting First National Bank, Account No. 111, for $230, by crediting Advances on Behalf of Clients, Account No. 131, for $5, and by crediting Legal Fees Revenue, Account No. 411, for $225.

Mr. Cameron directed that Check No. 365 for $49.75 be issued to the Gilbert Department Store in payment of his personal account.

Since this transaction is a disbursement in payment of a personal account of Mr. Cameron, it was recorded in the combined cash journal by debiting Donald L. Cameron, Drawing, Account No. 031, and by crediting the First National Bank, Account No. 111.

Mr. Cameron has been engaged by Thelma Baldwin to administer the estate of Nicholas Baldwin, deceased. Minimum fee is $500. A check for $75 was received as a retainer. Case No. 161.

Thursday, December 28

Issued Check No. 366 for $375 to M. J. Horn, CPA, in payment of her statement covering auditing service rendered to Mr. Cameron's client, F. E. Lyons. Case No. 156.

Received a check in the amount of $250 from T. S. Edwards in settlement of account. Case No. 155.

Issued Check No. 367 for $60 to the Jackson Department Store to remit a partial collection from James H. Moore in the amount of $90, less a 33⅓% collection fee. Collection No. 19.

Friday, December 29

Mr. Cameron withdrew $900 for personal use. Check No. 368.

Issued the following checks in payment of salaries for the second half of the month:

No. 369 for $258.80 to Joan Larsen, part-time law clerk, in payment of her salary in the amount of $325, less $19.50 withheld for FICA tax and $46.70 withheld for income tax.

No. 370 for $239.90 to Henrietta Duncan, the office secretary, in payment of her salary in the amount of $300, less $18 withheld for FICA tax and $42.10 withheld for income tax.

PAGE 33 — COMBINED CASH JOURNAL

First National Bank Deposits 111 DR	First National Bank Checks 111 CR	CK. NO.	DAY	DESCRIPTION	POST. REF.
				AMOUNTS FORWARDED Balance 9,100.27	
	450 00	351	1	Rent Expense	513
200 00			1	Quality Mfg. Corp. Case #157	✓
	25 25	352	4	Miscellaneous Expense	519
175 00			4	Marian Gardner, Trust Agreement	✓
	43 18	353	5	Telephone Expense	514
150 00			5	W. C. Macomber Case #149	✓
510 00			6	Adams Mfg. Co. Case #152	✓
	89 74	354	6	Automobile Expense	516
250 00			7	Woods & Meyer, Partnership Agreement	✓
150 00			8	M. Cohen Adv. Agency, Inc. Case #158	✓
1435 00	608 17				
32 18			11	Accts. Pay.—Nina Rogers Co. Coll. #17 9,927.10	211
	886 34	355	12	Law Library	141
	25 00	356	13	Charitable Contributions Expense	518
75 00			13	Toland & Harrison Plbg. Co. Mech. Lien	✓
	70 00	357	14	Miscellaneous Expense	519
50 00			14	Marsha Wong, Lease	✓
	327 60	358	14	Employees Income Tax Payable	221
				FICA Tax Payable	231
	218 12	359	14	Accts. Pay.—Nina Rogers Co. Coll. #17	211
	865 00	360	15	Donald L. Cameron, Drawing	031
	258 80	361	15	Salary Expense	511
	239 90	362	15	Salary Expense	511
725 00			15	R. E. Olds Co. Case #151	✓
				Advances on Behalf of Clients 8,213.52	131
2612 18	3498 93				
	45 70	363	18	Office Supplies Expense	515
8500 00			18	Albert O. Foster Case #143	✓
75 00			19	Ruth Hamilton, Will	✓
100 00			20	Melvin Robertson Case #159	✓
	620 18	364	20	Office Equipment	151
90 00			21	Accts. Pay.—Jackson Dept. Store Coll. #19	211
675 00			21	M. Cohen Adv. Agency Inc. Case #158	✓
100 00			22	Carolyn Hill Case #160	✓
12152 18	4164 81			Carried Forward 17,087.64	
12152 18	4164 81				

Donald L. Cameron, Attorney at Law — Combined Cash Journal (Left Page)

Chapter 5 — Accounting for Personal Service (Attorneys) — 123

FOR MONTH OF December 1978 — PAGE 33

#	GENERAL DEBIT	GENERAL CREDIT	REVENUE LEGAL FEES 411 CR.	REVENUE COLL. FEES 412 CR.	WAGE DEDUCTIONS EMP. INC. TAX PAY. 221 CR.	WAGE DEDUCTIONS FICA TAX PAY. 231 CR.
1						
2	45000					
3			20000			
4	2525					
5			17500			
6	4318					
7			15000			
8			51000			
9	8974					
10			25000			
11			15000			
12	60817	21812	143500	10906		
13	88634					
14	2500					
15			7500			
16	7000					
17			5000			
18	17760					
19	15000					
20	21812					
21	86500					
22	32500				4670	1950
23	30000				4210	1800
24			50000			
25		22500				
26	362523 4570	44312	206000	10906	8880	3750
27			850000			
28			7500			
29			10000			
30	62018					
31		6000		3000		
32			67500			
33			10000			
34	429111 429111	50312 50312	1151000 1151000	13906 13906	8880 8880	3750 3750

Donald L. Cameron, Attorney at Law — Combined Cash Journal (Right Page)

COMBINED CASH JOURNAL — PAGE 34

	FIRST NATIONAL BANK		CK. NO.	DAY	DESCRIPTION	POST. REF.
	DEPOSITS 111 DR.	CHECKS 111 CR.				
1	1,215.18	416.48		22	AMOUNTS FORWARDED Balance 17,087.64	✓
2	230.00			27	Quality Mfg. Corp. Case #157	✓
3					Advances on Behalf of Clients	131
4		49.75	365	27	Donald L. Cameron, Drawing	031
5	75.00			27	Thelma Baldwin Case #161	✓
6		375.00	366	28	Advances on Behalf of Clients Case #156	131
7	250.00			28	Marvin Edwards Case #155	✓
8		60.00	367	28	Accts. Pay. – Jackson Dept. Store Coll. #19	211
9		900.00	368	29	Donald L. Cameron, Drawing	031
10		258.80	369	29	Salary Expense	511
11		239.90	370	29	Salary Expense	511
12		37.52	371	29	Advances on Behalf of Clients	131
13					Donald L. Cameron, Drawing	031
14					Office Supplies Expense	515
15					Automobile Expense	516
16					Charitable Contributions Expense	518
17					Miscellaneous Expense	519
18				29	Payroll Taxes Expense	512
19					FICA Tax Payable 15,721.67	✓
20	1,270.18 1,270.18	6,085.78 6,085.78				
21	(111)	(111)				

Donald L. Cameron, Attorney at Law — Combined Cash Journal (Left Page) *(concluded)*

Issued Check No. 371 for $37.52 to replenish the petty cash fund. The following statement provided the information needed in recording this transaction in the combined cash journal:

STATEMENT OF PETTY CASH DISBURSEMENTS FOR DECEMBER

Advances on Behalf of Clients	$10.00
Donald L. Cameron, Drawing	8.00
Office Supplies Expense	5.95
Automobile Expense	3.72
Charitable Contributions Expense	3.00
Miscellaneous Expense	6.85
Total disbursements	$37.52

Made an entry in the combined cash journal for the employer's portion of the FICA tax for the month of December by debiting

Chapter 5   Accounting for Personal Service (Attorneys)   **125**

	GENERAL		REVENUE		WAGE DEDUCTIONS	
	DEBIT	CREDIT	LEGAL FEES 411 CR.	COLL. FEES 412 CR.	EMP. INC. TAX PAY. 221 CR.	FICA TAX PAY. 231 CR.
1	4291 11	503 12	1151 00	139 06	88 80	37 50
2			225 00			
3		5 00				
4	49 75					
5			75 00			
6	375 00					
7			250 00			
8	60 00					
9	900 00					
10	325 00				46 70	19 50
11	300 00				42 10	18 00
12	10 00					
13	8 00					
14	5 95					
15	3 72					
16	3 00					
17	6 85					
18	75 00					
19						75 00
20	6413 38 / 6413 38	508 12 / 508 12	1206 00 / 1206 00	139 06 / 139 06	177 60 / 177 60	150 00 / 150 00
21	(✓)	(✓)	(411)	(412)	(221)	(231)

Donald L. Cameron, Attorney at Law — Combined Cash Journal (Right Page) *(concluded)*

Payroll Taxes Expense and by crediting FICA Tax Payable for $75. Both of Mr. Cameron's employees' wages have exceeded $6,000, and there is therefore no expense in the month of December for federal or state unemployment taxes.

Proved the footings, entered the totals, and ruled the combined cash journal. Compared the bank balance in the combined cash journal with the balance in the checkbook ($15,721.67). Completed the individual postings from the General Debit and Credit columns of the combined cash journal to the ledger accounts. Since this was the end of the month, the summary posting was completed, and the account numbers were written immediately below the totals of the columns in the combined cash journal. A trial balance of the general ledger accounts which have balances on December 31 appears on page 130.

Account: First National Bank — Account No. 111

DATE	ITEM	POST. REF.	DEBIT	CREDIT	BALANCE DEBIT	BALANCE CREDIT
1978 Dec. 1	Balance	✓			9100 27	
29		CG34	12707 18			
29		CG34		6035 78	15721 67	

Account: Petty Cash Fund — Account No. 112

DATE	ITEM	POST. REF.	DEBIT	CREDIT	BALANCE DEBIT	BALANCE CREDIT
1978 Dec. 1	Balance	✓			50 00	

Account: Advances on Behalf of Clients — Account No. 131

DATE	ITEM	POST. REF.	DEBIT	CREDIT	BALANCE DEBIT	BALANCE CREDIT
1978 Dec. 1	Balance	✓			285 00	
15		CG33		225 00		
27		CG34		5 00		
28		CG34	375 00			
29		CG34	10 00		440 00	

Account: Law Library — Account No. 141

DATE	ITEM	POST. REF.	DEBIT	CREDIT	BALANCE DEBIT	BALANCE CREDIT
1978 Dec. 1	Balance	✓			8965 74	
12		CG33	886 34		9852 08	

Account: Accumulated Depreciation — Law Library — Account No. 014

DATE	ITEM	POST. REF.	DEBIT	CREDIT	BALANCE DEBIT	BALANCE CREDIT
1978 Dec. 1	Balance	✓				2724 13

Account: Office Equipment — Account No. 151

DATE	ITEM	POST. REF.	DEBIT	CREDIT	BALANCE DEBIT	BALANCE CREDIT
1978 Dec. 1	Balance	✓			2321 87	
20		CG33	620 18		2942 05	

Account: Accumulated Depreciation — Office Equip. — Account No. 015

DATE	ITEM	POST. REF.	DEBIT	CREDIT	BALANCE DEBIT	BALANCE CREDIT
1978 Dec. 1	Balance	✓				394 71

Donald L. Cameron, Attorney at Law — General Ledger

Account: Automobile — Account No. 161

DATE	ITEM	POST. REF.	DEBIT	CREDIT	BALANCE DEBIT	BALANCE CREDIT
1978 Dec. 1	Balance	✓			3650 23	

Account: Accumulated Depreciation — Automobile — Account No. 016

DATE	ITEM	POST. REF.	DEBIT	CREDIT	BALANCE DEBIT	BALANCE CREDIT
1978 Dec. 1	Balance	✓				1368 83

Account: Accounts Payable — Account No. 211

DATE	ITEM	POST. REF.	DEBIT	CREDIT	BALANCE DEBIT	BALANCE CREDIT
1978 Dec. 11		CJ33		218 12		
14		CJ33	218 12			
21		CJ33		60 00		
28		CJ34	60 00		—0—	—0—

Account: Employees Income Tax Payable — Account No. 221

DATE	ITEM	POST. REF.	DEBIT	CREDIT	BALANCE DEBIT	BALANCE CREDIT
1978 Dec. 1	Balance	✓				177 60
14		CJ33	177 60		—0—	—0—
29		CJ34		177 60		177 60

Account: FICA Tax Payable — Account No. 231

DATE	ITEM	POST. REF.	DEBIT	CREDIT	BALANCE DEBIT	BALANCE CREDIT
1978 Dec. 1	Balance	✓				150 00
14		CJ33	150 00		—0—	—0—
29		CJ34		150 00		150 00

Account: FUTA Tax Payable — Account No. 241

DATE	ITEM	POST. REF.	DEBIT	CREDIT	BALANCE DEBIT	BALANCE CREDIT
1978 Dec. 1	Balance	✓				84 00

Account: State Unemployment Tax Payable — Account No. 251

DATE	ITEM	POST. REF.	DEBIT	CREDIT	BALANCE DEBIT	BALANCE CREDIT
1978 Dec. 1	Balance	✓				20 25

Donald L. Cameron, Attorney at Law — General Ledger *(continued)*

Account: Donald L. Cameron, Capital — Account No. 311

DATE	ITEM	POST. REF.	DEBIT	CREDIT	BALANCE DEBIT	BALANCE CREDIT
1978 Dec. 1	Balance	✓				2221369

Account: Donald L. Cameron, Drawing — Account No. 031

DATE	ITEM	POST. REF.	DEBIT	CREDIT	BALANCE DEBIT	BALANCE CREDIT
1978 Dec. 1	Balance	✓			2103025	
15		CJ33	86500			
27		CJ34	4975			
29		CJ34	90000			
29		CJ34	800		2285300	

Account: Expense and Revenue Summary — Account No. 321

DATE	ITEM	POST. REF.	DEBIT	CREDIT	BALANCE DEBIT	BALANCE CREDIT

Account: Legal Fees Revenue — Account No. 411

DATE	ITEM	POST. REF.	DEBIT	CREDIT	BALANCE DEBIT	BALANCE CREDIT
1978 Dec. 1	Balance	✓				3972000
29		CJ34		1206000		5178000

Account: Collection Fees Revenue — Account No. 412

DATE	ITEM	POST. REF.	DEBIT	CREDIT	BALANCE DEBIT	BALANCE CREDIT
1978 Dec. 1	Balance	✓				142135
29		CJ34		13906		156041

Account: Salary Expense — Account No. 511

DATE	ITEM	POST. REF.	DEBIT	CREDIT	BALANCE DEBIT	BALANCE CREDIT
1978 Dec. 1	Balance	✓			1375000	
15		CJ33	32500			
15		CJ33	30000			
29		CJ34	32500			
29		CJ34	30000		1500000	

Donald L. Cameron, Attorney at Law — General Ledger *(continued)*

Chapter 5 — Accounting for Personal Service (Attorneys) — 129

ACCOUNT Payroll Taxes Expense — **ACCOUNT NO.** 512

DATE	ITEM	POST. REF.	DEBIT	CREDIT	BALANCE DEBIT	BALANCE CREDIT
1978 Dec. 1	Balance	✓			1233 00	
29		CJ34	75 00		1308 00	

ACCOUNT Rent Expense — **ACCOUNT NO.** 513

DATE	ITEM	POST. REF.	DEBIT	CREDIT	BALANCE DEBIT	BALANCE CREDIT
1978 Dec. 1	Balance	✓			4950 00	
1		CJ33	450 00		5400 00	

ACCOUNT Telephone Expense — **ACCOUNT NO.** 514

DATE	ITEM	POST. REF.	DEBIT	CREDIT	BALANCE DEBIT	BALANCE CREDIT
1978 Dec. 1	Balance	✓			508 20	
5		CJ33	43 18		551 38	

ACCOUNT Office Supplies Expense — **ACCOUNT NO.** 515

DATE	ITEM	POST. REF.	DEBIT	CREDIT	BALANCE DEBIT	BALANCE CREDIT
1978 Dec. 1	Balance	✓			332 40	
18		CJ33	45 70			
29		CJ34	5 95		384 05	

ACCOUNT Automobile Expense — **ACCOUNT NO.** 516

DATE	ITEM	POST. REF.	DEBIT	CREDIT	BALANCE DEBIT	BALANCE CREDIT
1978 Dec. 1	Balance	✓			1540 20	
6		CJ33	89 74			
29		CJ34	3 72		1633 66	

ACCOUNT Depreciation Expense — **ACCOUNT NO.** 517

DATE	ITEM	POST. REF.	DEBIT	CREDIT	BALANCE DEBIT	BALANCE CREDIT

ACCOUNT Charitable Contributions Expense — **ACCOUNT NO.** 518

DATE	ITEM	POST. REF.	DEBIT	CREDIT	BALANCE DEBIT	BALANCE CREDIT
1978 Dec. 1	Balance	✓			288 00	
13		CJ33	25 00			
29		CJ34	3 00		316 00	

Donald L. Cameron, Attorney at Law — General Ledger *(continued)*

ACCOUNT	Miscellaneous Expense				ACCOUNT NO. 519	
DATE	ITEM	POST. REF.	DEBIT	CREDIT	BALANCE DEBIT	CREDIT
1978 Dec. 1	Balance	✓			269 40	
4		CJ33	25 25			
14		CJ33	70 00			
29		CJ34	6 85		371 50	

Donald L. Cameron, Attorney at Law — General Ledger *(concluded)*

DONALD L. CAMERON, ATTORNEY AT LAW
Trial Balance
December 31, 1978

First National Bank	111	15,721.67	
Petty Cash Fund	112	50.00	
Advances on Behalf of Clients	131	440.00	
Law Library	141	9,852.08	
Accumulated Depreciation — Law Library	014		2,724.13
Office Equipment	151	2,942.05	
Accumulated Depreciation — Office Equipment	015		394.71
Automobile	161	3,650.23	
Accumulated Depreciation — Automobile	016		1,368.83
Employees Income Tax Payable	221		177.60
FICA Tax Payable	231		150.00
FUTA Tax Payable	241		84.00
State Unemployment Tax Payable	251		20.25
Donald L. Cameron, Capital	311		22,213.69
Donald L. Cameron, Drawing	031	22,853.00	
Legal Fees Revenue	411		51,780.00
Collection Fees Revenue	412		1,560.41
Salary Expense	511	15,000.00	
Payroll Taxes Expense	512	1,308.00	
Rent Expense	513	5,400.00	
Telephone Expense	514	551.38	
Office Supplies Expense	515	384.05	
Automobile Expense	516	1,633.66	
Charitable Contributions Expense	518	316.00	
Miscellaneous Expense	519	371.50	
		80,473.62	80,473.62

Report No. 5-1

Complete Report No. 5-1 in the study assignments and submit your working papers to the instructor for approval. After completing the report, you may continue with the textbook discussion in Chapter 6 until the next report is required.

6

Accounting for Personal Service (Physicians and Dentists)

Accounting for physicians and dentists has much in common with accounting for attorneys. Indeed, there are many similarities in accounting for any type of personal service whether professional or business; but each type of service also has its own peculiarities. Some of the items peculiar to accounting for physicians and dentists will be explained in this chapter.

As with attorneys, the most valuable asset the physician or dentist has is time. A daily service record should be kept showing as a minimum the name of the patient, the kind of service, and the charge to the patient's account or the amount of cash received.

The cash basis of accounting for physicians and dentists

Most physicians and dentists use the cash basis of accounting. Usually income is not recognized until cash is received and expenses are not recorded until they are paid. The revenue for services performed in one month may be accounted for in a later month, and expenses incurred in one month may be paid in the following month, or sometimes several months later.

Chart of accounts

As a means of explaining some of the peculiarities of accounting for persons in the medical and dental professions, a system of accounts for Linda Engle and Douglas Brenner, physicians and surgeons, is presented. The chart of accounts appears on page 132. All asset accounts have numbers beginning with 1; liability accounts begin with 2; owner's equity accounts begin with 3; revenue accounts begin with 4; expense accounts begin with 5; and contra accounts begin with 0. If new accounts are needed, they may be added without disturbing the numerical order of the existing accounts.

ENGLE AND BRENNER, PHYSICIANS AND SURGEONS
CHART OF ACCOUNTS

Assets *	*Revenue*
111 Clermont Bank	411 Professional Fees
112 Petty Cash Fund	
131 Office Equipment	*Expenses*
013 Accumulated Depreciation — Office Equipment	511 Automobile Expense
	512 Charitable Contributions Expense
141 Medical Equipment	513 Depreciation Expense
014 Accumulated Depreciation — Medical Equipment	517 Dues and Subscriptions Expense
	518 Electricity, Gas & Water Expense
151 X-Ray Equipment	519 Insurance Expense
015 Accumulated Depreciation — X-Ray Equipment	520 Laundry and Dry Cleaning Expense
161 Automobiles	521 Legal Expense
016 Accumulated Depreciation — Automobiles	522 Medical Library Expense
	523 Medical Supplies Expense
171 Prepaid Insurance	524 Office Supplies Expense
	525 Payroll Taxes Expense
Liabilities	526 Postage Expense
211 FICA Tax Payable	527 Rent Expense
221 Employees Income Tax Payable	528 Repairs and Maintenance Expense
231 FUTA Tax Payable	529 Salary Expense
241 State Unemployment Tax Payable	530 Surgical Instruments Expense
	531 Surgical Supplies Expense
Owner's Equity	532 Telephone Expense
311 Linda Engle, Capital	533 Miscellaneous Expense
031 Linda Engle, Drawing	
321 Douglas Brenner, Capital	
032 Douglas Brenner, Drawing	
331 Expense and Revenue Summary	

*Words in italics represent headings and not account titles.

Some of the accounts which appear in the chart of accounts are discussed in the following paragraphs.

Professional Fees, Account No. 411. Drs. Engle and Brenner use only one general ledger account in which to record their professional fees. In the daily service record there are columns headed Office Calls and Surgery. The totals of these columns at the end of the month will show the amounts entered for office calls and for surgery. If it is desired, separate accounts could be kept for as many types of service as are rendered. For example, office calls might be assigned the number 411, surgery the number 412, and laboratory work the number 413. A dentist could use one account for professional fees, or separate accounts could be used for different types of service rendered to patients.

Medical Library Expense, Account No. 522. The number of reference books a professional person may have in a personal library may vary according to the person's needs. For example, a lawyer may require quick and easy access to a large number of references and thus would need an extensive library. A doctor, on the other hand, may have a limited number of references in a personal library if there happens to be a complete reference library at a nearby hospital. The amount of money a professional person invests in current and classic reference materials can determine how to account for the investment. A large annual investment in reference books is usually treated as an asset and depreciated at the end of the year. On the other hand, an occasional purchase of a reference book is usually treated as an expense at the time of the purchase.

Medical Supplies Expense, Account No. 523; Office Supplies Expense, Account No. 524; Surgical Supplies Expense, Account No. 531; Surgical Instruments Expense, Account No. 530. Supplies and instruments are charged to expense when paid for.

Books of account

Drs. Engle and Brenner use the following books of account:

(a) General books
    (1) Combined cash journal
    (2) General ledger

(b) Auxiliary records
    (1) Petty cash disbursements record
    (2) Daily service record
    (3) Patients ledger
    (4) Employee's earnings record
    (5) Checkbook

Combined Cash Journal. Drs. Engle and Brenner use one book of original entry, a combined cash journal. The combined cash journal, reproduced on pages 144 to 147, contains two money columns to the left of the Description column and six to the right of the Description column. The column headings are as listed below and on page 134.

(a) Clermont Bank
    (1) Deposits 111 Dr.
    (2) Checks 111 Cr.
(b) General
    (1) Debit
    (2) Credit
(c) Professional Fees 411 Cr.

(d) Salary Expense 529 Dr.
(e) Wage Deductions
   (1) Employees Income Tax Payable 221 Cr.
   (2) FICA Tax Payable 211 Cr.

General Ledger. Drs. Engle and Brenner use a four-column account form for the general ledger accounts. The ledger is reproduced on pages 149 to 155. In each case the balance as of April 1 has been entered. The accounts in the general ledger are arranged in the order given in the chart of accounts on page 132. Posting to the general ledger is from the combined cash journal. A trial balance is taken at the end of each month to prove the equality of the general ledger balances. The trial balance as of April 30 appears on page 156.

Auxiliary Records. Drs. Engle and Brenner use a petty cash disbursements record, a daily service record, a patients ledger, employees' earnings records, and a checkbook as auxiliary records. The employee's earnings record kept for each employee is similar to the one illustrated on pages 80 and 81.

Petty Cash Disbursements Record. A petty cash fund of $100 is maintained. The petty cash disbursements record is similar to that illustrated on pages 50 and 51.

Daily Service Record. A portion of the daily service record is illustrated on page 135. Note that the daily service record is not set up as a double-entry record. There is nothing to offset the Payments column under Patients' Accounts. The amounts in the Charges column are posted to the Charges column in the appropriate patients' ledger accounts, and the amounts in the Payments column are posted to the Payments column in the patients' ledger accounts. The total cash received from patients will be shown in the columns headed "Patients' Accounts — Payments" and "Cash Services." The total cash received should be recorded in the combined cash journal in the Clermont Bank Deposits Dr. column and the Professional Fees Cr. column.

Patients Ledger. The patients' accounts are kept in a file rather than in a bound book to permit using a copying machine to reproduce the accounts as monthly statements. Information in the Charges column of the daily service record is posted to the individual patients' accounts. Credits to the patients' accounts are also posted from the Payments column of the daily service record. A model patient's account for Joan Amos is reproduced on page 136.

Chapter 6   Accounting for Personal Service (Physicians and Dentists)   **135**

DAILY SERVICE RECORD FOR MONTH OF April 1978

Day	Name of Patient	KIND OF SERVICE - Office Calls	KIND OF SERVICE - Surgery	PATIENTS' ACCOUNTS - Charges	PATIENTS' ACCOUNTS - Payments	Cash Services
	Amounts Forwarded					
1	Dorothy Colton		400 00	400 00		
1	Frank Ballou	25 00				25 00
1	Helen Miller — S. Joseph	20 00				20 00
1	Harry Williams		1,550 00	1,550 00		
1	Jean Smith	25 00		25 00		
3	Donald Henderson				100 00	
3	Joan Amos				350 00	
3	Frank Jones — D. Helen		350 00	350 00		
3	Diane Brown	25 00		25 00		
3	Louis Nelson	25 00		25 00		
4	Stanley Richter	25 00				25 00
4	Thomas Foster		850 00	850 00		
4	Mrs. William Hall				25 00	
4	Gary Peters				550 00	
4	Charlene Carroll		500 00	500 00		
5	Elmer Salo — D. Kathie	12 00				12 00
5	Elizabeth Hoffman				850 00	
5	Julia Kenyon		1,600 00	1,600 00		
5	Timothy Abbott	25 00		25 00		
5	Wilbur Page				735 00	
6	Judith Myers		350 00	350 00		
6	Emily Hamilton	25 00				25 00
7	John Bancroft	12 00				12 00
7	Grace Sarvela				900 00	
7	John Raeburn — S. Jim	12 00				12 00
7	Roberta Mullins				250 00	
7	Harriet Wells				435 00	
8	Margaret Thomas		400 00	400 00		
8	Marilyn Abrams				100 00	
8	Helen Chen	25 00		25 00		
8	Robert Feldman	12 00		12 00		
10	Otto Haskins	25 00				25 00
26	Margaret Thomas				400 00	
26	Edward Conley	12 00				12 00
27	Georgia Stanton				175 00	
27	Jean Smith				25 00	
28	William Lindsey				300 00	
29	Allen Jackson		800 00	800 00		
		1,255 00	21,950 00	22,561 00	20,615 00	644 00

Daily Service Record for Month of April

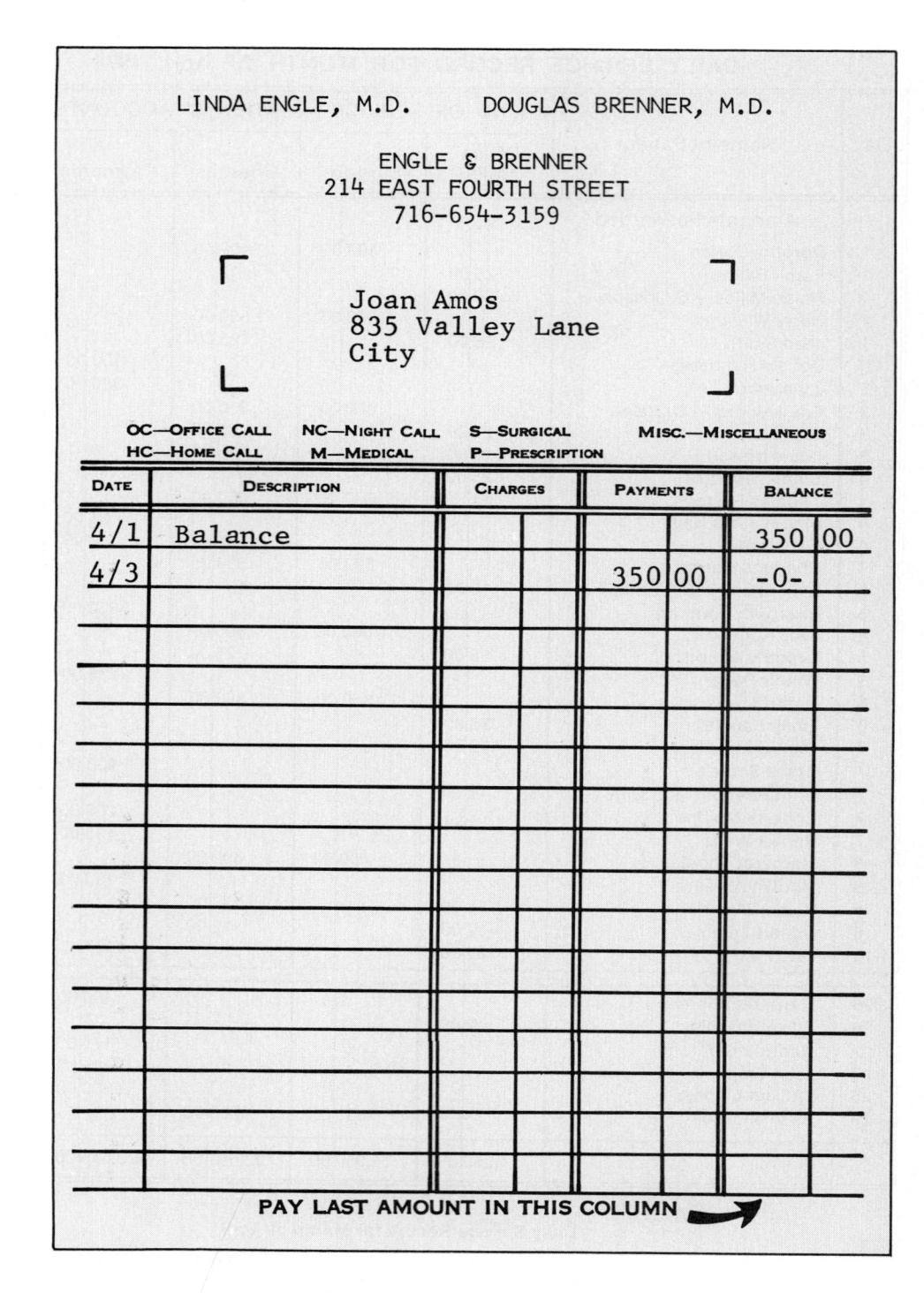

Accounting for Personal Service (Physicians and Dentists)

LINDA ENGLE, M.D.   DOUGLAS BRENNER, M.D.

ENGLE & BRENNER
214 EAST FOURTH STREET
716-654-3159

Joan Amos
835 Valley Lane
City

OC—Office Call   NC—Night Call   S—Surgical   Misc.—Miscellaneous
HC—Home Call   M—Medical   P—Prescription

Date	Description	Charges	Payments	Balance
4/1	Balance			350 00
4/3			350 00	-0-

PAY LAST AMOUNT IN THIS COLUMN ➤

Illustration of Patient's Account

Following is a narrative of transactions completed by Drs. Engle and Brenner during the month of April. These transactions are recorded in the combined cash journal on pages 144 to 147.

ENGLE AND BRENNER, PHYSICIANS AND SURGEONS

Narrative of Transactions

Saturday, April 1

Issued Check No. 529 for $1,500 payable to the White Realty Corporation for rent of the office for the month of April.

> The transaction was recorded in the combined cash journal by debiting Rent Expense, Account No. 527, in the General Dr. column and crediting Clermont Bank, Account No. 111.

Monday, April 3

Issued Check No. 530 for $175.18 payable to Sherman's Garage for the garage bill for March.

> This transaction was recorded in the combined cash journal by debiting Automobile Expense, Account No. 511, and crediting Clermont Bank, Account No. 111.

Issued Check No. 531 for $65.18 to the Columbia Electric Co. for electricity consumed during March.

> This transaction was recorded in the combined cash journal by debiting Electricity, Gas and Water Expense, Account No. 518, and by crediting Clermont Bank, Account No. 111.

Issued Check No. 532 for $76.32 to the Bell Telephone Co. for March service.

Tuesday, April 4

Issued Check No. 533 for $54.35 to the Union Natural Gas Corporation for gas consumed during March.

Issued Check No. 534 for $47.80 to the Acme Laundry for laundry service for the month of March.

Issued Check No. 535 for $80.15 to Physicians' Supply Corporation for medical supplies purchased in March.

Wednesday, April 5

Issued Check No. 536 for $25.30 to the Medical Equipment Co. for an equipment repair.

> This transaction was recorded in the combined cash journal by debiting Repairs and Maintenance Expense, Account No. 528, and by crediting Clermont Bank, Account No. 111.

Issued Check No. 537 for $3,516 to the Evans Insurance Agency for a one-year physicians' liability insurance policy.

> This transaction was recorded in the combined cash journal by debiting Prepaid Insurance, Account No. 171, and by crediting Clermont Bank.

Thursday, April 6

Issued Check No. 538 for $96 to the Peerless Cleaning Co. for services rendered during March.

> This transaction was recorded in the combined cash journal by debiting Laundry and Dry Cleaning Expense, Account No. 520, and by crediting Clermont Bank.

Friday, April 7

Issued Check No. 539 for $287.35 to the Quality Instrument Co. for surgical instruments purchased in March.

> This transaction was recorded in the combined cash journal by debiting Surgical Instruments Expense, Account No. 530, and by crediting Clermont Bank.

Saturday, April 8

Dr. Brenner has given the account of Helen Janos in the amount of $375 and the account of Robert Becker in the amount of $1,200 to Donald L. Cameron, an attorney, for collection. If Mr. Cameron collects all or part of these accounts, his fee will be 33⅓ percent. No entry is needed at this time.

Footed the amount columns in the daily service record and obtained the following totals:

Kind of service:	
Office calls	$ 268
Surgery	6,000
Total	$6,268
Patients' accounts — charges	$6,137
Cash services	131
Total	$6,268

Posted all entries in the Patients' Accounts Charges and Payments columns to the appropriate individual accounts in the patients ledger.

The total cash received from patients for the week was found to be:

Payments	$4,295
Cash services	131
Total	$4,426

Recorded the total cash received ($4,426) in the combined cash journal by entering the words "Total receipts" in the Description column and the amount in both the Clermont Bank Deposits Dr. column and the Professional Fees Cr. column.

Footed the amount columns of the combined cash journal and checked the cash balance in the checkbook ($18,619.70) by starting with the checkbook balance on April 1 ($20,117.33) and adding the total of the Clermont Bank Dr. column and subtracting the total of the Clermont Bank Cr. column. Completed the individual postings from the General Dr. and Cr. columns of the combined cash journal. As each item was posted, the account number was entered in the Posting Reference column of the combined cash journal. The page number of the combined cash journal was entered in the Posting Reference column of the accounts to which items from the combined cash journal were posted.

Monday, April 10

Issued Check No. 540 for $10 to the American Medical Association for a subscription to a professional journal.

Tuesday, April 11

Issued Check No. 541 for $45 to the Johnson Supply Company for surgical supplies.

Wednesday, April 12

Issued Check No. 542 for $20.15 to the Stone County Water Authority for March service.

Thursday, April 13

Issued Check No. 543 for $75.49 to the Scientific Publishing Co. for medical books.

> This transaction was recorded by debiting Medical Library Expense, Account No. 522, and crediting Clermont Bank.

Friday, April 14

Issued Check No. 544 for $79.80 to the Jackson Department Store in payment of Dr. Brenner's personal account.

> Since this transaction is a personal expense, it is recorded in the combined cash journal by debiting Douglas Brenner, Drawing, Account No. 032, and by crediting Clermont Bank.

Saturday, April 15

Dr. Engle withdrew $800 for personal use. Check No. 545.
Dr. Brenner withdrew $850 for personal use. Check No. 546.

Issued the following checks in payment of salaries for the first half of the month:

No. 547 for $324.30 to Teresa Mantia, R.N., in payment of salary in the amount of $400, less $24 withheld for FICA tax and $51.70 withheld for federal income tax.

No. 548 for $277.70 to David Reitz, typist, in the amount of $350, less $21 withheld for FICA tax and $51.30 withheld for federal income tax.

No. 549 for $349.10 to Rebecca McBaron, secretary-bookkeeper, in the amount of $450, less $27 withheld for FICA tax and $73.90 withheld for federal income tax.

No. 550 for $337 to Michael Coleman, X-Ray and laboratory technician, in the amount of $425, less $25.50 withheld for FICA tax and $62.50 withheld for federal income tax.

> Drs. Engle and Brenner are subject to the tax imposed under the federal unemployment tax act and to the state unemployment tax. These taxes are collected entirely from the employer on the first $6,000 of each employee's earnings during the year. No deductions are made from the salaries of the employees for unemployment taxes.

Footed the amount columns in the daily service record and obtained the following totals:

Kind of service:	
Office calls	$ 257
Surgery	4,850
Total	$5,107
Patients' accounts — charges	$4,989
Cash services	118
Total	$5,107

Posted all entries in the Patients' Accounts Charges and Payments columns to the appropriate individual accounts in the patients ledger.

The total cash received from patients for the week was found to be:

Payments	$3,875
Cash services	118
Total	$3,993

Recorded the total cash received ($3,993) in the combined cash journal by entering the words "Total receipts" in the Description column and the amount in both the Clermont Bank Deposits Dr. column and the Professional Fees Cr. column.

Footed the amount columns of the combined cash journal and checked the cash balance in the checkbook ($19,444.16) by adding the total of the Clermont Bank Dr. column to the checkbook balance on April 1 ($20,117.33) and subtracting the total of the Clermont Bank Cr. column. Completed the individual postings from the General Dr. and Cr. columns of the combined cash journal.

Monday, April 17

Issued Check No. 551 for $168.90 to the Emerson Office Equipment Co. in payment for a new filing cabinet.

Tuesday, April 18

Issued Check No. 552 for $25.90 to the Sanders Stationery Company for stationery and supplies.

Issued Check No. 553 for $145.17 to Physicians' Supply Co. for medical supplies.

Wednesday, April 19

Issued Check No. 554 for $100 to the United Fund in payment of the part of the pledge due in April.

> This transaction was recorded in the combined cash journal by debiting Charitable Contributions Expense, Account No. 512, and by crediting Clermont Bank.

Thursday, April 20

Issued Check No. 555 for $368.80 to the Evans Insurance Agency in payment of the renewal premium on an insurance policy on Dr. Linda Engle's car.

> Since the car is used exclusively for business purposes, the cost of the policy is debited to Prepaid Insurance, Account No. 171.

Friday, April 21

Issued Check No. 556 for $12 to the Clermont Bank in payment of the annual rental of a safe deposit box for use of the partnership.

> This transaction was recorded by debiting Miscellaneous Expense, Account No. 533, and by crediting Clermont Bank.

Saturday, April 22

Issued Check No. 557 for $20.75 to the Emerson Office Equipment Co. for typewriter repairs.

Footed the amount columns in the daily service record and obtained the totals shown on page 142.

Kind of service:

Office calls	$ 385
Surgery	5,320
Total	$5,705
Patients' accounts — charges	$5,530
Cash services	175
Total	$5,705

Posted all entries in the Patients' Accounts Charges and Payments columns to the appropriate individual accounts in the patients ledger.

The total cash received from patients for the week was:

Payments	$6,810
Cash services	175
Total	$6,985

Recorded the total cash received ($6,985) in the combined cash journal.

Footed the amount columns of the combined cash journal and checked the cash balance in the checkbook ($25,587.64). Completed the individual postings from the General Dr. and Cr. columns of the combined cash journal.

Monday, April 24

Issued Check No. 558 for $500 to the American Cancer Society.

Tuesday, April 25

Issued Check No. 559 for $1,890.15 to Baker Medical Equipment Co. for medical equipment.

Received $250 from Donald Cameron representing collection of the account of Helen Janos in the amount of $375. Mr. Cameron deducted his fee of $125 and remitted the balance, $250.

> This transaction was recorded in the combined cash journal by debiting Clermont Bank for $250 and Legal Expense, Account No. 521, for $125, and by crediting Professional Fees, Account No. 411, for $375. In order to avoid a duplication of the $375 credit to Professional Fees, this payment was not entered in the daily service record. An entry was therefore made in Helen Janos' account in the patients ledger crediting the account for $375.

Wednesday, April 26

Issued Check No. 560 for $60.28 to the Quality Equipment Co. for repairs to the X-Ray equipment.

Thursday, April 27

Issued Check No. 561 for $225.50 to the Physicians' Publishing Co. for medical books.

Friday, April 28

Received $200 from Donald Cameron to apply on the account of Robert Becker. Mr. Cameron collected $300 from Mr. Becker and remitted $200 after deducting the fee of $100.

> This transaction was recorded in the combined cash journal by debiting Clermont Bank for $200 and Legal Expense, Account No. 521, for $100, and by crediting Professional Fees, Account No. 411, for $300. An entry was also made in Robert Becker's account in the patients ledger crediting the account for $300.

Issued Check No. 562 for $200 in payment of the annual dues for Drs. Engle and Brenner to the Stone County Medical Society.

Saturday, April 29

Dr. Engle withdrew $900 for personal use. Check No. 563.
Dr. Brenner withdrew $850 for personal use. Check No. 564.

Issued the following checks in payment of salaries for the second half of the month:

No. 565 for $324.30 to Teresa Mantia, R.N., in payment of salary in the amount of $400, less $24 withheld for FICA tax and $51.70 withheld for federal income tax.

No. 566 for $277.70 to David Reitz, typist, in the amount of $350, less $21 withheld for FICA tax and $51.30 withheld for federal income tax.

No. 567 for $349.10 to Rebecca McBaron, secretary-bookkeeper, in the amount of $450, less $27 withheld for FICA tax and $73.90 withheld for federal income tax.

No. 568 for $337 to Michael Coleman, X-Ray and laboratory technician, in the amount of $425, less $25.50 withheld for FICA tax and $62.50 withheld for federal income tax.

Issued Check No. 569 for $868.80 to the Clermont Bank in payment of the following payroll taxes based on wages paid during the month of March.

Employees' income tax withheld from wages		$478.80
FICA tax:		
Withheld from employees' wages	$195.00	
Imposed on employer	195.00	390.00
Amount of check		$868.80

> Form 501 accompanied this deposit to the Clermont Bank. Form 501 had also been sent to the Clermont Bank in February and March in payment of employees' income tax and FICA tax payable for the months of January and February. Since March was the third month of the first quarter, Form 941 was filed with the Internal Revenue Service.

Issued Check No. 570 for $263.25 to the State Unemployment Bureau for the state unemployment tax for the first quarter.

Combined Cash Journal — Page 42

DEPOSITS 111 DR.	CHECKS 111 CR.	CK. NO.	DAY	DESCRIPTION	POST. REF.
				AMOUNTS FORWARDED Balance 20,117.33	
	1500 00	529	1	Rent Expense	527
	175 18	530	3	Automobile Expense	511
	65 18	531	3	Electricity, Gas & Water Expense	518
	76 32	532	3	Telephone Expense	532
	54 35	533	4	Electricity, Gas & Water Expense	518
	47 80	534	4	Laundry & Dry Cleaning Expense	520
	80 15	535	4	Medical Supplies Expense	523
	25 30	536	5	Repairs & Maintenance Expense	528
	3516 00	537	5	Prepaid Insurance	171
	96 00	538	6	Laundry & Dry Cleaning Expense	520
	287 35	539	7	Surgical Instruments Expense	530
4426 00			8	Total receipts	✓
4426 00	5923 63				
	10 00	540	10	Dues & Subscriptions Expense 13,619.70	517
	45 00	541	11	Surgical Supplies Expense	531
	20 15	542	12	Electricity, Gas & Water Expense	518
	75 49	543	13	Medical Library Expense	522
	79 80	544	14	Douglas Brenner, Drawing	032
	800 00	545	15	Linda Engle, Drawing	031
	850 00	546	15	Douglas Brenner, Drawing	032
	324 30	547	15	Teresa Mantia	✓
	277 70	548	15	David Reitz	✓
	349 10	549	15	Rebecca McBaron	✓
	337 00	550	15	Michael Coleman	✓
3993 00			15	Total receipts	✓
8419 00	9092 17			19,444.16	
	168 90	551	17	Office Equipment	131
	25 90	552	18	Office Supplies Expense	524
	145 17	553	18	Medical Supplies Expense	523
	100 00	554	19	Charitable Contributions Expense	512
	368 80	555	20	Prepaid Insurance	171
	12 00	556	21	Miscellaneous Expense	533
	20 75	557	22	Repairs & Maintenance Expense	528
6985 00			22	Total receipts	✓
15404 00	9933 69			25,587.64	
15404 00	9933 69			Carried forward	

Engle & Brenner — Combined Cash Journal (Left Page)

Chapter 6 Accounting for Personal Service (Physicians and Dentists) **145**

FOR MONTH OF April 19 78   PAGE 42

GENERAL DEBIT	GENERAL CREDIT	PROFESSIONAL FEES 411 CR.	SALARY EXPENSE 529 DR.	EMP. INC. TAX PAY. 221 CR.	FICA TAX PAY. 211 CR.
150000					
17518					
6518					
7632					
5435					
4780					
8015					
2530					
351600					
9600					
28735					
592363		442600			
1000		442600			
4500					
2015					
7549					
7980					
80000					
85000					
			40000	5170	2400
			35000	5130	2100
			45000	7390	2700
			42500	6250	2550
		399300			
780407		541900	162500	23940	9750
16890					
2590					
14517					
10000					
36880					
1200					
2075					
		698500			
864559		1540400	162500	23940	9750
864559		1540400	162500	23940	9750

Engle & Brenner — Combined Cash Journal (Right Page)

PAGE 43 — COMBINED CASH JOURNAL

Clermont Bank Deposits 111 DR.	Checks 111 CR.	Ck. No.	Day	Description	Post. Ref.
15404 00	9933 69		22	AMOUNTS FORWARDED Balance 25,587.64	✓
	500 00	558	24	Charitable Contributions Expense	512
	1890 15	559	25	Medical Equipment	141
250 00			25	Legal Expense — Helen Janos	521
	60 28	560	26	Repairs & Maintenance Expense	528
	225 50	561	27	Medical Library Expense	522
200 00			28	Legal Expense — Robert Becker	521
	200 00	562	28	Dues & Subscriptions Expense	517
	900 00	563	29	Linda Engle, Drawing	031
	850 00	564	29	Douglas Brenner, Drawing	032
	324 30	565	29	Teresa Mantia	✓
	277 70	566	29	David Reitz	✓
	349 10	567	29	Rebecca Mc Baron	✓
	337 00	568	29	Michael Coleman	✓
	868 80	569	29	Employees Income Tax Payable	221
				FICA Tax Payable	211
	263 25	570	29	State Unemployment Tax Payable	241
5855 00			29	Total receipts	✓
			29	Payroll Taxes Expense	525
				FICA Tax Payable	✓
				FUTA Tax Payable	231
				State Unemployment Tax Pay.	241
	76 75	571	29	Linda Engle, Drawing	031
				Douglas Brenner, Drawing	032
				Automobile Expense	511
				Miscellaneous Expense	533
				Office Supplies Expense	524
				Postage Expense	526
21709 00	17056 52			24,769.81	
21709 00	17056 52				
(111)	(111)				

Engle & Brenner — Combined Cash Journal (Left Page) *(concluded)*

Chapter 6 — Accounting for Personal Service (Physicians and Dentists) — 147

FOR MONTH OF April 19 78 PAGE 43

	GENERAL DEBIT	GENERAL CREDIT	PROFESSIONAL FEES 411 CR.	SALARY EXPENSE 529 DR.	EMP. INC. TAX PAY. 221 CR.	FICA TAX PAY. 211 CR.	
1	8645 59		15404 00	1625 00	239 40	97 50	1
2	500 00						2
3	1890 15						3
4	125 00			375 00			4
5	60 28						5
6	225 50						6
7	100 00			300 00			7
8	200 00						8
9	900 00						9
10	850 00						10
11				400 00	51 70	24 00	11
12				350 00	51 30	21 00	12
13				450 00	73 90	27 00	13
14				425 00	62 50	25 50	14
15	478 80						15
16	390 00						16
17	263 25						17
18				5855 00			18
19	305 50						19
20						195 00	20
21		22 75					21
22		87 75					22
23	12 50						23
24	16 90						24
25	7 25						25
26	9 30						26
27	4 80						27
28	26 00						28
29	15010 82	110 50	21934 00	3250 00	478 80	390 00	29
30	(✓)	(✓)	(411)	(529)	(221)	(211)	30

Engle & Brenner — Combined Cash Journal (Right Page) *(concluded)*

Since the FUTA tax will not reach $100 until the second quarter of the year, no payment is necessary at the end of April.

Footed the amount columns in the daily service record and obtained the following totals:

Kind of service:	
Office calls	$ 345
Surgery	5,780
Total	$6,125
Patients' accounts — charges	$5,905
Cash services	220
Total	$6,125

Posted all entries in the Patients' Accounts Charges and Payments columns to the appropriate individual accounts in the patients ledger.

The total cash received from patients for the week was found to be:

Payments	$5,635
Cash services	220
Total	$5,855

Recorded the total cash received ($5,855) in the combined cash journal.

Made an entry in the combined cash journal for the payroll taxes imposed on Drs. Engle and Brenner for the month of April by debiting Payroll Taxes Expense, Account No. 525, for $305.50 and by crediting FICA Tax Payable, Account No. 211, for $195 ($3,250 times 6%), FUTA Tax Payable, Account No. 231, for $22.75 ($3,250 times .7%), and State Unemployment Tax Payable, Account No. 241, for $87.75 ($3,250 times 2.7%).

Issued Check No. 571 for $76.75 to replenish the petty cash fund.

The following statement provided the information needed in recording this transaction in the combined cash journal:

STATEMENT OF PETTY CASH DISBURSEMENTS FOR APRIL

Linda Engle, Drawing	$12.50
Douglas Brenner, Drawing	16.90
Automobile Expense	7.25
Miscellaneous Expense	9.30
Office Supplies Expense	4.80
Postage Expense	26.00
Total disbursements	$76.75

Footed the amount columns of the combined cash journal and checked the cash balance in the checkbook ($24,769.81).

Chapter 6   Accounting for Personal Service (Physicians and Dentists)   **149**

Completed the individual postings from the general columns of the combined cash journal. Since this was the end of the month, the summary posting was completed and the account numbers were written immediately below the totals of the columns in the combined cash journal. A trial balance of the general ledger accounts which have balances on April 30 appears on page 156.

ACCOUNT Clermont Bank   **ACCOUNT NO.** 111

DATE	ITEM	POST. REF.	DEBIT	CREDIT	BALANCE DEBIT	BALANCE CREDIT
1973 Apr. 1	Balance	✓			20117 33	
29		CJ43	21709 00			
29		CJ43		17056 52	24769 81	

ACCOUNT Petty Cash Fund   **ACCOUNT NO.** 112

DATE	ITEM	POST. REF.	DEBIT	CREDIT	BALANCE DEBIT	BALANCE CREDIT
1973 Apr. 1	Balance	✓			100 00	

ACCOUNT Office Equipment   **ACCOUNT NO.** 131

DATE	ITEM	POST. REF.	DEBIT	CREDIT	BALANCE DEBIT	BALANCE CREDIT
1973 Apr. 1	Balance	✓			5773 40	
17		CJ42	168 90		5942 30	

ACCOUNT Accumulated Depreciation – Office Equipt.   **ACCOUNT NO.** 013

DATE	ITEM	POST. REF.	DEBIT	CREDIT	BALANCE DEBIT	BALANCE CREDIT
1973 Apr. 1	Balance	✓				1735 10

ACCOUNT Medical Equipment   **ACCOUNT NO.** 141

DATE	ITEM	POST. REF.	DEBIT	CREDIT	BALANCE DEBIT	BALANCE CREDIT
1973 Apr. 1	Balance	✓			15615 73	
25		CJ43	1890 15		17505 88	

ACCOUNT Accumulated Depreciation – Medical Equipt.   **ACCOUNT NO.** 014

DATE	ITEM	POST. REF.	DEBIT	CREDIT	BALANCE DEBIT	BALANCE CREDIT
1973 Apr. 1	Balance	✓				2184 72

Engle & Brenner — General Ledger

ACCOUNT X-Ray Equipment — ACCOUNT NO. 151

DATE	ITEM	POST. REF.	DEBIT	CREDIT	BALANCE DEBIT	BALANCE CREDIT
1978 Apr. 1	Balance	✓			3087549	

ACCOUNT Accumulated Depreciation—X-Ray Equip. — ACCOUNT NO. 015

DATE	ITEM	POST. REF.	DEBIT	CREDIT	BALANCE DEBIT	BALANCE CREDIT
1978 Apr. 1	Balance	✓				649238

ACCOUNT Automobiles — ACCOUNT NO. 161

DATE	ITEM	POST. REF.	DEBIT	CREDIT	BALANCE DEBIT	BALANCE CREDIT
1978 Apr. 1	Balance	✓			847509	

ACCOUNT Accumulated Depreciation—Automobiles — ACCOUNT NO. 016

DATE	ITEM	POST. REF.	DEBIT	CREDIT	BALANCE DEBIT	BALANCE CREDIT
1978 Apr. 1	Balance	✓				201877

ACCOUNT Prepaid Insurance — ACCOUNT NO. 171

DATE	ITEM	POST. REF.	DEBIT	CREDIT	BALANCE DEBIT	BALANCE CREDIT
1978 Apr. 1	Balance	✓			80000	
5		CJ42	351600			
20		CJ42	36880		468480	

ACCOUNT FICA Tax Payable — ACCOUNT NO. 211

DATE	ITEM	POST. REF.	DEBIT	CREDIT	BALANCE DEBIT	BALANCE CREDIT
1978 Apr. 1	Balance	✓				39000
29		CJ43	39000			
29		CJ43		39000		39000

ACCOUNT Employees Income Tax Payable — ACCOUNT NO. 221

DATE	ITEM	POST. REF.	DEBIT	CREDIT	BALANCE DEBIT	BALANCE CREDIT
1978 Apr. 1	Balance	✓				47880
29		CJ43	47880			
29		CJ43		47880		47880

Engle & Brenner — General Ledger *(continued)*

ACCOUNT: FUTA Tax Payable — ACCOUNT NO. 231

DATE	ITEM	POST. REF.	DEBIT	CREDIT	BALANCE DEBIT	BALANCE CREDIT
1978 Apr. 1	Balance	✓				68 25
29		CJ43		22 75		91 00

ACCOUNT: State Unemployment Tax Payable — ACCOUNT NO. 241

DATE	ITEM	POST. REF.	DEBIT	CREDIT	BALANCE DEBIT	BALANCE CREDIT
1978 Apr. 1	Balance	✓				263 25
29		CJ43	263 25			
29		CJ43		87 75		87 75

ACCOUNT: Linda Engle, Capital — ACCOUNT NO. 311

DATE	ITEM	POST. REF.	DEBIT	CREDIT	BALANCE DEBIT	BALANCE CREDIT
1978 Apr. 1	Balance	✓				16776 30

ACCOUNT: Linda Engle, Drawing — ACCOUNT NO. 031

DATE	ITEM	POST. REF.	DEBIT	CREDIT	BALANCE DEBIT	BALANCE CREDIT
1978 Apr. 1	Balance	✓			5250 00	
15		CJ42	800 00			
29		CJ43	900 00			
29		CJ43	12 50		6962 50	

ACCOUNT: Douglas Brenner, Capital — ACCOUNT NO. 321

DATE	ITEM	POST. REF.	DEBIT	CREDIT	BALANCE DEBIT	BALANCE CREDIT
1978 Apr. 1	Balance	✓				12551 29

ACCOUNT: Douglas Brenner, Drawing — ACCOUNT NO. 032

DATE	ITEM	POST. REF.	DEBIT	CREDIT	BALANCE DEBIT	BALANCE CREDIT
1978 Apr. 1	Balance	✓			5627 83	
14		CJ42	79 80			
15		CJ42	850 00			
29		CJ43	850 00			
29		CJ43	16 90		7424 53	

Engle & Brenner — General Ledger (*continued*)

ACCOUNT: Expense and Revenue Summary — ACCOUNT NO. 331

DATE	ITEM	POST. REF.	DEBIT	CREDIT	BALANCE DEBIT	BALANCE CREDIT

ACCOUNT: Professional Fees — ACCOUNT NO. 411

DATE	ITEM	POST. REF.	DEBIT	CREDIT	BALANCE DEBIT	BALANCE CREDIT
1978 Apr. 1	Balance	✓				68052 00
29		CJ43		21934 00		89986 00

ACCOUNT: Automobile Expense — ACCOUNT NO. 511

DATE	ITEM	POST. REF.	DEBIT	CREDIT	BALANCE DEBIT	BALANCE CREDIT
1978 Apr. 1	Balance	✓			347 85	
3		CJ42	175 18			
29		CJ43	7 25		530 28	

ACCOUNT: Charitable Contributions Expense — ACCOUNT NO. 512

DATE	ITEM	POST. REF.	DEBIT	CREDIT	BALANCE DEBIT	BALANCE CREDIT
1978 Apr. 1	Balance	✓			180 00	
19		CJ42	100 00			
24		CJ43	500 00		780 00	

ACCOUNT: Depreciation Expense — ACCOUNT NO. 513

DATE	ITEM	POST. REF.	DEBIT	CREDIT	BALANCE DEBIT	BALANCE CREDIT

ACCOUNT: Dues and Subscriptions Expense — ACCOUNT NO. 517

DATE	ITEM	POST. REF.	DEBIT	CREDIT	BALANCE DEBIT	BALANCE CREDIT
1978 Apr. 1	Balance	✓			115 00	
10		CJ42	10 00			
28		CJ43	200 00		325 00	

Engle & Brenner — General Ledger (continued)

Chapter 6 — Accounting for Personal Service (Physicians and Dentists) — 153

ACCOUNT Electricity, Gas and Water Expense **ACCOUNT NO.** 518

DATE	ITEM	POST. REF.	DEBIT	CREDIT	BALANCE DEBIT	BALANCE CREDIT
1978 Apr. 1	Balance	✓			28045	
3		CJ42	6518			
4		CJ42	5435			
12		CJ42	2015		42013	

ACCOUNT Insurance Expense **ACCOUNT NO.** 519

DATE	ITEM	POST. REF.	DEBIT	CREDIT	BALANCE DEBIT	BALANCE CREDIT

ACCOUNT Laundry and Dry Cleaning Expense **ACCOUNT NO.** 520

DATE	ITEM	POST. REF.	DEBIT	CREDIT	BALANCE DEBIT	BALANCE CREDIT
1978 Apr. 1	Balance	✓			28540	
4		CJ42	4780			
6		CJ42	9600		42920	

ACCOUNT Legal Expense **ACCOUNT NO.** 521

DATE	ITEM	POST. REF.	DEBIT	CREDIT	BALANCE DEBIT	BALANCE CREDIT
1978 Apr. 1	Balance	✓			17500	
25		CJ43	12500			
28		CJ43	10000		40000	

ACCOUNT Medical Library Expense **ACCOUNT NO.** 522

DATE	ITEM	POST. REF.	DEBIT	CREDIT	BALANCE DEBIT	BALANCE CREDIT
1978 Apr. 1	Balance	✓			25620	
13		CJ42	7549			
27		CJ43	22550		55719	

ACCOUNT Medical Supplies Expense **ACCOUNT NO.** 523

DATE	ITEM	POST. REF.	DEBIT	CREDIT	BALANCE DEBIT	BALANCE CREDIT
1978 Apr. 1	Balance	✓			57238	
4		CJ42	8015			
18		CJ42	14517		79770	

Engle & Brenner — General Ledger (continued)

Accounting for Personal Service (Physicians and Dentists) — Chapter 6

ACCOUNT Office Supplies Expense   **ACCOUNT NO.** 524

DATE	ITEM	POST. REF.	DEBIT	CREDIT	BALANCE DEBIT	BALANCE CREDIT
1978 Apr. 1	Balance	✓			89 42	
18		CJ42	25 90			
29		CJ43	4 80		120 12	

ACCOUNT Payroll Taxes Expense   **ACCOUNT NO.** 525

DATE	ITEM	POST. REF.	DEBIT	CREDIT	BALANCE DEBIT	BALANCE CREDIT
1978 Apr. 1	Balance	✓			916 50	
29		CJ43	305 50		1222 00	

ACCOUNT Postage Expense   **ACCOUNT NO.** 526

DATE	ITEM	POST. REF.	DEBIT	CREDIT	BALANCE DEBIT	BALANCE CREDIT
1978 Apr. 1	Balance	✓			84 50	
29		CJ43	26 00		110 50	

ACCOUNT Rent Expense   **ACCOUNT NO.** 527

DATE	ITEM	POST. REF.	DEBIT	CREDIT	BALANCE DEBIT	BALANCE CREDIT
1978 Apr. 1	Balance	✓			4500 00	
1		CJ42	1500 00		6000 00	

ACCOUNT Repairs and Maintenance Expense   **ACCOUNT NO.** 528

DATE	ITEM	POST. REF.	DEBIT	CREDIT	BALANCE DEBIT	BALANCE CREDIT
1978 Apr. 1	Balance	✓			211 98	
5		CJ42	25 30			
22		CJ42	20 75			
26		CJ43	60 28		318 31	

Engle & Brenner — General Ledger *(continued)*

ACCOUNT **Salary Expense** ACCOUNT NO. 529

DATE	ITEM	POST. REF.	DEBIT	CREDIT	BALANCE DEBIT	BALANCE CREDIT
1978 Apr. 1	Balance	✓			9750 00	
29		CJ43	3250 00		13000 00	

ACCOUNT **Surgical Instruments Expense** ACCOUNT NO. 530

DATE	ITEM	POST. REF.	DEBIT	CREDIT	BALANCE DEBIT	BALANCE CREDIT
1978 Apr. 1	Balance	✓			263 30	
7		CJ42	287 35		550 65	

ACCOUNT **Surgical Supplies Expense** ACCOUNT NO. 531

DATE	ITEM	POST. REF.	DEBIT	CREDIT	BALANCE DEBIT	BALANCE CREDIT
1978 Apr. 1	Balance	✓			137 80	
11		CJ42	45 00		182 80	

ACCOUNT **Telephone Expense** ACCOUNT NO. 532

DATE	ITEM	POST. REF.	DEBIT	CREDIT	BALANCE DEBIT	BALANCE CREDIT
1978 Apr. 1	Balance	✓			149 87	
3		CJ42	76 32		226 19	

ACCOUNT **Miscellaneous Expense** ACCOUNT NO. 533

DATE	ITEM	POST. REF.	DEBIT	CREDIT	BALANCE DEBIT	BALANCE CREDIT
1978 Apr. 1	Balance	✓			60 34	
21		CJ42	12 00			
29		CJ43	9 30		81 64	

Engle & Brenner — General Ledger (concluded)

ENGLE AND BRENNER, PHYSICIANS AND SURGEONS
Trial Balance
April 30, 1978

Clermont Bank	111	24,769.81	
Petty Cash Fund	112	100.00	
Office Equipment	131	5,942.30	
Accumulated Depreciation — Office Equipment	031		1,735.10
Medical Equipment	141	17,505.88	
Accumulated Depreciation — Medical Equipment	014		2,184.72
X-Ray Equipment	151	30,875.49	
Accumulated Depreciation — X-Ray Equipment	015		6,492.38
Automobiles	161	8,475.09	
Accumulated Depreciation — Automobiles	016		2,018.77
Prepaid Insurance	171	4,684.80	
FICA Tax Payable	211		390.00
Employees Income Tax Payable	221		478.80
FUTA Tax Payable	231		91.00
State Unemployment Tax Payable	241		87.75
Linda Engle, Capital	311		16,776.30
Linda Engle, Drawing	031	6,962.50	
Douglas Brenner, Capital	321		12,551.29
Douglas Brenner, Drawing	032	7,424.53	
Professional Fees	411		89,986.00
Automobile Expense	511	530.28	
Charitable Contributions Expense	512	780.00	
Dues and Subscriptions Expense	517	325.00	
Electricity, Gas and Water Expense	518	420.13	
Laundry and Dry Cleaning Expense	520	429.20	
Legal Expense	521	400.00	
Medical Library Expense	522	557.19	
Medical Supplies Expense	523	797.70	
Office Supplies Expense	524	120.12	
Payroll Taxes Expense	525	1,222.00	
Postage Expense	526	110.50	
Rent Expense	527	6,000.00	
Repairs and Maintenance Expense	528	318.31	
Salary Expense	529	13,000.00	
Surgical Instruments Expense	530	550.65	
Surgical Supplies Expense	531	182.80	
Telephone Expense	532	226.19	
Miscellaneous Expense	533	81.64	
		132,792.11	132,792.11

Report No. 6-1

Complete Report No. 6-1 in the study assignments and submit your working papers to the instructor for approval. After completing the report, you will then be given instructions as to the work to be done next.

7

The Periodic Summary

One of the major reasons for keeping accounting records is to accumulate information that will make it possible to prepare periodic summaries of both (1) the revenue and expenses of the business during a specified period and (2) the assets, liabilities, and owner's equity of the business at a specified date. A trial balance of the general ledger accounts will provide most of the information that is required for these summaries (the income statement and the balance sheet). However, the trial balance does not supply the data in a form that is easily interpreted, nor does it reflect changes in the accounting elements that have not been represented by ordinary business transactions. Therefore, at the end of a fiscal period it is necessary, first, to determine the kind and amounts of changes that the accounts do not reflect and to adjust the accounts accordingly and, second, to recast the information into the form of an income statement and a balance sheet. These two steps are often referred to as "the periodic summary."

END-OF-PERIOD WORK SHEET

An end-of-period **work sheet** is a device that assists the accountant in three ways. It facilitates (1) the preparing of the financial statements, (2) the making of needed adjustments in the accounts, and (3) the closing of the temporary owner's equity accounts. When a number of adjustments are to be made at the end of a period, a work sheet is especially helpful in determining the balance of the accounts after adjustment.

Work sheets are not financial statements; they are devices used to assist the accountant in performing certain tasks. Ordinarily it is only the accountant who uses (or even sees) a work sheet.

A work sheet for an attorney

Although an end-of-period work sheet can be in any of several forms, a common and widely used arrangement involves ten amount columns. The amount columns are used in pairs. The first pair of amount columns is for the trial balance. The data to be recorded consist of the name, number, and debit or credit balance of each account. Debit balances should be entered in the left-hand column and credit balances in the right-hand column. The second pair of amount columns is used to record needed end-of-period adjustments. The third pair of amount columns is used to show the account balances as adjusted. This pair of amount columns is headed "Adjusted Trial Balance" because its purpose is to show that the debit and credit account balances as adjusted are equal in amount. The fourth pair of amount columns is for the adjusted balances of the expense and revenue accounts. This pair of columns is headed "Income Statement" since the amounts shown will be reported in that statement. The fifth, and last, pair of amount columns is headed "Balance Sheet" and shows the adjusted account balances that will be reported in that statement.

To illustrate the preparation and use of the end-of-period work sheet, the example of the accounts of Donald L. Cameron, Attorney at Law, will be continued. The journal and ledger for Mr. Cameron for the month of December were reproduced in Chapter 5. In this chapter the income statement for the year and the balance sheet at the end of the year will be reproduced, showing the use of a work sheet as a device for summarizing the data to be presented in those statements.

The work sheet for Donald L. Cameron, Attorney at Law

The end-of-year work sheet for Mr. Cameron is reproduced on page 159. Following is a description and discussion of the steps that were followed in the preparation of this work sheet. Each step should be studied carefully with frequent reference to the work sheet itself.

Trial Balance Columns. The trial balance of the general ledger accounts as of December 31 was entered in the first pair of amount columns. This trial balance is the same as the one shown on page 130 except that all of the account titles were included in the work sheet list even though certain of the accounts had no balance at this point.

The Trial Balance Debit and Credit columns were totaled. The totals should be equal. If not, the cause of any discrepancy must be found and corrected before the preparation of the work sheet can proceed.

Chapter 7   The Periodic Summary

Donald L. Cameron, Attorney at Law
Work Sheet
For the Year Ended December 31, 1978

	Acct. No.	Trial Balance Debit	Trial Balance Credit	Adjustments Debit	Adjustments Credit	Adj. Trial Balance Debit	Adj. Trial Balance Credit	Income Statement Debit	Income Statement Credit	Balance Sheet Debit	Balance Sheet Credit
First National Bank	111	1572167				1572167				1572167	
Petty Cash Fund	112	5000				5000				5000	
Advances on Behalf of Clients	131	44000				44000				44000	
Law Library	141	985208				985208				985208	
Accum. Deprec.—Law Library	014		272413		(a) 298858		571271				571271
Office Equipment	151	294205				294205				294205	
Accum. Deprec.—Office Equip.	015		39471		(b) 23219		62690				62690
Automobile	161	365023				365023				365023	
Accum. Deprec.—Automobile	016		136813		(c) 91256		228139				228139
Accounts Payable	211										
Employees Income Tax Payable	221		17760				17760				17760
F.I.C.A. Tax Payable	231		15000				15000				15000
FUTA Tax Payable	241		8400				8400				8400
State Unemployment Tax Pay.	251		2025				2025				2025
Donald L. Cameron, Capital	311		2221369				2221369				2221369
Donald L. Cameron, Drawing	031	2285300				2285300				2285300	
Expense and Revenue Summary	032										
Legal Fees Revenue	411		5178000				5178000		5178000		
Collection Fees Revenue	412		15604				15604		15604		
Salary Expense	511	1500000				1500000		1500000			
Payroll Taxes Expense	512	130800				130800		130800			
Rent Expense	513	540000				540000		540000			
Telephone Expense	514	55138				55138		55138			
Office Supplies Expense	515	38405				38405		38405			
Automobile Expense	516	163366				163366		163366			
Depreciation Expense	517			(a) 298858 (b) 23219 (c) 91256		298858 23219 91256		298858 23219 91256			
Charitable Contributions Exp.	518	31600				31600		31600			
Miscellaneous Expense	519	37150				37150		37150			
		8047362	8047362	413333	413333	8460695	8460695	2909792	5334041	5550903	3126654
Net Income								2424249			2424249
								5334041	5334041	5550903	5550903

Donald L. Cameron, Attorney at Law — Ten-Column Work Sheet

Adjustments Columns. The second pair of amount columns on the work sheet was used to record certain entries necessary to reflect the depreciation that had occurred during the year.

Three entries were made in the Adjustments columns to reflect these changes. When the account was debited, the amount was entered in the Adjustments Debit column on the same horizontal line as the name of the account. Amounts credited were entered, of course, in the Credit column. Each entry made on the work sheet was identified by a small letter in parentheses to facilitate cross-reference. Following is an explanation of each of the entries.

Entry (a): This entry recorded the depreciation expense for the year on the law library by debiting Depreciation Expense, Account No. 517, for $2,988.58 and by crediting Accumulated Depreciation — Law Library, Account No. 014, for $2,988.58. Law Library, Account No. 141, shows that additional law books were purchased on December 12 at a cost of $886.34. Mr. Cameron follows the practice of not taking depreciation on assets that have been owned for less than a month, so the debit to Depreciation Expense is based on the balance of $8,965.74 in Account No. 141 on December 1. The depreciation rate used for the law library is 33⅓ percent, and 33⅓ percent of $8,965.74 is $2,988.58. Law books will last physically for a long time; however, they become outdated very quickly, and this accounts for the use of a high rate of depreciation.

Entry (b): This entry recorded the depreciation expense for the year on office equipment by debiting Depreciation Expense, Account No. 517, for $232.19 and by crediting Accumulated Depreciation — Office Equipment, Account No. 015, for $232.19. Office Equipment, Account No. 151, shows that an electric typewriter was purchased on December 20 at a cost of $620.18. As with the purchase of law books in December, no depreciation is taken on assets that have been owned for less than a month; so the debit to Depreciation Expense is based on the December 1 balance of $2,321.87 in Account No. 151. The depreciation rate used for office equipment is 10 percent, and 10 percent of $2,321.87 is $232.19.

Entry (c): This entry recorded the depreciation expense on the automobile by debiting Depreciation Expense, Account No. 517, for $912.56 and crediting Accumulated Depreciation — Automobile, Account No. 016, for $912.56.

The automobile has been owned for the entire year. The original cost of the automobile was $3,650.23. The depreciation rate is 25 percent; therefore, the depreciation expense is 25 percent of $3,650.23, or $912.56.

After making the required entries in the Adjustments columns of the work sheet, the columns were totaled to prove the equality of the debit and credit entries.

Adjusted Trial Balance Columns. The third pair of amount columns of the work sheet was used for the *adjusted trial balance*. To determine the balance of each account after making the required adjustments, it was necessary to take into consideration the amounts recorded in the first two pairs of amount columns. When an account balance was not affected by entries in the Adjustments columns, the amount in the Trial Balance columns was extended directly to the Adjusted Trial Balance columns.

When an account balance was affected by an entry in the Adjustments columns, the balance recorded in the Trial Balance columns was increased or decreased, as the case might be, by the amount of the adjusting entry. For example, Accumulated Depreciation — Office Equipment was listed in the Trial Balance Credit column as $394.71. Since there was an entry of $232.19 in the Adjustments Credit column, the amount extended to the Adjusted Trial Balance Credit column was the total of $394.71 and $232.19, or $626.90.

A rule which can always be followed in combining figures in the Trial Balance columns and the Adjustments columns is that if there are debits in both columns or credits in both columns, the two amounts are added and the total is carried to the Adjusted Trial Balance columns. If there is a debit in one column and a credit in the other, the smaller amount is subtracted from the larger and the difference will be a debit or a credit depending on whether the debit or the credit is the larger amount. If the debit is the larger amount, the amount carried to the Adjusted Trial Balance columns will be placed in the Debit column. If the credit is the larger amount, the difference will be placed in the Adjusted Trial Balance Credit column. The Adjusted Trial Balance columns were totaled to prove the equality of the debits and credits.

Income Statement Columns. The fourth pair of amount columns in the work sheet was used to show the amounts that will be reported in the income statement. The amounts for legal fees revenue and collection fees revenue were extended to the Income Statement Credit column from the Adjusted Trial Balance Credit column. The amounts of the expenses were extended to the Income Statement Debit column.

The Income Statement columns were totaled. The difference between the totals of these columns is the amount of the increase or the decrease in owner's equity due to net income or net loss during the accounting period. If the total of the credits exceeds the total of the debits, the difference represents the increase in owner's equity due to net income; if the total of the debits exceeds the total of the credits, the difference represents the decrease in owner's equity due to net loss.

Reference to the Income Statement columns of Mr. Cameron's work sheet will show that the total of the credits amounted to $53,340.41 and the total of the debits amounted to $29,097.92. The difference, amounting to $24,242.49, was the amount of the net income for the year.

Balance Sheet Columns. The fifth pair of amount columns of the work sheet was used to show the amounts that will be reported in the balance sheet. The amounts were extended to the Balance Sheet Debit and Credit columns from the Adjusted Trial Balance columns. The Balance Sheet columns were totaled. The difference between the totals of these columns also is the amount of the net income or the net loss for the accounting period. If the total of the debits exceeds the total of the credits, the difference represents a net income for the accounting period; if the total of the credits exceeds the total of the debits, the difference represents a net loss for the period. This difference should be the same as the difference between the totals of the Income Statement columns.

Reference to the Balance Sheet columns of the work sheet will show that the total of the debits amounted to $55,509.03 and the total of the credits amounted to $31,266.54. The difference of $24,242.49 represented the amount of the net income for the year.

Completing the Work Sheet. The difference between the totals of the Income Statement columns and the totals of the Balance Sheet columns should be recorded on the next horizontal line below the column totals. If the difference represents net income, it should be so designated and recorded in the Income Statement Debit and in the Balance Sheet Credit columns. If, instead, a net loss has been the result, the amount should be so designated and entered in the Income Statement Credit and in the Balance Sheet Debit columns. Finally, the totals of the Income Statement and Balance Sheet columns, after the net income (or net loss) has been recorded, are entered, and a double line is ruled immediately below the totals.

Proving the Work Sheet. The fact that the difference between the Income Statement columns and the difference between the Balance Sheet columns are the same amount is not a coincidence. This occurs because an excess of revenue over expenses results in net income. Likewise, an excess of expenses over revenue results in a net loss. It is also true, but not quite so obvious, that if there is a net income, it will result in an increase in assets in the Balance Sheet columns in the form of additional cash, accounts receivable, or other assets. Sometimes cash received is used to pay liabilities, so that the assets at the end of the period may not have increased in total, but the liabilities have decreased. The increase in owner's equity, however, which results from profitable operations has not yet been recorded in the permanent owner's equity account at the time the work sheet is prepared. The balance of the owner's capital account is the amount of owner's equity at the beginning of the period, because the day by day changes are recorded in the temporary owner's equity accounts — the revenue and expense accounts.

When the amount of the net income is added to the Income Statement Debit column, the total of expenses and net income is equal to the revenue items in the Income Statement Credit column; and when the amount of net income is added to the Balance Sheet Credit column, the total assets equal the total liabilities and owner's equity, which is the accounting equation presented on page 5. After the temporary accounts are closed at the end of the period and the net amount of income for the period has been transferred to the owner's capital account, that account includes the net income for the period.

Report No. 7-1

> Complete Report No. 7-1 in the study assignments and submit your working papers to the instructor for approval. After completing the report, continue with the following textbook discussion until the next report is required.

THE FINANCIAL STATEMENTS

The financial statements usually consist of (1) an income statement and (2) a balance sheet.

The income statement

An **income statement** is a formal statement of the results of the operation of an enterprise during an accounting period. Other titles sometimes used for this statement include *profit and loss statement, income and expense statement, revenue and expense statement,* *operating statement*, and *report of earnings*. Whatever the title, the purpose of the statement or report is to show the types and amounts of revenue and expenses that the business had during the period involved, and the resulting net income or net loss for this accounting period.

Importance of the Income Statement. The income statement is generally considered to be one of the most important financial statements of a business. A business cannot exist indefinitely unless it has profit or net income. The income statement is essentially a "report card" of the enterprise. The statement provides a basis for judging the overall effectiveness of the management. Decisions as to whether to continue a business, to expand it, or to contract it are often based upon the results as reported in the income statement. Actual and potential creditors are interested in income statements because one of the best reasons for extending credit or for making a loan is that the business is profitable.

Various government agencies are interested in income statements of businesses for a variety of reasons. Regulatory bodies are concerned with the earnings of the enterprises they regulate, because a part of the regulation usually relates to the prices, rates, or fares that may be charged. If the enterprise is either exceptionally profitable or unprofitable, some change in the allowed prices or rates may be needed. Income tax authorities, both federal and local, have an interest in business income statements. Net income determination for tax purposes differs somewhat from the calculation of net income for other purposes; but, for a variety of reasons, the tax authorities are interested in both sets of calculations.

Form of the Income Statement. The form of the income statement depends in part upon the type of enterprise. For a professional practice, the professional revenue is listed first, the professional expenses are listed next, and the total of the professional expenses is subtracted from the professional revenue to determine the net professional income. The amounts of any revenue from other sources, such as dividend revenue from investments, are added to, and the amounts of any other expenses, such as interest on a loan from the bank, are subtracted from, the net professional income to arrive at the final amount of net income (or net loss).

It is essential that the income statement be properly headed. The name of the business (or of the individual if the enterprise is a professional practice or if the business is operated in the owner's name) should be shown first. The name of the statement is placed on the second line, and the period of time that the statement covers appears on the third line. An income statement always covers a period of time; and if the period is a year, it may be stated, for example, "For the Year Ended December 31, 19--."

The income statement presented to the owner (or owners) of an enterprise and to potential creditors or other interested parties is usually typewritten. The income statement for Mr. Cameron for the year ended December 31, 1978, is shown below. The information needed to prepare the statement was obtained from the work sheet shown on page 159.

```
                DONALD L. CAMERON, ATTORNEY AT LAW
                          Income Statement
                  For the Year Ended December 31, 1978

Professional revenue:
   Legal fees revenue .........................            $51,780.00
   Collection fees revenue ....................              1,560.41
      Total professional revenue ..............             $53,340.41

Professional expenses:
   Salary expense..............................  $15,000.00
   Payroll taxes expense ......................    1,308.00
   Rent expense................................    5,400.00
   Telephone expense...........................      551.38
   Office supplies expense ....................      384.05
   Automobile expense..........................    1,633.66
   Depreciation expense........................    4,133.33
   Charitable contributions expense ...........      316.00
   Miscellaneous expense.......................      371.50
      Total professional expenses .............                29,097.92
Net income .....................................              $24,242.49
```

Donald L. Cameron, Attorney at Law — Income Statement

The balance sheet

A formal statement of the assets, liabilities, and owner's equity in an enterprise at a specified date is known as a **balance sheet**. The title of the statement had its origin in the equality of the elements; that is, in the balance between the sum of the assets and the sum of the liabilities and owner's equity. Sometimes the balance sheet is called a *statement of financial condition* or a *statement of financial position*.

Importance of the Balance Sheet. The balance sheet of a business is of considerable interest to various parties for several reasons. The owner or owners of a business are interested in the kinds and amounts of assets and liabilities and the amount of the owner's equity or capital element.

Persons considering buying an ownership interest in a business are greatly interested in the character and amount of the assets and liabilities, though this interest is probably secondary to their concern about the future earnings possibilities.

Finally, various regulatory bodies are interested in the financial condition of the businesses that are under their jurisdiction. Examples of regulated businesses include banks, insurance companies, public utilities, railroads, and airlines.

Form of the Balance Sheet. Traditionally, balance sheets have been presented either in **account form** or in **report form**. When the account form is followed, the assets are listed on the left side of the page (or on the left of two facing pages) and the liabilities and owner's equity on the right. This form is similar to the debit-side and credit-side arrangement of the standard ledger account. The balance sheet of Donald L. Cameron, Attorney at Law, as of December 31, 1978, in account form is reproduced below and on page 167. The data for the preparation of the statement were secured from the work sheet.

When the report form of the balance sheet is followed, the assets, liabilities, and owner's equity elements are listed underneath each other. This arrangement is usually preferable when the statement is typed on letter-size paper (8½" × 11").

DONALD L. CAMERON,
Balance
December

Assets			
Current assets:			
Cash in bank		$15,721.67	
Petty cash fund		50.00	
Advances on behalf of clients		440.00	
Total current assets			$16,211.67
Long-lived assets:			
Law library	$ 9,852.08		
Less accumulated depreciation—law library	5,712.71	$ 4,139.37	
Office equipment	$ 2,942.05		
Less accumulated depreciation—office equipment	626.90	2,315.15	
Automobile	$ 3,650.23		
Less accumulated depreciation—automobile	2,281.39	1,368.84	
Total long-lived assets			7,823.36
Total assets			$24,035.03

Donald L. Cameron, Attorney at Law — Balance Sheet (Left Side)

Whichever form is used, it is essential that the statement have the proper heading. This means that three things must be shown: **(1)** the name of the business (or name of the individual if the business or professional practice is carried on in the name of an individual); followed by **(2)** the name of the statement — usually just "Balance Sheet"; and finally, **(3)** the date — month, day, and year. Sometimes the expression "As of Close of Business December 31, 1978" (or whatever date is involved) is included. It must be remembered that a balance sheet relates to a particular moment of time. This is in contrast to the income statement which always refers to a certain period of time.

Classification of Data in the Balance Sheet. The purpose of the balance sheet and of all other financial statements and reports is to convey as much information as possible. This aim is furthered by some classification of the data being reported. It has become almost universal practice to classify both assets and liabilities in the balance sheet as either **(1)** *current* or **(2)** *noncurrent* or *long-lived*.

Current Assets. **Current assets** include cash and all other assets that may be reasonably expected to be realized in cash or sold or consumed during the normal operating cycle of the business. In a professional practice, the current assets may include cash and receivables, such as advances on behalf of clients.

```
ATTORNEY AT LAW
Sheet
31, 1978
                              Liabilities

Current liabilities:
   Employees income tax payable.......    $    177.60
   FICA tax payable ..................         150.00
   FUTA tax payable ..................          84.00
   State unemployment tax payable.....          20.25
       Total current liabilities .......              $    431.85

                           Owner's Equity

Donald L. Cameron, capital:
   Capital, January 1 ................               $22,213.69
   Net income........................  $24,242.49
      Less withdrawals...............   22,853.00     1,389.49
   Capital, December 31 .............                              23,603.18


Total liabilities and owner's equity                              $24,035.03
```

Donald L. Cameron, Attorney at Law — Balance Sheet (Right Side)

Long-Lived Assets. Property that is used in the operation of a professional practice may include such assets as land, buildings, office equipment, professional equipment, professional libraries, and automobiles. Such assets are called **long-lived assets** because they have a useful life that is comparatively long. Of these assets only land, however, is really permanent.

Reference to the balance sheet of Donald L. Cameron will show that his long-lived assets consist of a law library, office equipment, and an automobile. In each case, the amount of the accumulated depreciation is shown as a deduction from the cost of the depreciable asset. The difference between the cost of the asset and the accumulated depreciation is the **book value** of the asset. The book value represents the undepreciated amount of the asset. In future periods, the book value of a specific asset will decrease as depreciation expense is realized and the amount of accumulated depreciation increases.

Current Liabilities. **Current liabilities** include those obligations that will be due in a short time and paid with monies provided by the current assets. As of December 31, Mr. Cameron's current liabilities consisted of employees income tax payable, FICA tax payable, FUTA tax payable, and state unemployment tax payable.

Long-Term Liabilities. **Long-term liabilities** (sometimes called *fixed liabilities*) include those obligations that will not be due for a relatively long time. The most common of the long-term liabilities is mortgages payable.

A **mortgage payable** is a debt or an obligation that is secured by a **mortgage**, which provides for the conveyance of certain property upon failure to pay the debt at maturity. When the debt is paid, the mortgage becomes void. It will be seen, therefore, that a mortgage payable differs little from an account payable or a note payable except that the creditor holds the mortgage as security for the payment of the debt. Usually debts secured by mortgages run for a longer period of time than ordinary notes payable or accounts payable. A mortgage payable should be classified as a long-term liability if the maturity date extends beyond the normal operating cycle of the business (usually a year). Mr. Cameron has no long-term liabilities.

Owner's Equity. As previously explained, accounts relating to the owner's equity element may be either permanent or temporary owner's equity accounts. The permanent owner's equity accounts used in recording the operations of a particular enterprise depend upon the type of organization; that is, whether the enterprise is organized as a sole proprietorship, as a partnership, or as a corporation.

In the case of a sole proprietorship, one or more accounts representing the owner's interest or equity in the assets may be kept. Reference to the chart of accounts shown on page 109 will show that the following accounts are classified as owner's equity accounts:

>Account No. 311, Donald L. Cameron, Capital
>Account No. 031, Donald L. Cameron, Drawing
>Account No. 321, Expense and Revenue Summary

Account No. 311 reflects the amount of Mr. Cameron's equity. It may be increased by additional investments or by the practice of not withdrawing cash or other assets in an amount as large as the net income of the enterprise. It may be decreased by withdrawals in excess of the amount of the net income or by sustaining a net loss during one or more accounting periods. Usually there will be no changes in the balance of this account during the accounting period, in which case the balance represents the owner's investment in the business as of the beginning of the accounting period and until the books are closed at the end of the accounting period.

Account No. 031 is Mr. Cameron's drawing account. This account is debited for any withdrawals of cash or other property for personal use. It is a temporary account in which is kept a record of the owner's personal drawings during the accounting period. Ordinarily such drawings are made in anticipation of earnings rather than as withdrawals of capital. The balance of the account, as shown by the trial balance at the close of an accounting period, represents the total amount of the owner's drawings during the period.

Reference to the work sheet shown on page 159 will reveal that the balance of Mr. Cameron's drawing account is listed in the Balance Sheet Debit column. This is because there is no provision on a work sheet for making deductions from owner's equity except by listing them in the Debit column. Since the balance of the owner's capital account is listed in the Balance Sheet Credit column, the listing of the balance of the owner's drawing account in the Debit column is equivalent to deducting the amount from the balance of the owner's capital account.

Account No. 321 is used only at the close of the accounting period for the purpose of summarizing the temporary owner's equity accounts. Sometimes this account is referred to as a **clearing account**. No entries should appear in the account before the books are closed at the end of the accounting period.

The owner's equity section of Mr. Cameron's balance sheet is arranged to show the major changes that took place during the year in the owner's equity element of the law practice. Mr. Cameron's interest in the practice amounted to $22,213.69 at the beginning of the year. His interest was increased $24,242.49 as the result of profitable operations and decreased $22,853 as the result of withdrawals during the year. Thus, the owner's equity increased by $1,389.49 because withdrawals were less than the income for the period. Mr. Cameron's anticipation of income was less than the amount actually earned. The owner's equity element on December 31 amounted to $23,603.18.

Report No. 7-2

Complete Report No. 7-2 in the study assignments and submit your working papers to the instructor for approval. After completing the report, you may continue with the textbook discussion in Chapter 8 until the next report is required.

8

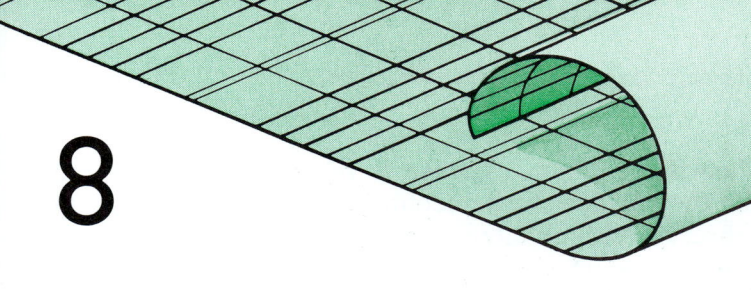

Adjusting and Closing Accounts at End of Accounting Period

As explained in the preceding chapter, the adjustment of certain accounts at the end of the accounting period is required because of changes that have occurred during the period that are not reflected in the accounts. Since the purpose of the temporary owner's equity accounts is to assemble information relating to a specified period of time, at the end of the period the balances of these accounts must be removed to allow the accounts to be ready to perform their function in the following period. Accounts of this type must be "closed."

ADJUSTING ENTRIES

In preparing the work sheet for Donald L. Cameron, Attorney at Law (reproduced on page 159), adjustments were made to accomplish the following purposes:

(a) To record the estimated amount of depreciation of the law library for the year.
(b) To record the estimated amount of depreciation of the office equipment for the year.
(c) To record the estimated amount of depreciation of the automobile for the year.

Note that each of the adjusting entries affects both the balance sheet and the income statement. If an adjusting entry increases an

172 Adjusting and Closing Accounts at End of Accounting Period Chapter 8

expense, as when depreciation expense is recorded in entries (a), (b), and (c), then the balance sheet accounts Accumulated Depreciation — Law Library, Accumulated Depreciation — Office Equipment, and Accumulated Depreciation — Automobile are also increased. It should also be noted that adjusting entries for accumulated depreciation do not affect cash because the long-lived asset has already been paid for. Depreciation, as explained in Chapter 5, is simply a way of allocating the original cost of the asset to the periods in which it is used up.

The effect of these adjustments was reflected in the financial statements reproduced on pages 165, 166, and 167. To bring the ledger into agreement with the financial statements, the adjustments should be recorded in the proper accounts. It is customary, therefore, at the end of each accounting period to journalize the adjustments and to post them to the accounts.

Journalizing the adjusting entries

Adjusting entries may be recorded in either a general journal or a combined cash journal. If the entries are made in a combined cash journal, the only amount columns used are the General Debit and Credit columns. A portion of a page of a combined cash journal showing Mr. Cameron's adjusting entries is reproduced below. Note that when the adjusting entries are recorded in the combined cash journal, they are entered in exactly the same manner as they would be entered in a general journal. Since the heading "Adjusting Entries" explains the nature of the entries, a separate explanation of each adjusting entry is unnecessary. The information needed in journalizing the adjustments was obtained from the Adjustments col-

COMBINED CASH JOURNAL FOR MONTH OF *December* 19 78   PAGE **35**

DAY	DESCRIPTION	POST. REF.	GENERAL DEBIT	GENERAL CREDIT
	AMOUNTS FORWARDED			
31	Adjusting Entries			
	Depreciation Expense	517	2988 58	
	Accum. Deprec.-Law Library	014		2988 58
	Depreciation Expense	517	232 19	
	Accum. Deprec.-Office Equip.	015		232 19
	Depreciation Expense	517	912 56	
	Accum. Deprec.-Automobile	016		912 56
			4133 33	4133 33

Donald L. Cameron, Attorney at Law — Adjusting Entries

Chapter 8   Adjusting and Closing Accounts at End of Accounting Period   **173**

umns of the work sheet shown on page 159. The account numbers were not entered in the Posting Reference column at the time of journalizing; they were entered as the posting was completed.

Posting the adjusting entries

The adjusting entries should be posted individually to the proper general ledger accounts. The accounts of Mr. Cameron that were affected by the adjusting entries are reproduced below. The entries in the accounts for December transactions that were posted prior to posting the adjusting entries are the same as appeared in the accounts reproduced on pages 126–129. The number of the combined cash journal page on which the adjusting entries were recorded was entered in the Posting Reference column of the general ledger accounts affected, and the account numbers were entered in the Posting Reference column of the combined cash journal as the posting was completed. This provided a cross-reference in both books.

ACCOUNT: Accumulated Depreciation—Law Library   ACCOUNT NO. 014

DATE	ITEM	POST. REF.	DEBIT	CREDIT	BALANCE DEBIT	BALANCE CREDIT
1978 Dec. 1	Balance	✓				2724 13
31		CJ35		2988 58		5712 71

ACCOUNT: Accumulated Depreciation—Office Equip.   ACCOUNT NO. 015

DATE	ITEM	POST. REF.	DEBIT	CREDIT	BALANCE DEBIT	BALANCE CREDIT
1978 Dec. 1	Balance	✓				394 71
31		CJ35		232 19		626 90

ACCOUNT: Accumulated Depreciation—Automobile   ACCOUNT NO. 016

DATE	ITEM	POST. REF.	DEBIT	CREDIT	BALANCE DEBIT	BALANCE CREDIT
1978 Dec. 1	Balance	✓				1368 83
31		CJ35		912 56		2281 39

ACCOUNT: Depreciation Expense   ACCOUNT NO. 517

DATE	ITEM	POST. REF.	DEBIT	CREDIT	BALANCE DEBIT	BALANCE CREDIT
1978 Dec. 31		CJ35	2988 58			
31		CJ35	232 19			
31		CJ35	912 56		4133 33	

**Donald L. Cameron, Attorney at Law —
General Ledger Accounts After Posting Adjusting Entries**

Report No. 8-1

> Complete Report No. 8-1 in the study assignments and submit your working papers to the instructor for approval. Continue with the following textbook discussion until Report No. 8-2 is required.

CLOSING PROCEDURE

After the adjusting entries have been posted, all of the temporary owner's equity accounts should be closed. This means that the accountant must remove ("close out") **(1)** the balance of every account that enters into the calculation of the net income (or net loss) for the accounting period and **(2)** the balance of the owner's drawing account. The purpose of the closing procedure is to transfer the balances of the temporary owner's equity accounts to the permanent owner's equity account. This could be accomplished simply by debiting or crediting each account involved, with an offsetting credit or debit to the permanent owner's equity account. However, it is considered better practice to transfer the balances of all accounts that enter into the net income or net loss determination to a summarizing account called **Expense and Revenue Summary** (sometimes called *Income Summary, Profit and Loss Summary*, or just *Profit and Loss*). Then the resulting balance of the expense and revenue summary account (which will be the amount of the net income or net loss for the period) is transferred to the permanent owner's equity account.

The final step in the closing procedure is to transfer the balance of the owner's drawing account to the permanent owner's equity account. After this is done, only the asset accounts, the liability accounts, and the permanent owner's equity account have balances. If there has been no error, the sum of the balances of the asset accounts (less balances of any contra accounts) will be equal to the sum of the balances of the liability accounts plus the balance of the permanent owner's equity account. The accounts will agree exactly with what is shown by the balance sheet as of the close of the period. Reference to the balance sheet of Donald L. Cameron reproduced on pages 166 and 167 will show that the assets, liabilities, and owner's equity as of December 31 may be expressed in equation form as follows:

ASSETS	=	LIABILITIES	+	OWNER'S EQUITY
$24,035.03		$431.85		$23,603.18

Chapter 8 Adjusting and Closing Accounts at End of Accounting Period **175**

Journalizing the closing entries

Closing entries, like adjusting entries, may be recorded in either a general journal or a combined cash journal. If the entries are made in a combined cash journal, only the General Debit and Credit columns are used. A portion of a page of a combined cash journal showing the closing entries for Mr. Cameron is reproduced below. Since the heading "Closing Entries" explains the nature of the entries, a separate explanation of each closing entry is not necessary. The information required in preparing the closing entries was obtained from the work sheet illustrated on page 159.

COMBINED CASH JOURNAL FOR MONTH OF December 19 78   PAGE 36

DAY	DESCRIPTION	POST. REF.	GENERAL DEBIT	GENERAL CREDIT
	AMOUNTS FORWARDED			
31	Closing Entries			
	Legal Fees Revenue	411	51780 00	
	Collection Fees Revenue	412	1560 41	
	Expense & Revenue Summary	321		53340 41
	Expense and Revenue Summary	321	29097 92	
	Salary Expense	511		15000 00
	Payroll Taxes Expense	512		1308 00
	Rent Expense	513		5400 00
	Telephone Expense	514		551 38
	Office Supplies Expense	515		384 05
	Automobile Expense	516		1633 66
	Depreciation Expense	517		4133 33
	Charitable Contributions Expense	518		316 00
	Miscellaneous Expense	519		371 50
	Expense and Revenue Summary	321	24242 49	
	Donald L. Cameron, Capital	311		24242 49
	Donald L. Cameron, Capital	311	22853 00	
	Donald L. Cameron, Drawing	031		22853 00
			129533 82	129533 82

Donald L. Cameron, Attorney at Law — Closing Entries

The first closing entry was made to close the revenue accounts, Legal Fees Revenue and Collection Fees Revenue. Since these accounts have credit balances, each account must be debited for the amount of its balance in order to close it. The debits to these two accounts are offset by a credit of $53,340.41 to Expense and Revenue Summary.

The second closing entry was made to close the expense accounts. Since these accounts have debit balances, each account must be credited for the amount of its balance in order to close it. The credits to these accounts are offset by a debit of $29,097.92 to Expense and Revenue Summary.

The posting of the first two closing entries causes the expense and revenue summary account to have a credit balance of $24,242.49, the net income for the year. The account has now served its purpose and must be closed. The third closing entry closes the expense and revenue summary account by debiting that account and crediting Donald L. Cameron, Capital, for $24,242.49.

The final closing entry was made to close the Donald L. Cameron drawing account. Since this account has a debit balance, it must be credited to close it. The offsetting entry is a debit of $22,853 to Donald L. Cameron, Capital.

The account numbers shown in the Posting Reference column were not entered at the time the closing entries were made — they were entered as the posting was completed.

Posting the closing entries

Closing entries should be posted in the usual manner. Proper cross-references are provided by using the Posting Reference columns of the combined cash journal and the ledger accounts. After all the closing entries have been posted, the accounts affected appear as shown below and on pages 177 to 179. The income statement accounts are now in balance.

ACCOUNT *Donald L. Cameron, Capital* — ACCOUNT NO. 311

DATE	ITEM	POST. REF.	DEBIT	CREDIT	BALANCE DEBIT	BALANCE CREDIT
1978 Dec. 1	Balance	✓				22213 69
31		CJ36		24242 49		
31		CJ36	22853 00			23603 18

ACCOUNT *Donald L. Cameron, Drawing* — ACCOUNT NO. 031

DATE	ITEM	POST. REF.	DEBIT	CREDIT	BALANCE DEBIT	BALANCE CREDIT
1978 Dec. 1	Balance	✓			21030 25	
15		CJ33	865 00			
27		CJ34	49 75			
29		CJ34	900 00			
29		CJ34	8 00		22853 00	
31		CJ36		22853 00	—0—	—0—

Donald L. Cameron, Attorney at Law — Partial General Ledger

Expense and Revenue Summary — Account No. 321

DATE	ITEM	POST. REF.	DEBIT	CREDIT	BALANCE DEBIT	BALANCE CREDIT
1978 Dec. 31		CJ36		5334041		
31		CJ36	2909792			
31		CJ36	2424249		—0—	—0—

Legal Fees Revenue — Account No. 411

DATE	ITEM	POST. REF.	DEBIT	CREDIT	BALANCE DEBIT	BALANCE CREDIT
1978 Dec. 1	Balance	✓				3972000
29		CJ34		1206000		5178000
31		CJ36	5178000		—0—	—0—

Collection Fees Revenue — Account No. 412

DATE	ITEM	POST. REF.	DEBIT	CREDIT	BALANCE DEBIT	BALANCE CREDIT
1978 Dec. 1	Balance	✓				142135
29		CJ34		13906		156041
31		CJ36	156041		—0—	—0—

Salary Expense — Account No. 511

DATE	ITEM	POST. REF.	DEBIT	CREDIT	BALANCE DEBIT	BALANCE CREDIT
1978 Dec. 1	Balance	✓			1375000	
15		CJ33	32500			
15		CJ33	30000			
29		CJ34	32500			
29		CJ34	30000		1500000	
31		CJ36		1500000	—0—	—0—

Payroll Taxes Expense — Account No. 512

DATE	ITEM	POST. REF.	DEBIT	CREDIT	BALANCE DEBIT	BALANCE CREDIT
1978 Dec. 1	Balance	✓			123300	
29		CJ34	7500		130800	
31		CJ36		130800	—0—	—0—

Donald L. Cameron, Attorney at Law — Partial General Ledger (continued)

ACCOUNT Rent Expense   **ACCOUNT NO.** 513

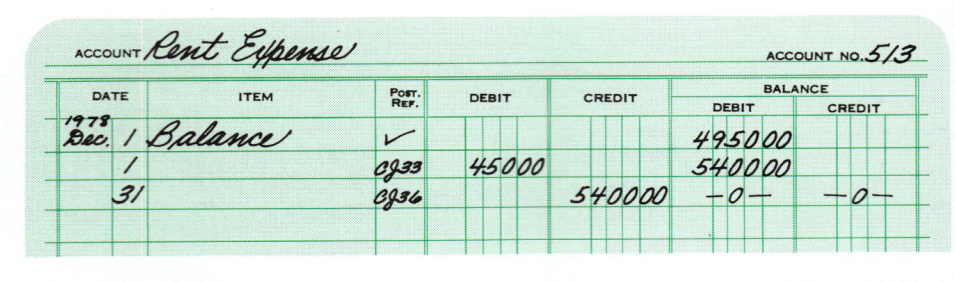

DATE	ITEM	POST. REF.	DEBIT	CREDIT	BALANCE DEBIT	BALANCE CREDIT
1978 Dec. 1	Balance	✓			4950 00	
1		CJ33	450 00		5400 00	
31		CJ36		5400 00	—0—	—0—

ACCOUNT Telephone Expense   **ACCOUNT NO.** 514

DATE	ITEM	POST. REF.	DEBIT	CREDIT	BALANCE DEBIT	BALANCE CREDIT
1978 Dec. 1	Balance	✓			508 20	
5		CJ33	43 18		551 38	
31		CJ36		551 38	—0—	—0—

ACCOUNT Office Supplies Expense   **ACCOUNT NO.** 515

DATE	ITEM	POST. REF.	DEBIT	CREDIT	BALANCE DEBIT	BALANCE CREDIT
1978 Dec. 1	Balance	✓			332 40	
18		CJ33	45 70			
29		CJ34	5 95		384 05	
31		CJ36		384 05	—0—	—0—

ACCOUNT Automobile Expense   **ACCOUNT NO.** 516

DATE	ITEM	POST. REF.	DEBIT	CREDIT	BALANCE DEBIT	BALANCE CREDIT
1978 Dec. 1	Balance	✓			1540 20	
6		CJ33	89 74			
29		CJ34	3 72		1633 66	
31		CJ36		1633 66	—0—	—0—

ACCOUNT Depreciation Expense   **ACCOUNT NO.** 517

DATE	ITEM	POST. REF.	DEBIT	CREDIT	BALANCE DEBIT	BALANCE CREDIT
1978 Dec. 31		CJ35	2988 58			
31		CJ35	232 19			
31		CJ35	912 56		4133 33	
31		CJ36		4133 33	—0—	—0—

Donald L. Cameron, Attorney at Law — Partial General Ledger *(continued)*

Charitable Contributions Expense — Account No. 518

DATE	ITEM	POST. REF.	DEBIT	CREDIT	BALANCE DEBIT	BALANCE CREDIT
1978 Dec. 1	Balance	✓			288 00	
13		CJ33	25 00			
29		CJ34	3 00		316 00	
31		CJ36		316 00	—0—	—0—

Miscellaneous Expense — Account No. 519

DATE	ITEM	POST. REF.	DEBIT	CREDIT	BALANCE DEBIT	BALANCE CREDIT
1978 Dec. 1	Balance	✓			269 40	
4		CJ33	25 25			
14		CJ33	70 00			
29		CJ34	6 85		371 50	
31		CJ36		371 50	—0—	—0—

Donald L. Cameron, Attorney at Law — Partial General Ledger *(concluded)*

After the income statement accounts have been closed, the accounts still open are the balance sheet accounts; that is, the asset, liability, and permanent owner's equity accounts. If a new general ledger is to be opened in which to record the transactions of the new year, the balances of the open accounts which have debit balances should be entered in the Debit Balance columns. The balances of the open accounts which have credit balances should be entered in the Credit Balance columns. The date will be January 1, even though the new ledger may be opened a few days after January 1.

If the old general ledger is to be used for the new year, the December 31 balances of the open accounts automatically become the balances on January 1. The number of the new year should be entered when the first entry is made in the new year.

Trial balance after closing

A trial balance of the general ledger accounts that remain open after the temporary owner's equity accounts have been closed is usually referred to as a **post-closing trial balance**. The purpose of the post-closing trial balance is to prove that the general ledger is in balance at the beginning of a new accounting period. It is advisable to know that such is the case before any transactions for the new accounting period are recorded.

The post-closing trial balance should contain the same accounts and amounts as appear in the Balance Sheet columns of the work sheet, except that (1) the owner's drawing account is omitted because it has been closed and (2) the owner's capital account has been adjusted for the amount of the net income (or net loss) and the amount of the owner's drawings.

A post-closing trial balance of Mr. Cameron's general ledger is shown below. Some accountants advocate that the post-closing trial balance should be dated as of the close of the old accounting period, while others advocate that it should be dated as of the beginning of the new accounting period. In this illustration the trial balance is dated December 31, the end of the period.

DONALD L. CAMERON, ATTORNEY AT LAW
Post-Closing Trial Balance
December 31, 1978

First National Bank	111	15,721.67	
Petty Cash Fund	112	50.00	
Advances on Behalf of Clients	131	440.00	
Law Library	141	9,852.08	
Accumulated Depreciation — Law Library	014		5,712.71
Office Equipment	151	2,942.05	
Accumulated Depreciation — Office Equipment	015		626.90
Automobile	161	3,650.23	
Accumulated Depreciation — Automobile	016		2,281.39
Employees Income Tax Payable	221		177.60
FICA Tax Payable	231		150.00
FUTA Tax Payable	241		84.00
State Unemployment Tax Payable	251		20.25
Donald L. Cameron, Capital	311		23,603.18
		32,656.03	32,656.03

Donald L. Cameron, Attorney at Law — Post-Closing Trial Balance

The accounting cycle

The steps involved in handling the effect of all transactions and events completed during an accounting period, beginning with entries in the books of original entry and ending with the post-closing trial balance, are known as the **accounting cycle**. The following is a list of the steps in the accounting cycle.

(a) Journalizing the transactions.
(b) Posting to the ledger accounts.
(c) Taking a trial balance.
(d) Determining the needed adjustments.
(e) Completing an end-of-period work sheet.

(f) Preparing an income statement and a balance sheet.
(g) Journalizing and posting the adjusting and closing entries.
(h) Taking a post-closing trial balance.

In visualizing the accounting cycle, it is important to realize that steps (c) through (h) in the foregoing list are performed *as of the last day of the accounting period*. This does not mean that they necessarily are done *on* the last day. The accountant or bookkeeper may not be able to do any of these things until the first few days of the next period. Nevertheless, the work sheet, statements, and entries are prepared or recorded as of the closing date. While the journalizing of transactions in the new period proceeds in regular fashion, it is not usual to post to the general ledger any entries relating to the new period until the steps relating to the period just ended have been completed.

Income and self-employment taxes

An unincorporated business or professional practice is not subject to income taxes. The owner — not the business or practice — is subject to income taxes. The amounts of business or professional revenue and expenses must be reported in the owner's personal income tax return regardless of the amount of money or other property the owner has actually withdrawn from the enterprise during the year. In the case of a sole proprietorship or a partnership, there is no legal distinction between the enterprise and the owner.

In order to bring a large class of self-employed individuals into the federal social security program, the law requires all self-employed persons (except those specifically exempted) to pay a self-employment tax. The rate of tax is 2.1 percent more than the prevailing FICA rate, but the base of the "self-employment income tax" is the same as the base for the FICA tax. (If it is assumed that the combined FICA tax rate is 6 percent, the self-employment income tax rate would be 8.1 percent on the assumed base of $18,000.) The actual rate and base of the tax may be changed by Congress at any time. In general, **self-employment income** means the net income of a professional practice or business conducted by an individual or a partner's distributive share of the net income of a partnership whether or not any cash is distributed. Earnings of less than $400 from self-employment are ignored.

A taxable year for the purpose of the tax on self-employment income is the same as the taxpayer's taxable year for federal income tax purposes. The self-employment tax is reported along with the regular federal income tax. For calendar-year taxpayers, the tax return and full or final payment is due on April 15 following the close of the year. Like the personal income tax, the self-employment tax is treated as a personal expense of the owner. If the taxes are paid with business funds, the amount should be charged to the owner's drawing account.

Report No. 8-2

Complete Report No. 8-2 in the study assignments and submit your working papers to the instructor for approval. You will then be given instructions as to the work to be done next.

5-8

Practical Accounting Problems

Problem 5-A   Mr. Paul Ortiz, Miss Helen Courtney, and Mr. Carlos Holscher have decided to form a partnership for the practice of law. The firm will be known as Ortiz, Courtney, and Holscher. John Leonard has been hired as a typist, and Rita Jensen has been hired as a secretary-bookkeeper. It has been decided that the firm's books will be kept on the cash basis and that the accounting records will be a combined cash journal and a general ledger. There are several auxiliary records which are not involved in this problem. The following transactions were completed during the month of July:

July 1. The partners invested the following amounts in the enterprise and opened an account in the Security National Bank:

Paul Ortiz..	$25,000
Helen Courtney	$22,000
Carlos Holscher...	$10,000

Mr. Holscher also contributed an automobile valued at $5,200. (In the combined cash journal, debit Automobile and credit Carlos Holscher, Capital.)

1. Paid W. L. Morse for rent for July, $800.
2. Purchased supplies for cash, $185.10.
6. Received payment for drawing a will for Louise Kirk, $50.
8. Paid the State Bar Association for annual dues for the three partners, $150.
12. The firm was engaged to represent Acme Products Co. in the lawsuit of Acme Products Co. against George Henderson. Received retainer, $200.
15. Paid wages of employees for first half of month as follows:

Rita Jensen, $500, less income tax payable, $80.10, and FICA tax payable, $30.

John Leonard, $400, less income tax payable, $49.40, and FICA tax payable, $24.

July 19. Paid Modern Law Book Co. for law books purchased, $6,227.35.
21. Drafted a partnership agreement for Kelly and Hanson, stockbrokers. Received $250.
23. Paid City Oil Co. for repairs on automobile used for professional purposes, $73.20.
27. Paid Quality Office Furniture Co. for office furniture and equipment purchased, $6,877.92.
29. Paid Richards Insurance Agency for a one-year insurance policy on the law library and furniture and equipment, $122.35.
31. Paid wages of employees for second half of month as follows:
Rita Jensen, $500, less income tax payable, $80.10, and FICA tax payable, $30.
John Leonard, $400, less income tax payable, $49.40, and FICA tax payable, $24.

REQUIRED: (1) Record each transaction in the combined cash journal using the following accounts:

111 Security National Bank	311 Paul Ortiz, Capital
121 Supplies	321 Helen Courtney, Capital
131 Law Library	331 Carlos Holscher, Capital
141 Office Furniture and Equipment	411 Legal Fees
	511 Automobile Expense
151 Automobile	512 Insurance Expense
221 Employees Income Tax Payable	513 Miscellaneous Expense
	514 Rent Expense
231 FICA Tax Payable	515 Salary Expense

For the combined cash journal, use a sheet of paper like that shown in the illustration on pages 122 and 123. A column for collection fees will not be needed in this problem. Number the page of the journal. (2) Prove the combined cash journal by footing the amount columns; then total and rule the journal. (3) Open the necessary accounts using account forms like those illustrated on pages 126–130. Post the combined cash journal entries for July and enter the account balances. (4) Take a trial balance as of July 31, using a sheet of two-column journal paper.

Problem 5-B   The law firm of Kennedy and Fagin has 17 employees. The employees are paid by check on the 15th and last business day of each month. The entry to record each payroll includes the liabilities for the amounts withheld. The employer's payroll taxes are recorded on each payday. The social security and withheld income taxes exceed $2,000 on each payday, and it is therefore necessary for Kennedy and Fagin to deposit the taxes within three banking days of each payday. Thus the taxes for salaries paid January 15 and January 31 must be paid within three banking days following January 15 and January 31.

Following is a narrative of the transactions completed during the month of February of the current year that relate to payrolls and payroll taxes:

Feb. 2. Paid $2,497.57 for January 31 payroll taxes:
- Employees' income tax withheld $1,259.32
- FICA tax 1,238.25

15. Payroll for the first half of month:
- Total salaries $10,383.33
- Less amounts withheld:
  - Employees' income tax................. $1,229.40
  - FICA tax 623.00   1,852.40
- Net amount paid........................... $ 8,530.93

15. Social security taxes imposed on employer:
- FICA tax @ 6.0%
- State unemployment tax @ 2.5%
- FUTA tax @ .7%

28. Payroll for the second half of month:
- Total salaries $10,423.33
- Less amounts withheld:
  - Employees' income tax................. $1,237.80
  - FICA tax 625.40   1,863.20
- Net amount paid........................... $ 8,560.13

28. Social security taxes imposed on employer:
All salaries taxable; rates same as on February 15.

REQUIRED: **(1)** Journalize the foregoing transactions, using two-column general journal paper. **(2)** Foot the debit and credit amount columns as a means of proof.

Problem 5-C

Janet Wilke and Jean Yablonski are partners engaged in the practice of law. They employ a secretary and a secretary-bookkeeper. The books, which are kept on the cash basis, consist of a combined cash journal and a general ledger. For the combined cash journal, use a sheet of paper like that shown in the illustration on pages 122 and 123. A column for collection fees will not be needed in this journal. Number the page of the journal using number 29. The trial balance taken as of May 31, 19-- appears on page 186.

NARRATIVE OF TRANSACTIONS FOR JUNE

June 1. Paid rent for June, $800.
    2. Paid the following bills:
- Telephone bill, $165.82
- Electric bill, $17.63

WILKE AND YABLONSKI, ATTORNEYS AT LAW
Trial Balance
May 31, 19--

Cash	111	19,560.03	
Petty Cash	112	50.00	
Law Library	131	10,835.41	
Accumulated Depreciation — Law Library	013		3,145.18
Furniture and Equipment	141	5,927.42	
Accumulated Depreciation — Furn. and Equip.	014		1,123.27
Employees Income Tax Payable	221		235.60
FICA Tax Payable	231		228.00
State Unemployment Tax Payable	241		102.60
FUTA Tax Payable	251		66.50
Janet Wilke, Capital	311		16,027.46
Janet Wilke, Drawing	031	9,000.00	
Jean Yablonski, Capital	321		13,929.29
Jean Yablonski, Drawing	032	7,500.00	
Legal Fees	411		35,122.00
Insurance Expense	511	954.62	
Payroll Taxes Expense	512	893.00	
Rent Expense	513	4,000.00	
Salary Expense	514	9,500.00	
Stationery and Supplies Expense	515	880.22	
Utilities Expense	516	879.20	
		69,979.90	69,979.90

June 3. Received $1,500 from the U.S. Government. Ms. Wilke acted as an expert witness before a government committee.

7. Received $2,275 from Philip Meloni for balance due on Case No. 221.

9. Paid cash for office supplies, $35.10.

10. Received $900 for work in connection with the incorporation of the Thomas Manufacturing Corporation.

14. Paid $463.60 for May payroll taxes:

Employees' income tax withheld	$235.60
FICA tax	228.00
	$463.60

15. Paid wages of employees for first half of month as follows:

$550, less income tax payable, $61.50, and FICA tax payable, $33.

$400, less income tax payable, $56.30, and FICA tax payable, $24.

17. Received $780 from Ramsay and Shulman for balance due on Case No. 219.

21. Paid for additions to the law library, $227.81.

23. Received $750 for work in connection with planning the estate of A.G. Hermann.

June 24. Received $50 for drawing a will for D.S. Sanchez.
25. Received $50.35 for overcharge on law books purchased in May. (Law Library, Account No. 131, had been debited for the total amount of the invoice.)
28. Received $1,700 for work in connection with preparing a pension plan for the Star Manufacturing Co.
30. Paid wages of employees for the second half of month as follows:
$550, less income tax payable, $61.50, and FICA tax payable, $33.
$445, less income tax payable, $65.60, and FICA tax payable, $26.70.
30. Ms. Wilke withdrew $1,800 for personal use.
30. Mrs. Yablonski withdrew $1,500 for personal use.
30. Replenished the petty cash fund. The following disbursements had been made:

Stationery and Supplies Expense	$12.49
Utilities Expense — collect telegram	2.27
Jean Yablonski, Drawing	18.56
Total disbursements	$33.32

30. Made an entry in the combined cash journal for the employer's portion of the FICA tax, for the state unemployment tax, and for the FUTA tax for the month of June by debiting Payroll Taxes Expense for $182.84 and crediting FICA Tax Payable for $116.70, State Unemployment Tax Payable for $52.52, and FUTA Tax Payable for $13.62.

REQUIRED: **(1)** Record each transaction in the combined cash journal. **(2)** Prove the combined cash journal by footing the amount columns; total and rule the journal. **(3)** Open the necessary general ledger accounts using account forms like those illustrated on pages 126–130. Record the June 1 balances as shown in the May 31 trial balance and complete the individual posting from the combined cash journal. Determine the balances of the accounts. **(4)** Take a trial balance as of June 30, using a sheet of two-column journal paper.

Problem 5-D   The law firm of Larson and Collins has three employees: David Evans, a legal assistant; Dorothy Frantz, a secretary-bookkeeper; and Louise Lauer, a secretary. The employees are paid semimonthly. On August 15, 19--, the total payroll was $1,550. Income tax withheld amounted to $220.40, and FICA tax deductions were $93. On August 31 the total payroll was $1,588.94. Income tax withheld amounted to $230, and FICA tax deductions were $95.34. All employees have earned more than $6,000 prior to the month of August; so the employer is not liable for state unemployment tax or FUTA tax on the August wages.

Mr. Evans resigned at the end of August, and Miss Esther Lipscomb was hired to take Mr. Evans' place effective September 1. Miss Lipscomb's salary is $1,100 per month payable semimonthly. On September 15 the total payroll was $1,500. Income tax withheld amounted to $237, and FICA tax deductions were $90. On September 29 the total payroll was $1,551.92. Income tax withheld amounted to $248.20 and FICA tax deductions were $93.12. The state unemployment tax rate is assumed to be 2.7%, and the FUTA rate is assumed to be .7%.

REQUIRED: **(1)** Prepare entries in general journal form to record the payment of the salaries on August 15 and on August 31. **(2)** Prepare an entry in general journal form to record the employer's payroll taxes for the month of August. **(3)** Prepare entries in general journal form to record the payment of the salaries on September 15 and on September 29. **(4)** Prepare an entry in general journal form to record the employer's payroll taxes for September. **(5)** Foot the debit and credit amount columns as a means of proof.

Problem 6-A   Dr. Philip Oliveri is engaged in the practice of medicine and surgery. The only book of original entry is a combined cash journal. A general ledger is kept and also several auxiliary records including a daily service record and a patients ledger. Dr. Oliveri has one employee, a secretary, Alma Weaver, who also keeps the books. The books are kept on the cash basis. The trial balance as of January 31 appears on page 189.

NARRATIVE OF TRANSACTIONS FOR FEBRUARY

Feb. 1. Paid rent for February, $800.
    3. Paid oil company bill for January, $129.70.
    4. Paid for professional equipment, $3,515.82.
    6. The amount columns in the daily service record for the week ended February 6 contained the following totals:

Kind of service:	
Office calls	$ 260.00
Surgery	2,250.00
Total	$2,510.00
Patients' accounts — charges	$2,460.00
Cash services	50.00
Total	$2,510.00

The total cash received from patients during the week ended February 6 was as shown on page 189.

DR. PHILIP OLIVERI, PHYSICIAN AND SURGEON
Trial Balance
January 31, 19--

Account	No.	Debit	Credit
First National Bank	111	3,418.46	
Professional Equipment	121	20,142.15	
Accumulated Depreciation — Prof. Equip.	012		8,829.82
Office Equipment	131	3,721.35	
Accumulated Depreciation — Office Equip.	013		960.48
Automobile	141	5,807.91	
Accumulated Depreciation — Automobile	014		1,051.72
Employees Income Tax Payable	211		131.20
FICA Tax Payable	221		108.00
FUTA Tax Payable	231		6.30
Philip Oliveri, Capital	311		17,066.85
Philip Oliveri, Drawing	031	1,810.15	
Professional Fees	411		9,125.00
Automobile Expense	511	145.72	
Laundry Expense	512	65.25	
Miscellaneous Expense	513	19.85	
Payroll Taxes Expense	514	60.30	
Professional Supplies Expense	515	126.64	
Rent Expense	516	800.00	
Salary Expense	517	900.00	
Stationery and Supplies Expense	518	30.95	
Telephone Expense	519	55.49	
Utilities Expense	520	175.15	
		37,279.37	37,279.37

Feb. 6.	Payments	$2,800.00
	Cash services	50.00
	Total	$2,850.00

    8. Paid laundry bill for January, $62.27.
   10. Paid the following bills:
       Gas and electric bill, $145.32.
       Water bill, $22.48.
   10. Paid for professional supplies, $61.22.
   13. The amount columns in the daily service record contained the following totals:

Kind of service:		
	Office calls	$ 275.00
	Surgery	2,200.00
	Total	$2,475.00
	Patients' accounts — charges	$2,455.00
	Cash services	20.00
	Total	$2,475.00

Feb. 13. The total cash received from patients during the week ended February 13 was:

Payments	$1,895.00
Cash services	20.00
Total	$1,915.00

15. Paid $239.20 for January payroll taxes:

Employees income tax withheld	$131.20
FICA tax	108.00
	$239.20

15. Paid salary to Alma Weaver for first half of month: $450, less income tax payable, $65.60, and FICA tax payable, $27.
17. Paid for professional supplies, $70.15.
18. Paid telephone bill, $64.67.
19. Paid for automobile repairs, $85.35.
20. The amount columns in the daily service record contained the following totals:

Kind of service:

Office calls	$ 225.00
Surgery	1,885.00
Total	$2,110.00
Patients' accounts — charges	$1,998.00
Cash services	112.00
Total	$2,110.00

The total cash received from patients during the week ended February 20 was:

Payments	$2,935.00
Cash services	112.00
Total	$3,047.00

24. Paid for office supplies, $25.70.
26. Paid the American Medical Association for a subscription to a professional journal, $15. (Debit Miscellaneous Expense.)
27. Dr. Oliveri withdrew $1,800 for personal use.
27. Paid salary to Alma Weaver for second half of the month: $488.94, less income tax payable, $75.20, and FICA tax payable, $29.34.
27. The amount columns in the daily service record contained the following totals:

Kind of service:

Office calls	$ 110.00
Surgery	1,820.00
Total	$1,930.00

Feb. 27.	Patients' accounts — charges	$1,850.00
	Cash services	80.00
	Total	$1,930.00

The total cash received from patients for the week ended February 27 was:

Payments	$2,150.00
Cash services	80.00
Total	$2,230.00

27. Made an entry in the combined cash journal for the employer's portion of the FICA tax and for the FUTA tax for the month of February by debiting Payroll Taxes Expense and by crediting FICA Tax Payable for $56.34 and FUTA Tax Payable for $6.57.

REQUIRED: **(1)** Record the transactions in the combined cash journal using a sheet of paper like that illustrated on pages 144–147. **(2)** Prove the journal by footing the amount columns; total and rule the journal. **(3)** Open the necessary general ledger accounts using account forms like those illustrated on pages 149–155. Record the February 1 balances as shown on the January 31 trial balance and complete the posting from the combined cash journal. Determine the balances of the accounts. **(4)** Take a trial balance using a sheet of two-column journal paper.

Problem 6-B

John C. Lang and Theresa A. Lang, physicians and surgeons, operate a clinic known as the Lang Clinic. They employ five other physicians and seven other employees. The books are closed each year as of December 31, but interim statements are prepared monthly. The following information is presented so that certain entries can be made in the month of April:

(a) Apr. 18.	Employees' income tax withheld from wages paid on April 15		$2,257.80
	FICA tax:		
	Withheld from employees' wages	$751.00	
	Imposed on employer	751.00	1,502.00
			$3,759.80

The Lang Clinic is required to deposit the income and FICA taxes withheld and the employer's share of the FICA tax within three banking days of the 15th and of the last day of each month, since the cumulative unpaid tax is more than $2,000 on the fifteenth and on the last day of the month.

  (b) Apr. 29. FUTA tax for the quarter ending March 31.. $520.18

The Lang Clinic is required to deposit the FUTA tax owed by the employer at the end of the first quarter, since the cumulative unpaid tax is more than $100.

  (c) Apr. 29. State unemployment tax due for quarter ending March 31 .... $1,958.60

  (d)   30. Payroll taxes expense for the month of April:
    FICA tax $1,501.00
    State unemployment tax on wages of employees who have earned less than $6,000 in the current year 337.50
    FUTA tax on wages of employees who have earned less than $6,000 in the current year 87.50

  (e)   30. Statement of petty cash disbursements for April:
    Theresa Lang, Drawing $14.85
    Automobile Expense........................ 13.50
    Miscellaneous Expense 40.27
    Professional Supplies Expense........... 10.16
    Stationery and Supplies Expense........ 5.77
    Total disbursements..................... $84.55

REQUIRED: Prepare entries in general journal form to record the information given.

Problem 6-C Dr. Ramona Burton, a physician and surgeon, keeps her books on the cash basis. A trial balance taken as of August 31, 19--, does not balance. A check of the records reveals the following information:

(1) The correct total of the First State Bank Dr. column in the combined cash journal is $5,694. This amount was posted in the cash account in the general ledger as $5,649.

(2) The combined cash journal was out of balance by $169 because a payment for professional supplies was debited to the proper account but was not entered in the First State Bank Cr. column.

(3) The balance in the office equipment account was entered in the trial balance as $260 instead of the correct figure of $2,600.
(4) The miscellaneous expense account in the amount of $114 was omitted from the trial balance.
(5) All accounts have normal balances.

DR. RAMONA BURTON
Trial Balance
August 31, 19--

First State Bank	12,368.00	
Professional Equipment	13,215.00	
Accumulated Depreciation — Professional Equip.		4,660.41
Office Equipment	260.00	
Accumulated Depreciation — Office Equipment		792.00
Employees Income Tax Payable		112.60
FICA Tax Payable		96.00
FUTA Tax Payable		47.99
Ramona Burton, Capital		9,110.00
Ramona Burton, Drawing	12,250.00	
Professional Fees		44,215.00
Payroll Taxes Expense		276.00
Professional Supplies Expense		1,300.00
Rent Expense	9,600.00	
Salary Expense	6,855.00	
Utilities Expense	580.00	
	55,128.00	60,610.00

REQUIRED: Prepare a corrected trial balance.

Problem 6-D   Dr. James Litwin is a dentist. The only book of original entry is a combined cash journal. The accounts are kept in a general ledger. Dr. Litwin has two employees, Michael Schneider, a dental hygienist, and Marie Dubois, a secretary-bookkeeper. There is an auxiliary record for the patients seen by Dr. Litwin and for the patients seen by the hygienist, but these records are not involved in this problem. The books are kept on the cash basis. Dr. Litwin requests that patients pay cash for the services of the hygienist, and most do. The trial balance as of June 30 is shown on page 194.

NARRATIVE OF TRANSACTIONS FOR JULY

July 1. Paid rent for July, $1,100.
   3. Paid telephone bill for June, $47.85.
   5. Paid the Acme Dental Laboratory for laboratory work done in June, $3,019.

DR. JAMES LITWIN, DENTIST
Trial Balance
June 30, 19--

Security State Bank	111	9,501.57	
Professional Equipment	121	18,195.20	
Accumulated Depreciation — Prof. Equip.	012		7,337.27
Office Equipment	131	3,462.95	
Accumulated Depreciation — Office Equip.	013		1,677.20
Employees Income Tax Payable	211		199.20
FICA Tax Payable	221		204.00
State Unemployment Tax Payable	231		137.70
FUTA Tax Payable	241		71.40
James Litwin, Capital	311		12,439.67
James Litwin, Drawing	031	10,800.00	
Professional Fees — Dentistry	411		45,850.00
Professional Fees — Oral Hygiene	412		11,700.00
Laboratory Expense	511	18,630.00	
Laundry Expense	512	147.80	
Miscellaneous Expense	513	31.27	
Payroll Taxes Expense	514	958.80	
Professional Supplies Expense	515	215.75	
Rent Expense	516	6,600.00	
Salary Expense	517	10,200.00	
Stationery and Supplies Expense	518	145.10	
Telephone Expense	519	269.80	
Utilities Expense	520	458.20	
		79,616.44	79,616.44

July 8. The amount columns in the daily service records kept by Dr. Litwin and Mr. Schneider for the week ended July 8 contained the following totals:

Kind of service:
Dentistry — Dr. Litwin	$1,785.00
Oral hygiene — Mr. Schneider	360.00
Total	$2,145.00

The total cash received from patients during the week ended July 8 was:
Dentistry	$1,825.00
Oral hygiene	330.00
Total	$2,155.00

10. Paid laundry bill for June, $25.27.
11. Paid the following bills:
    Gas and electric bill, $30.18.
    Water bill, $24.92.
15. The amount columns in the daily service records contained the totals given at the top of the next page.

July 15. Kind of service:
    Dentistry $2,010.00
    Oral hygiene 435.00
        Total $2,445.00

The total cash received from patients during the week ended July 15 was:
    Dentistry $2,645.00
    Oral hygiene 450.00
        Total $3,095.00

15. Paid salary to Michael Schneider for first half of month: $450, less income tax payable, $43.30, and FICA tax payable, $27; and to Marie Dubois, $400, less income tax payable, $56.30, and FICA tax payable, $24.
18. Paid for professional supplies, $42.77.
20. Paid $60 for dues to the state dental society. Debit Miscellaneous Expense.
22. The amount columns in the daily service records contained the following totals:

    Kind of service:
        Dentistry $1,837.00
        Oral hygiene 375.00
            Total $2,212.00

The total cash received from patients during the week ended July 22 was:
    Dentistry $2,127.00
    Oral hygiene 420.00
        Total $2,547.00

24. Paid for office supplies, $21.63.
26. Paid for subscriptions to magazines for the waiting room, $30. Debit Miscellaneous Expense.
29. Paid $403.20 for June payroll taxes:
    Employees' income tax withheld $199.20
    FICA tax 204.00
        Total $403.20

29. Paid state unemployment tax for the second quarter, $137.70.
31. The amount columns in the daily service records contained the following totals:

    Kind of service:
        Dentistry $1,982.00
        Oral hygiene 405.00
            Total $2,387.00

July 31. The total cash received from patients for the period July 24–31 was:

Dentistry	$1,720.00
Oral hygiene	390.00
Total	$2,110.00

31. Paid salary to Michael Schneider for second half of month: $450, less income tax payable, $43.30, and FICA tax payable, $27; and to Marie Dubois, $427.69, less income tax payable, $60.80, and FICA tax payable, $25.66.
31. Dr. Litwin withdrew $1,800 for personal use.
31. Made an entry in the combined cash journal for the employer's portion of the FICA tax for the month of July by debiting Payroll Taxes Expense and crediting FICA Tax Payable for $103.66.
31. Made an entry in the combined cash journal for the state unemployment tax and the FUTA tax based on the earnings, $1,427.69, in July which do not exceed $6,000 in the current year by debiting Payroll Taxes Expense and crediting State Unemployment Tax Payable and FUTA Tax Payable. The state unemployment tax rate is assumed to be 2.7% and the FUTA rate .7%.

REQUIRED: **(1)** Record each transaction in the combined cash journal using a sheet of paper like that illustrated on pages 144–147. Number the page of the journal using number 48. **(2)** Prove the combined cash journal by footing the amount columns; total and rule the journal. **(3)** Open the necessary general ledger accounts using account forms like those illustrated on pages 149–155. Record the July 1 balances as shown in the June 30 trial balance and complete the posting from the combined cash journal. Determine the balances of the accounts. **(4)** Take a trial balance as of July 31, using a sheet of two-column journal paper.

Problem 7-A   Albert Lewis and Anthony Sardis have formed a partnership for the practice of civil engineering. They employ ten engineers and drafters, a secretary, and a secretary-bookkeeper. The partners share profits and losses equally. The Trial Balance columns of the work sheet for the current year ended December 31 are shown on the next page.

REQUIRED: Prepare a ten-column work sheet making the necessary entries in the Adjustments columns to record the following:

Depreciation:
    Office equipment, 10% a year, $2,342.80.
    Professional equipment, 12½% a year, $2,751.70.
    Automotive equipment, 25% a year, $10,119.53.

LEWIS AND SARDIS, CIVIL ENGINEERS
Work Sheet
For the Year Ended December 31, 19--

Account	Acct. No.	Trial Balance Debit	Trial Balance Credit
Cash	111	47,264.38	
Petty Cash	112	50.00	
Office Equipment	141	23,427.98	
Accumulated Depreciation — Off. Equip.	014		11,845.02
Professional Equipment	151	22,013.62	
Accumulated Depreciation — Prof. Equip.	015		3,943.67
Automotive Equipment	161	40,478.13	
Accumulated Depreciation — Auto. Equip.	016		13,782.15
Employees Income Tax Payable	221		1,393.20
FICA Tax Payable	231		962.00
FUTA Tax Payable	241		
State Unemployment Tax Payable	251		
Albert Lewis, Capital	311		22,392.67
Albert Lewis, Drawing	031	32,415.30	
Anthony Sardis, Capital	321		21,849.73
Anthony Sardis, Drawing	032	33,689.20	
Expense and Revenue Summary	331		
Professional Fees	411		362,425.00
Automotive Expense	511	4,462.30	
Depreciation Expense	512		
Insurance Expense	513	2,550.35	
Miscellaneous Expense	514	372.93	
Payroll Taxes Expense	515	13,992.00	
Rent Expense	516	18,000.00	
Salary Expense	517	192,400.00	
Stationery, Supplies, and Blueprint Expense	518	4,170.55	
Telephone Expense	519	1,528.70	
Charitable Contributions Expense	520	1,778.00	
		438,593.44	438,593.44

NOTE: Problems 7-B and 8-A are based on the work sheet for Lewis and Sardis. If these problems are to be solved, the work sheet should be retained for reference until they are solved, at which time the solutions of all three problems may be submitted to the instructor.

Problem 7-B Refer to the work sheet for Lewis and Sardis (based on Problem 7-A) and from it prepare the following financial statements:

(1) An income statement for the year ended December 31.
(2) A balance sheet in account form as of December 31.

Problem 8-A Refer to the work sheet for Lewis and Sardis (based on Problem 7-A) and draft the general journal entries required:

(1) To adjust the general ledger accounts so they will be in agreement with the financial statements.
(2) To close the temporary owner's equity accounts on December 31.

Problem 8-B (Complete cycle problem) Angela Hamilton and Maria Leonardi for several years have been partners engaged in the practice of architecture. They share profits and losses equally. The accounting records consist of a combined cash journal and a general ledger. The column headings in the combined cash journal are as follows:

Provident National Bank Dr.	Stationery, Office, and Blueprint
Provident National Bank Cr.	Supplies Expense Dr.
General Dr.	Salary Expense Dr.
General Cr.	Employees Income Tax Payable Cr.
Professional Fees Cr.	FICA Tax Payable Cr.

The account forms in the general ledger are like those illustrated on pages 126–130.

The trial balance as of November 30 is on page 199. The trial balance includes all the accounts in the general ledger, some of which do not have balances as of November 30.

The firm employs seven persons, two architects, two drafters, two secretaries, and a secretary-bookkeeper.

NARRATIVE OF TRANSACTIONS FOR DECEMBER

Dec. 1. Paid the Grossman Realty Co. $3,000 for rent of the office for the month of December. Check No. 314.
    1. Received $5,559 from A. H. Wells Co. for work completed.
    4. Paid the Bell Telephone Co. bill, $280.13. Check No. 315.
    4. Paid the following payroll taxes based on wages paid during the month of November by sending Check No. 316 in the amount of $2,088.96 to the Provident National Bank. Since the amount is in excess of $2,000, it must be deposited within three business days following the end of the month.

Employees' income tax withheld from wages..............................		$1,649.00
FICA tax:		
Withheld from employees' wages..	$219.98	
Imposed on employer	219.98	439.96
Total		$2,088.96

A Federal Tax Deposit, Form 501, was filled out and sent with the check.

HAMILTON AND LEONARDI, ARCHITECTS
Trial Balance
November 30, 19--

Provident National Bank	111	50,413.60	
Petty Cash	112	75.00	
Office and Professional Equipment	141	46,314.28	
Acc. Dep. — Office and Prof. Equip.	014		14,926.12
Automobiles	151	16,687.67	
Accumulated Depreciation — Automobiles	015		4,021.36
Employees Income Tax Payable	221		1,649.00
FICA Tax Payable	231		439.96
FUTA Tax Payable	241		
State Unemployment Tax Payable	251		
Angela Hamilton, Capital	311		33,912.55
Angela Hamilton, Drawing	031	32,300.00	
Maria Leonardi, Capital	321		31,478.85
Maria Leonardi, Drawing	032	30,150.00	
Expense and Revenue Summary	331		
Professional Fees	411		281,026.59
Automobile Expense	511	3,760.14	
Charitable Contributions Expense	512	4,972.00	
Depreciation Expense	513		
Heat, Light, Power, and Water Expense	514	4,569.70	
Insurance Expense	515		
Miscellaneous Expense	516	341.70	
Payroll Taxes Expense	517	7,424.00	
Rent Expense	518	33,000.00	
Repairs and Maintenance Expense	519	1,830.50	
Salary Expense	520	122,433.37	
Stationery, Office, and Blueprint Sup. Exp.	521	5,420.72	
Telephone Expense	522	2,876.20	
Travel and Entertainment Expense	523	4,885.55	
		367,454.43	367,454.43

Dec. 6. Paid the Valley Gas and Electric Co. for November service, $225.15. Check No. 317.
   6. Paid for gasoline and oil used in the company cars during November, $78.35. Check No. 318.
   7. Received $2,525 from Superior Products Co. for work completed.
   8. Paid the Professional Supply Co. for blueprint supplies, $139.85. Check No. 319.
   8. Reimbursed Ms. Leonardi for expenses incurred in attending a professional meeting, $140.28. Check No. 320.
   11. Paid the Roberts Insurance Agency $2,786 for a one-year professional liability insurance policy. Check No. 321.
   13. Paid the Valley Country Club $40.25 for entertainment of a client. Check No. 322.
   14. Paid the Acme Cleaning Co. $245 for office cleaning services rendered during November. Check No. 323.

Dec. 14. Received $3,700 from Edward Murphy for work completed.
15. Paid salaries for the first half of the month, $5,083.33, less employees' withholding tax, $824.50, and FICA tax payable, $80. Checks No. 324–330 inclusive were issued for the net amounts payable to the employees.
15. Paid the Square Deal Garage $89.75 for repairs to one of the company cars. Check No. 331.
18. Paid the Harper Stationery Co. $145 for stationery and supplies. Check No. 332.
19. Received $8,300 from Jackson County in payment for work completed.
20. Contributed $25 to the Community Christmas Fund. Check No. 333. Debit Charitable Contributions Expense, Account No. 512.
21. Paid the Jackson County Water Authority $75.70 for November service. Check No. 334.
22. Received $7,000 from the Jackson County Airport for work completed.
26. Paid the balance due on the pledge to the United Fund, $500. Check No. 335. Debit Charitable Contributions Expense, Account No. 512.
26. Paid the Fine Line Furniture Co. $1,850 for office furniture. Check No. 336. Debit Office and Professional Equipment, Account No. 141.
28. Paid the Modern Stationery Co. $155.67 for office supplies. Check No. 337.
29. Paid the Provident National Bank $20 for annual rental of a safe deposit box for use of the partnership. Check No. 338. Debit Miscellaneous Expense, Account No. 516.
29. Paid the Sherwood Office Equipment Co. $25.50 for typewriter repairs. Check No. 339.
29. Mrs. Hamilton withdrew $2,800 for personal use. Check No. 340.
29. Ms. Leonardi withdrew $2,900 for personal use. Check No. 341.
29. Paid salaries for the second half of the month, $5,126.61, less employees' withholding tax, $833.80, and FICA tax payable, $82.60. Checks No. 342–348 inclusive were issued for the net amounts payable to the employees.
29. Issued Check No. 349 to replenish the petty cash fund. A statement of petty cash disbursements for December follows:

Angela Hamilton, Drawing	$10.00
Automobile Expense	12.25
Charitable Contributions Expense	5.00
Miscellaneous Expense	7.35
Stationery, Office, and Blueprint Supplies Expense	3.70
Travel and Entertainment Expense	32.86
Total disbursements	$71.16

Dec. 29. Made an entry in the combined cash journal for the employer's portion of the FICA tax for the month of December, $162.60.

REQUIRED: **(1)** Journalize the December transactions. **(2)** Open the necessary general ledger accounts and record the December 1 balances, using the November 30 trial balance as the source of the needed information. Complete the individual and summary posting from the combined cash journal. **(3)** Take a trial balance of the general ledger accounts and enter the figures in the first two columns of a ten-column work sheet. **(4)** Complete the ten-column work sheet making the required adjustments from the information given below.

Depreciation:
Office and professional equipment, 10% a year, $4,631.43, based on the balance at the beginning of the year. No depreciation is taken this year on the purchase of December 26.
Automobiles, 25% a year, $4,171.92.

(5) Prepare an income statement for the year ending December 31 and a balance sheet in report form as of December 31. **(6)** Record the adjusting entries in the combined cash journal and post. **(7)** Record the closing entries in the combined cash journal and post. The page numbers of the combined cash journal begin with No. 12. **(8)** Take a post-closing trial balance.

Appendix

Computer-Based Accounting Systems—Design and Use

Structure of accounting systems

The design of a system of forms, records, and reports depends in large measure on the nature of the business by which the system is used. The number of transactions to be recorded in a given time period has much to do with the planning and arrangement of the chart of accounts and of the procedures for gathering and processing transaction information. Physical location of factory buildings, warehouses, stores and offices, and the transaction volume at each location also influence the design of an accounting system.

The nature of the business, the plan of organization, the kinds of transactions to be recorded and summarized, the transaction volume, and the location of physical facilities together comprise the *structure* of an accounting system. All of these factors together make careful systems planning essential.

The language of computer-based systems

The original or *source documents* for many kinds of business transactions have been presented in this textbook. The source document is always the key record in a computer-based accounting system, just as it is in a manual accounting system. Whether a source document is prepared by hand or by machine, the data it contains must be collected and the recording process started by people.

Some modern businesses are quite large, and this relative size affects their accounting systems. Modern systems for relatively large businesses include computer equipment (hardware) that operates without human guidance other than pressing one or more buttons. The use of such equipment in an accounting system makes it a **computer-based accounting system**.

Computer-based accounting has brought about the development of a new language as well as new procedures. In computer-based accounting, facts and figures such as ledger account titles, dollar amounts, and physical quantities are known as **data**. The use of these data in different ways for different business purposes is known as **data processing**. Accounting involves the processing of data in several different forms. In fact, the original preparation of the source document for a business transaction is a form of data processing. Likewise, the recording of transactions in books of original entry, posting to ledger accounts, taking trial balances, and preparing financial statements are also forms of data processing.

Those who use computer equipment to process accounting records must apply accounting principles to each step. The same principles of debit and credit apply whether the work is done with computer equipment, with conventional accounting machines, or by the manual bookkeeper. Equipment and machines reduce routine manual work, increase the speed of producing records, and permit more accurate financial reporting.

Data processing is usually described in two ways. The processing of business transactions by means of simple office machines with card punches or tape writers attached is known as **integrated data processing (IDP)**. The processing of business transactions by means of an electronic computer is known as **electronic data processing (EDP)**.

Accounting systems review

No one can design and install an accounting system for a business that will function properly without a thorough knowledge of the operations of that business. When a business is first established, this may not be possible. What is more, expansion of a business into new areas of operation, new personnel, or increased transaction volume may cause its accounting system to become inadequate.

For any one of the foregoing reasons, a business may decide to review its accounting system on an almost continuous basis and to change one or more parts of the system at frequent intervals. Accounting systems review subdivides into three phases: **(1)** systems analysis, **(2)** systems design, and **(3)** systems implementation.

Systems analysis

Systems analysis has three major objectives:

(a) The determination of business needs for information.
(b) The determination of sources of such information.
(c) The shortcomings in the accounting systems and procedures presently in use.

The first step in systems analysis usually is a review of the organizational structure and the job descriptions of the personnel involved. The second step in systems analysis usually is a study of forms, records, and reports, and the processing methods and procedures used by the business. In this connection, a **systems manual**, which details instructions to employees and procedures to be followed, is extremely valuable to the systems analyst if it is available. The third step in systems analysis is to project management's plans for changes in such operational matters as sales volume, products, territories, sales agents, or customers into the near future.

Systems design

Accounting systems design changes are the result of systems analysis. A good systems designer needs to know the relative merits of various types of computer hardware and be able to evaluate the various alternatives open to the business, which may or may not involve computer hardware.

Creativity and imagination are important attributes of a successful systems designer. The following general principles also are important:

(a) The value of information produced by an accounting system should never be less than the cost of obtaining it, and preferably the value should be greater than the cost.
(b) Any accounting system needs sufficient built-in internal control to safeguard business assets and protect data reliability.
(c) Any accounting system needs to be flexible enough to absorb data volume increases and changes in procedures and data processing techniques without disruption of the system.

Systems implementation

A newly created or revised accounting system is worthless without the ability to carry out, or implement, the recommendations of the systems analyst. The new or revised forms, records, reports, procedures, and hardware recommended by the systems analyst must be installed, and obsolete items must be removed. Each and every employee who will have a hand in operating the system must be thoroughly trained and adequately supervised until the new system is operating smoothly.

A major systems change, such as from a manual accounting system to a computer-based accounting system, usually is spread over a rather long period of time. For a while during the changeover period, the old and new systems must function side by side at least in part, and care must be taken to avoid seriously affecting the reliability of the data produced by the system(s).

Flowcharts   One of the major tools of the systems analyst in the design of computer-based accounting systems is called the **flowchart**. In a flowchart, the major steps to be undertaken in processing a particular accounting transaction or series of closely related accounting transactions are shown in graphic form. The symbols most commonly used in preparing flowcharts are:

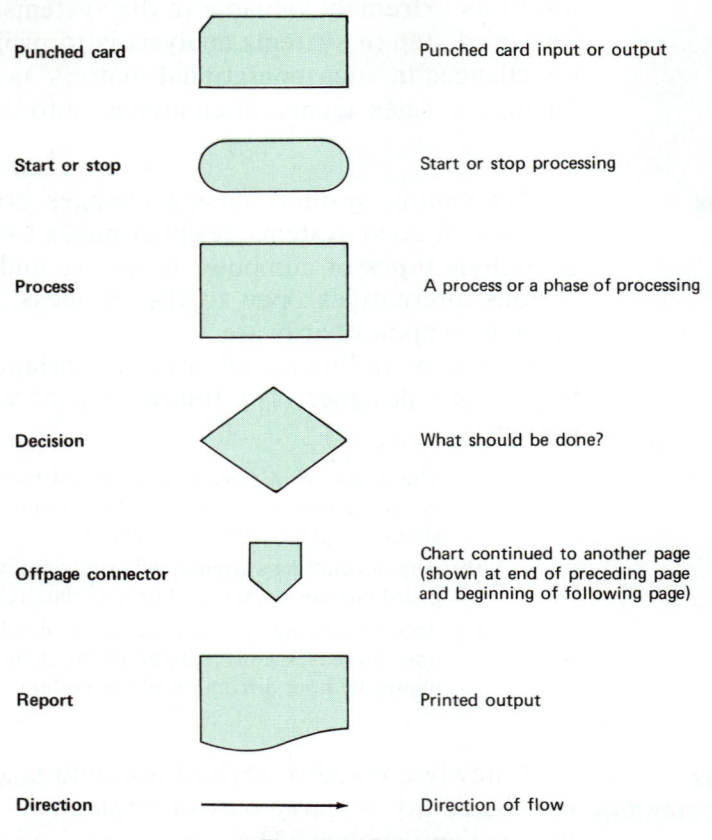

Symbol	Description
Punched card	Punched card input or output
Start or stop	Start or stop processing
Process	A process or a phase of processing
Decision	What should be done?
Offpage connector	Chart continued to another page (shown at end of preceding page and beginning of following page)
Report	Printed output
Direction	Direction of flow

Flowchart Symbols

Flowcharts usually are prepared to be read from left to right and from top to bottom, with the direction of the flow being shown by lines and arrows. A brief description of each step in processing usually is written inside each flowchart symbol. When one or more decisions are required at some stage in data processing, the questions to be answered usually are printed inside or next to each decision symbol. Most decisions involve comparison of two data items. If the items match, the decision is to go on with the process; if the two items do not match, the decision usually is to retrace some of the previously completed steps in the process.

The process involved in manually posting information from employee clock cards to a payroll register is shown in the flowchart reproduced below.

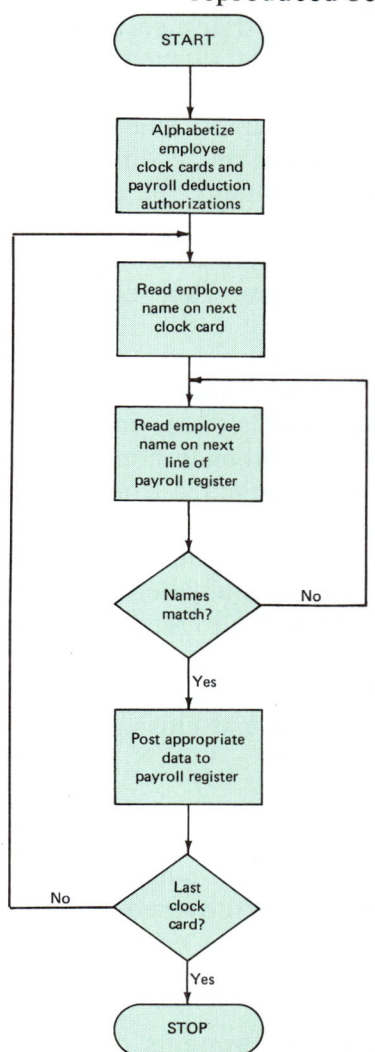

This flowchart correlates with the discussion on pages 77–78 in Chapter 4. The employee doing the work begins by arranging the completed clock cards and payroll deduction authorization forms in alphabetical order and clipping the related forms together for each employee. (The clock cards were in clock number or social security number order.) The name on the first clock card and the name on the first line of the payroll register are examined. If they match, the appropriate data is posted to the payroll register. If they do not match, each succeeding line of the register is examined until the right one is found. After posting the appropriate data to the right line, the name on the next clock card is matched to the register and the process is repeated until all clock cards have been posted. This assumes that there is only one clock card and set of related payroll deduction authorization forms per employee, and that each time a new employee is hired, a new clock card is prepared, related payroll deduction authorization forms are completed, and the payroll register listing of employees is revised. Otherwise, the flowchart would have to be extended to include the necessary correctional steps.

The amount of detail shown in a flowchart depends upon its purpose and the amount of detail desired. In implementing a computerized version of the payroll system illustrated at the left, information concerning hardware would have to be added, and more detailed information about adding new employees, dropping old employees, etc., would have to be included. The punched card symbol for input or output and the report symbol for printed output would then be pressed into use, as well as the connector symbol for flowcharts occupying two or more pages.

Flowchart — Posting Employee Clock Cards and Deduction Authorizations to Payroll Register

In a computer-based payroll system, the flowchart would be the basis for the development of the computer program. Each labeled symbol in the flowchart would constitute a programming step. A collection of computer programs is known as a **software** package.

The write-it-once principle as a labor-saving device

A source document, such as a purchase invoice or a sales ticket, usually is prepared manually by handwriting or typing on the document at the time of the transaction. The first step in computer-based accounting is the preparation of a punched card or a section of magnetic tape by a machine operator from a source document. (Optical character recognition (OCR) equipment that can read data from source documents directly into computers is rapidly emerging.)

If the operator types the source document on an office machine with a card punching or tape encoding attachment, the card or tape is being prepared at the same time that the source document is being typed. If the office machine used is not an integrated data processing machine, the card or tape must be prepared later as a separate operation.

The process of recording the basic information about a business transaction in a form that makes later hand copying unnecessary has been called the **write-it-once principle**. This first step in computer-based accounting makes it possible to save labor in completing the later steps of the accounting cycle. Once a punched card or a magnetic tape has been prepared by a machine operator or a source document has been "read" directly into the computer, the recorded information can be used over and over again when and where needed. The only further human effort needed is to feed the cards or tape into computer equipment. This equipment then performs automatically the functions of journalizing, posting, taking trial balances, preparing financial statements, and adjusting and closing ledger accounts.

Importance of locating errors in the write-it-once operation

If errors in the punching of cards, encoding of magnetic tape, or preparation of source documents are not discovered before the cards, tape, or documents are fed into computer equipment, such errors will be repeated in each step of the automated accounting cycle.

Designers of computer-based accounting systems have recognized the seriousness of the error problem. Errors in computer-based systems are normally located in either of two ways:

(a) Transaction information is verified as soon as it has been recorded.
(b) Automatic error-locating procedures built into the computer equipment are used later on in the accounting cycle.

Verifying transaction information already punched into cards is a process of running the cards through manually operated machines a second time. A different machine operator reads the information from the source document and goes through the same punching motions as did the original operator. If each punching stroke hits a hole in the card, the card passes right on through the machine. If a punching stroke hits a solid section of card, an error is indicated, and the machine notches the edge of the card next to the error. Notched cards are set aside and corrected later.

Businesses that find errors very difficult to control may decide not only to verify source document information before cards are processed but also to use automatic error-locating procedures later in the accounting cycle. Computer equipment also may be set up to locate certain errors electronically. When such errors are so located, an error light on the equipment usually goes on; and if the computer operator is not able to remedy the difficulty, the equipment stops running.

Basic phases of automated data processing

The automated processing of any data in the completion of the accounting cycle consists of five basic phases. These five phases are common to all computer equipment, regardless of manufacturer. They are:

(a) Input
(b) Control
(c) Storage
(d) Arithmetic and logic
(e) Output

A diagram of a basic computer system is shown at the left.

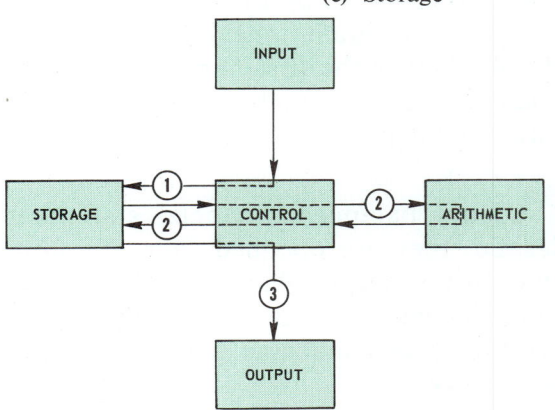

Diagram of Basic Computer System

Input. In order that computer equipment may complete the accounting process, the source document may have to be rewritten in a form that the equipment can interpret. Information about a business transaction in a form acceptable for use in automated data processing equipment is known as **input**. Any acceptable means for presenting this information to a computer is known as an **input device**.

Control. Control is the nerve center, or "action central," of the computer-based accounting system. It is like the central hall in a home or the lobby of a hotel. People must pass through the lobby of a hotel to get to their rooms. In the same way, transaction information must be routed through control in each step of automated data processing. Transaction information received as input is sent by control to storage, as shown by the flow line labeled "1" in the diagram on the preceding page.

Storage. Transaction information stops in **storage** to await further use in computer-based accounting. Storage is often called the CPU (central processing unit) by computer people. Because storage holds information for future use just as does the human mind, it is often referred to as "memory." But unlike the human mind, storage must be told in great detail what to do with each item of transaction information that it holds. A detailed list of steps to be followed in completing the computerized accounting cycle is known as a **program**. A person who designs programs is called a **programmer**. The detailed work of arranging transaction information in the most efficient manner for computer processing is called **programming** and is usually preceded by a flowchart, as mentioned earlier.

Arithmetic and Logic. The primary work of computer-based accounting is done in the **arithmetic and logic** phase. Transaction information is routed from storage through control to arithmetic and logic. In the arithmetic phase, addition, subtraction, multiplication, or division is performed as needed; and the result is returned by control to storage. This round trip is shown by the flow line labeled "2" in the basic computer system diagram. The logic phase can compare two numbers and tell whether the first number is smaller than, equal to, or larger than the second number. This feature is useful in controlling inventories and expenses.

Output. When ledger account balances, financial statement items, or other data are desired, they are obtained from the automated data processing system in the output phase. Business information in a form acceptable for human use is known as **output**. Any acceptable means for converting coded machine information into English is known as an **output device**.

Business information requested by management from the data processing system is routed from storage through control to output, as shown by the flow line labeled "3" in the basic computer system diagram. Output devices are prepared which are used later to print in English the particular business information requested, or output is produced directly on a high-speed printer attached to the CPU.

Input and output may be and often are handled by the same physical equipment, called I-O equipment by computer people.

Appendix Computer-Based Accounting Systems **A-9**

The punched card as an input device

At present, the punched card is the most frequently used initial input device. One form of punched card is the IBM (International Business Machines Corporation) card, illustrated below.

Standard IBM Card

Utility companies, oil companies, magazine publishers, and mail order houses use punched cards as statements of account. The federal government and many large private companies use punched cards for payroll checks and other remittance checks.

The small figures on the IBM card show that it has 80 columns, numbered from left to right. The large figures on the card show that it has ten rows, numbered 0 to 9 inclusive from top to bottom. In addition, as the illustration shows, the blank space at the top of the card provides room for two more rows, called the "twelve row" and the "eleven row."

As shown by the punches in the illustration, a single numerical digit may be formed by punching a small hole in a column at one of the ten positions numbered zero through nine. A single letter or symbol may be formed by punching two holes in a column. One of these holes is punched through a position numbered one through nine. The other hole is punched through a position numbered twelve, eleven, or zero, as shown in the illustration above. The three top rows on the card are called the "zone" rows, and a hole punched in one of these rows is called a "zone" punch.

Planning the Use of the Punched Card. The first step in the use of a punched card as an input device is to plan the arrangement of the information on the card. A punched card that is to be used as a statement of account will contain the information listed on page A-10.

(a) Customer's name and address
(b) Customer's account number
(c) Billing date
(d) Customer's previous balance
(e) Current sales to the customer
(f) Amount received on account
(g) Sales returns and allowances
(h) Customer's new balance

Each item of information requires that several holes be punched into the card. An estimate is made of the longest group of letters or numbers required for each of the eight items to be placed on any statement of account. The punched card (or cards if two are needed) is then subdivided into eight groups of columns of sufficient size.

A group of columns used for a single item of information on a punched card is known as a **field**. There is a field for the customer's name and address, and a field for each of the other seven items of information.

Punching Information Into the Punched Card. After the information for preparing a customer's statement of account has been provided by the computerized accounting system, a machine operator enters this information into a machine which in turn punches information holes into the card. One field on the card is used for each of the eight information items.

A machine used to punch information holes into punched cards from source documents is known as a **keypunch**. An IBM keypunch machine is illustrated here.

IBM Keypunch

Verifying the Information on the Punched Card. As soon as a batch of cards has been punched, the cards are checked in an attempt to avoid errors. A machine that looks exactly like a keypunch and is used to find punching errors is called a **verifier**. As mentioned earlier, another operator reading from the same source document as the keypunch operator enters the data into the verifier. The IBM verifier machine "feels" each card electronically to determine whether the correct holes have been punched. Each correct card is notched in a special "verify" position. If the verifier machine "feels" a missing hole or a hole in the wrong position, it notches a special "error" position on the card and the keyboard on the machine locks up.

Printing the Information on a Punched Card. The punched information on each IBM card is printed on a two-part statement card consisting of a statement and a stub. The printing is done by running the punched cards through an automatic printing machine that lists, totals, and prints information previously punched onto cards. This machine is called a **tabulator** or **high-speed printer**. The information may either be printed on the same punched card from which it comes or on a separate sheet of paper.

Completing a Punched Card Statement of Account. After each of the two-part statement cards has been tabulated, the customer's account number and balance due are punched into the stub portion of the card. The statement card is then ready to be mailed to the customer. A completed two-part statement card is illustrated below.

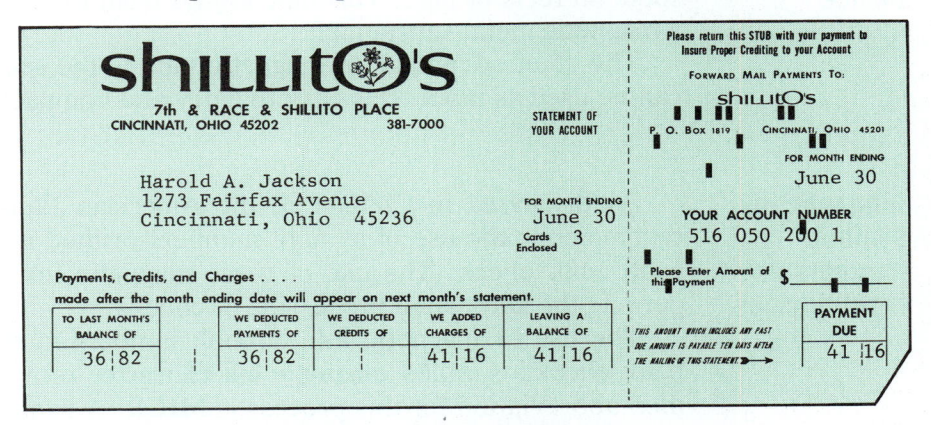

Punched Card Statement of Account

Sorting Customer Remittance Stubs. When the customer receives a statement like the one illustrated above, the stub is detached and returned with the remittance. When a remittance arrives, the amount received is keypunched into the stub that comes with the remittance. The stubs are then grouped into piles and run through a machine which sorts them by customer's account number.

A machine that automatically groups all punched cards of a similar kind and arranges them in some order is called a **sorter**. The stubs received from customers are placed in the hopper of the sorter. The sorted stubs drop into pockets. There is a "reject" pocket for cards that the machine is unable to sort.

Posting Customer Remittance Stubs. The final process in accounting for customer remittances is to run the stubs through the printer or tabulator in account number order. This machine process posts the remittances to individual customers' ledger account cards and determines the new account balances.

The same basic operations are followed in processing punched card checks, except that cash payment transactions are involved rather than cash receipt transactions. The transaction information must still be keypunched, verified, printed, sorted, and posted. These are basic data processing operations in computer-based accounting systems.

Magnetic tape as an input device

Magnetic tape usually is used as a repeat input device in EDP systems. It is prepared for input by depositing small magnetized spots on reels of tape. This tape comes from the factory coated with a magnetic metal substance.

The chief advantage of magnetic tape is the speed with which it can be used as input. It is easy to carry and compact to store.

Magnetic ink symbol numbers as input devices

As discussed in Chapter 3, the American Bankers Association recommends the use of symbol numbers printed in magnetic ink on each bank check. The use of these magnetic ink symbol numbers permits the automated processing of checks.

The use of magnetic ink symbol numbers in the processing of bank checks is called **magnetic ink character recognition**. The common abbreviation for this process is **MICR**. A bank check with magnetic ink symbol numbers printed across the bottom of the check is illustrated below:

Bank Check with Magnetic Ink Symbol Numbers

Note that the symbol numbers at the bottom of the check use a style that is different from regular Arabic numerals. This is because these numbers are read by a device that "feels" the surface area of each number and recognizes its shape. Regular Arabic numerals, especially 2, 5, 6, and 9, are too much alike to be easily distinguished one from the other by an electronic reading machine.

Encoding Symbol Numbers on Bank Checks. Magnetic ink symbol numbers are printed on checks using special printing machines. A machine for printing magnetic ink characters on checks is called an **encoder**.

Encoding may be done by the company that prints the blank checks or by the bank that supplies the checks to its depositors.

Clearing Encoded Bank Checks Through the Federal Reserve System. The first series of encoded numerals in the check illustration (0810-0459) is adapted from the ABA number in the upper right-hand corner of the check. Notice that the number 80, which represents the State of Missouri, has been dropped from the encoded symbol number. This is because 0810 locates the bank in the Eighth Federal Reserve District (08) and the Greater St. Louis area (10), and the State of Missouri is understood.

The Federal Reserve system sorts checks encoded with magnetic ink symbol numbers as follows:

Step 1. The bank in which the check is deposited forwards it to the Federal Reserve clearing house in its district.

Step 2. The Federal Reserve clearing house sorts the check along with other checks received from banks in its district on special sorting equipment using the first two encoded symbol numbers (08 in the illustration). This results in twelve batches of checks for the twelve Federal Reserve districts.

Step 3. Each Federal Reserve clearing house forwards the checks drawn on banks in other Federal Reserve districts to the proper districts. In this process, the check illustrated on the previous page is forwarded to the Eighth Federal Reserve District clearing house in St. Louis.

Step 4. The clearing house in St. Louis sorts on the next two encoded symbol numbers (10 in the illustration) for distribution of the checks to regional clearing houses. Since the bank on which the illustrated check is drawn is a Greater St. Louis bank, this check is not forwarded to a regional clearing house.

Step 5. Each district or regional clearing house sorts on the next four symbol numbers (0459 in the illustration) for distribution to individual banks. These four symbol numbers are individual bank numbers.

Step 6. Batches of sorted checks are forwarded to the banks on which they were drawn. The illustrated check is sent to St. Louis County National Bank.

Processing Encoded Bank Checks in Individual Banks. The second series of encoded numerals on the illustrated check (042-121-3) is the account number of the individual depositor at the bank. The depositor's bank sorts its own checks by account number. It uses the same type of MICR sorting equipment as that used in the Federal Reserve clearing houses. This equipment can sort as many as 90,000 checks per hour.

In smaller banks, checks sorted by depositor's account number are posted by using conventional bank posting machines. Larger banks having encoders of their own print the amount of each check in magnetic ink under the signature line. Encoding amounts of individual checks makes it possible to sort and post electronically to depositors' ledger accounts in one operation.

OCR Readers as Input Devices. As mentioned earlier, the use of optical character recognition (OCR) machines to "read" directly from source documents into computers is a growing practice, especially in conjunction with major credit-card systems. Special type is required, but it is not as stylized as MICR type. The only requirement is that all characters be printed at right angles and that all curves and diagonal lines be eliminated.

The control phase in automated accounting

The control phase of an electronic system receives electronic commands from input devices and sees that they are carried out. Each command refers to some item of transaction information which is in storage. The control phase searches storage locations one by one in carrying out commands from input devices and keeps track of the location of each command as it is carried out. This avoids skipping program steps.

The storage phase in automated accounting

In manual accounting, the journal, the ledger, and the trial balance are methods of temporarily storing transaction information. This information is stored permanently on the financial statements.

In computerized accounting, means of storage must be used which make it possible to complete the accounting cycle automatically. Means of storing journal entries, ledger account balances, and trial balance information must be found. Any means of storing accounting information in between the steps of the computerized accounting cycle is known as a **storage device**.

External Storage Devices. Storage devices physically removed from a computer system from which data can be fed into the system when desired are known as **external storage devices**. Both punched cards and magnetic tape are able to retain transaction information for long periods of time. For this reason, as well as the fact that they can be physically removed from the system, these input devices are used also as data (external) storage devices. (Magnetic disks, contained in a "phonograph-type" unit, are also used as external storage devices.)

Externally Stored Journal Entries. External storage devices may be used either for temporary storage or for permanent storage of transaction information. Punched cards are excellent storage devices for journal entries. This is because a separate punched card can be used to record each debit element of a journal entry and a separate punched card can be used to record each credit element of a journal entry. The cards can then be machine sorted by ledger account titles for machine posting.

Journal entries may also be stored on magnetic tape. However, reels of tape cannot be sorted in the same way that punched cards are sorted. Journal entries on reels of tape must be machine posted in the order in which they were recorded. This is the same order in which journal entries would be posted manually. The only advantage of machine posting is that it is faster and relatively free of error.

Internal Storage Devices. The internal storage phase of a computer system is contained within the machinery. The storage phase receives instructions from control, which have been passed on from input. These instructions are of four types:

(a) Take data from input
(b) Send data to arithmetic and logic
(c) Receive data from arithmetic and logic
(d) Send data to output

Devices for temporarily storing accounting information within a computer are known as **internal storage devices**.

Internally Stored Ledgers. Internal storage devices are used in computerized accounting to keep ledger accounts up-to-date. Each account in the ledger is assigned a storage address. Debits and credits are fed in on punched cards or reels of tape. Control instructs input to transfer a debit or a credit amount into storage from a card or tape reel.

The incoming debit or credit amount must go to a storage address different from the address assigned to the related ledger account. Since the storage address for the incoming debit or credit amount is needed only for the current posting operation, it is not permanently assigned. However, the accountant must keep a chart of permanent storage addresses (corresponding to a chart of accounts) in order to know at all times which addresses are assigned and which are open.

Automatic Posting. Automatic posting requires the following steps:

Step 1. Control instructs input to read the old balance of the ledger account from a master magnetic ledger tape into its assigned address in storage.

Step 2. Control instructs storage to transfer the old balance of the ledger account from its assigned address to the arithmetic and logic unit.

Step 3. Control instructs storage to transfer the related debit or credit amount, which has just come into storage from a punched card or transaction tape to arithmetic and logic.

Step 4. Control instructs arithmetic and logic either to add the debit amount to or subtract the credit amount from the old balance of the account.

Step 5. Control instructs storage to receive the new ledger account balance from arithmetic and logic and to store it in the assigned storage address for the particular ledger account. This is the same address in which the old ledger account balance was stored.

Step 6. Control instructs storage to transfer the new ledger account balance out to an updated master magnetic ledger tape.

In a computer-based accounting system, when a new item is stored electronically in the same internal storage address as a previous item, the new item replaces the old item at that address.

To illustrate the automated posting process, suppose that the cash account is assigned storage address number 10. The beginning cash balance, a debit of $1,200, becomes input by means of a punched card and is sent to address number 10 by the control unit. Suppose also that a debit to the cash account, in the amount of $50, is placed in input by means of another punched card and is sent by control to address number 100 for temporary storage.

The posting process will proceed as follows:

Step 1. Control instructs storage to transfer the beginning cash balance of $1,200 from address number 10 to arithmetic and logic.

Step 2. Control instructs storage to transfer the $50 debit to the cash account from address number 100 to arithmetic and logic.

Step 3. Control instructs arithmetic and logic to add the $50 cash debit to the beginning balance of $1,200.

Step 4. Control instructs storage to receive the new cash balance, $1,250, and to store it back in address number 10, the address assigned to the cash account in this program.

Limitations of Internal Storage. The illustration of automated posting demonstrates that internal storage may be used both for temporary storage of debits and credits to ledger accounts and for semipermanent storage of ledger account balances. A small business having relatively few ledger accounts could get along with a rather small amount of internal storage. However, a large business having a great many ledger accounts would need a rather large amount of internal storage. Internal storage either must be large enough to handle the ledger accounts and the posting operations of the computer-based accounting system in which it is used, or ledger account balances will have to be stored externally on magnetic tape, punched cards, or magnetic disks.

The arithmetic and logic phase in automated accounting

The arithmetic and logic phase of an electronic system receives instructions from control to add, subtract, multiply, or divide, or to compare two numbers. Arithmetic and logic works with only two numbers at a time, having received them from different storage locations. To avoid returning subtotals or partial products to storage, however, arithmetic and logic has a temporary electronic storage unit of its own. The electronic storage device in the arithmetic and logic phase of a computer system used to store subtotals and partial products for further processing is known as an **accumulator**.

The output phase in automated accounting

In many ways, the output phase in automated accounting is just the reverse of the input phase. Punched cards and magnetic tape have already been described as input devices and as storage devices. Cards and reels of tape may also be used effectively as output devices.

Upon request, control will instruct storage to punch out cards or to write on magnetic tape any information desired. This might be journal entries, ledger account balances, trial balances, or financial statements. The cards or tapes must then be converted to English language information.

The Tabulator as an Output Device. The tabulator has already been discussed in connection with the use of the punched card. As indicated, it can list, total, or print journal entries, ledger account balances, trial balances, or financial statements whenever desired. The tabulator prints a line at a time and can handle up to 90 lines a minute.

The High-Speed Printer as an Output Device. High-speed printing machines are now available into which punched cards, magnetic tape, or electronically readable source documents may be fed. These machines are capable of printing in excess of 1,200 lines of information per minute.

The use of automated accounting by professional persons

It is unlikely that lawyers or physicians, even large law firms or a number of physicians practicing in a clinic, will have sufficient accounting work to warrant the acquisition of automated equipment. This does not mean, however, that all work in such law firms or clinics must be done manually. Sometimes it is possible to have all or part of the accounting work done by a public accountant who has some form of automated equipment, or the work may be done by an organization known as an *automation company*. The public accountant or automation company will take the basic accounting data and process it. For example, financial statements, payroll reports, and income tax returns may be prepared and returned to the client.

In some localities it is possible for professional persons and persons engaged in business to have much of their accounting work done by the bank which handles their checking account. The bank must be provided with the account numbers used in the chart of accounts. Special checks and deposit tickets are then used which have spaces for the account numbers and amounts. Adjustment forms are used to correct accounts, delete or add accounts, or to handle items not reflected in activity in the checking account. For example, a person may wish to enter interest from savings into income classification. This may be done with the adjustment form without having to make a deposit. Cash purchases could be entered in the same way.

Based on the coded information, the bank prepares monthly statements of income and expense by category. These statements may show data for the month and year to date as well as a comparison with the previous year. Also, the data may be shown both by dollar amount and percentage.

If some of the accounting work is done by an outside organization, the secretary-bookkeeper in the employ of the professional person or persons will keep the basic records. This will usually be the information recorded in the book or books of original entry. In a physician's office, for example, the secretary-bookkeeper will probably keep the daily service record and the records of cash receipts and disbursements. This information together with supplementary data on such things as depreciation rates on the long-lived assets will make it possible for an accountant in public practice, or an automation company, or a bank to complete the accounting records and prepare the financial statements.

Systems using accounting boards

Another method of speeding up accounting work in a professional enterprise is through the use of a manual system which employs some type of accounting board. An **accounting board** is a device with posts on the left side. One or more printed forms with holes on the left side can be positioned on the board. When the forms are fitted over the posts, they are held in place and information written on the top form will also appear in the proper place on the forms below. For example, in recording payrolls, it is possible to create three records with one writing — the check, the payroll register, and the employee's earnings record. The use of a system designed for physicians can create the daily service record, the patient's individual account record, and the patient's receipt with just one writing. In the accounting board illustrated on page A-20, a disbursements journal is given for Hensel, Berry, and Moore, Attorneys at Law. Use of this accounting board enables the secretary-bookkeeper to record the entry in the disbursements journal while writing the check (see left side of journal). It also eliminates the need to fill in a check stub and address an envelope (see lower right corner of journal). Records prepared by using an accounting board system can also be sent to an outside accountant or automation company for further processing, if desired.

Hensel, Berry, & Moore — Accounting Board

Glossary

Account — The form of record kept for each asset, liability, owner's equity, revenue, and expense on the books of the enterprise.

Account form of balance sheet — A balance sheet in which the assets are presented on the left side and the liabilities and owner's equity are presented on the right side.

Accounting — The recording, classification, storage, summarization, reporting, and interpretation of financial information.

Accounting board — A device on which one or more printed forms can be positioned so that several records, such as checks, payroll registers, and employees' earnings records, are created with one writing.

Accounting cycle — The steps involved in handling all of the transactions and events completed during an accounting period, beginning with recording in a journal and ending with a post-closing trial balance.

Accounting equation — An equation stating the relationship between the three basic accounting elements: Assets = Liabilities + Owner's Equity.

Accounts payable — Unwritten promises to pay creditors for property, such as merchandise, supplies, and equipment, purchased on credit or for services rendered.

Accounts receivable — Unwritten promises by customers to pay for goods purchased on credit or for services rendered.

Accumulated depreciation — The accumulated portions of the cost of a long-lived asset which have been charged to depreciation expense.

Accumulator — The electronic storage device in the arithmetic and logic phase of a computer system used to store subtotals and partial products for further processing.

Additional withholding allowance — Additional income tax deductions granted to employees with large itemized deductions.

Adjusted trial balance — A trial balance which contains the balances of the ledger accounts after the required adjustments have been made.

Adjusting entries — Entries made to bring certain accounts up to date at the close of the accounting period.

Arithmetic and logic — The phase of computer-based accounting in which the primary work is done.

Assets — Properties of value that are owned by an enterprise.

Auditing — The testing and checking of the records of an enterprise to be certain that acceptable practices have been consistently followed.

Automatic teller machines — Machines which some banks use to provide machine-printed receipts for each deposit.

Automation companies — Business organizations engaged in data processing on a contract basis for other businesses of small and medium size.

Auxiliary record — A record that supplements the regular accounting records; for example, a petty cash disbursements record.

Balance sheet — A statement which shows the assets, liabilities, and owner's equity of a business or professional practice at a specified date; also referred to as a statement of financial condition or a statement of financial position.

Bank reconciliation — A statement showing the items causing the difference between the balance of an account reported by a bank and the balance on the depositor's books.

Bank service charge — A charge made by a bank for the handling of checks and other items.

Bank statement — A statement rendered by a bank to each depositor showing the activity in the account during the period of time covered by the statement.

Blank indorsement — The signature of a payee of a check on the back of a check without any additional notations.

Book of original entry — A record in which the first formal double-entry record of a transaction is made; also referred to as a journal.

Book value — The difference between the cost of a long-lived asset and the accumulated depreciation of the asset.

Capital — The amount by which the assets of the enterprise exceed its liabilities; also referred to as owner's equity, proprietorship, or net worth.

Cash — Currency and coins and, in a business, checks, drafts, and money orders.

Cash disbursements — Payments made by a business in cash or by bank check.

Cash receipts — The receipt of currency and coin and checks, drafts, and money orders payable to the business.

Charge — A word sometimes used as a substitute for the word "debit."

Chart of accounts — A list of the accounts in the ledger usually arranged in the order of assets, liabilities, owner's equity, revenue, and expense.

Check — A written negotiable form signed by the depositor ordering the bank to pay a specified sum of money to a designated person or enterprise from funds credited to the depositor's account.

Checkbook — Checks bound in the form of a book with two or three blank checks to a page, perforated so that they may be removed singly.

Check stub — That part of the check form that is bound permanently in the checkbook. It is used to record each cash payment and each deposit.

Clearing account — An account used only at the close of the accounting period for summarizing the revenue and expense accounts.

Closing entries — Entries made at the end of a fiscal period to transfer the balance of one account to another.

Combined cash journal — A journal with four or more columns which combines the features of a two-column general journal and a cash journal.

Compound entry — An entry that affects more than two accounts.

Constructive receipt — The recognition of revenue such as interest on a savings account which is available for withdrawal by the owner of the account. Such interest must be reported as revenue even though no cash is withdrawn from the account.

Contra accounts — Offsetting accounts with credit balances which are deducted from the related asset accounts in the balance sheet.

Control — The nerve center, or "action central," of the computer-based accounting system.

Credit — The right side of an account.

Credit advice — A form prepared by a bank advising a depositor that the depositor's account has been increased by an amount collected by the bank.

Credit entry — An entry recorded on the right side of an account.

Creditors — Those persons or businesses that supply goods and services which will be paid for later, or that lend money to the enterprise.

Current assets — Cash and all other assets that may be reasonably expected to be realized in cash or sold or consumed during the normal operating cycle of the enterprise.

Current liabilities — Obligations that will be due in a short time and paid with monies provided by the current assets.

Data processing — The use of data such as ledger account titles, dollar amounts, and physical quantities in different ways for different business purposes.

Debit — The left side of an account.

Debit entry — An entry recorded on the left side of an account.

Deposit in transit — A deposit recorded by the depositor and made by mail or placed in the night depository and not recorded by the bank until after the date of the bank statement.

Deposit ticket — A form banks provide depositors to use for a detailed listing of items being deposited.

Depreciation expense — The portion of the cost of a long-lived asset charged to expense in each accounting period.

Dishonored check — A check that a bank refuses to pay.

Double-entry bookkeeping — A recording system that involves the making of a record of each of the two or more aspects that are involved in every transaction.

Drawee — The bank in which the drawer of checks has money on deposit in a so-called "commercial" account.

Drawer — A depositor of funds in a bank who writes checks ordering the bank to pay specified sums of money to designated persons or enterprises.

Electronic data processing — The processing of business transactions by means of an electronic computer.

Employee's earnings record — A detailed account, recorded each pay period, of all items affecting payments made to each employee.

Employer identification number — A number required of all employers that is assigned to the employer by the Social Security Administration.

Encoder — A special machine for printing magnetic ink characters on checks.

Equity — Interest in, or claim on, the assets of a business.

Expense — A decrease in the owner's equity in an enterprise caused by a transaction other than a withdrawal by the owner.

Expense and revenue summary — An account to which the balances of the revenue and expense accounts are transferred when closing them at the end of the accounting period, a clearing account; also referred to as income summary, profit and loss summary, or summary account. The balance of the expense and revenue summary account represents the net income or net loss for the period.

External storage device — Storage devices physically removed from a computer system whose contents can be fed into the system when desired.

Fees — Charges made for services rendered by persons who are not employees of the enterprise for which the work is performed.

FICA tax — Federal Insurance Contributions Act tax. A social security tax paid to the federal government by both employees and employers to pay old age, survivors, disability, and health insurance benefits.

Field — A group of columns on a punched card used for a single item of information such as a customer's name and address.

Financial statements — Reports prepared to summarize and communicate economic information about the enterprise to interested persons.

Fiscal year — The annual accounting period, which may or may not be a calendar year, adopted by an enterprise.

Flowchart — A graphic presentation of the major steps to be undertaken in processing a particular accounting transaction or series of closely related transactions.

Footing — The process of totaling the debit and credit amounts in each account before taking a trial balance.

FUTA tax — Federal Unemployment Tax Act tax. Tax assessed by the federal government on employers and used for paying administrative expenses for the state and federal unemployment programs.

General journal — A two-column journal in which all kinds of entries may be recorded.

General ledger — A group of related accounts for a specific enterprise; sometimes called the ledger.

High-speed printer — High-speed printing machine which lists, totals, and prints information previously punched onto cards.

Imprest method — A method of handling a petty cash fund in which the fund is always reimbursed for an amount which will restore the fund to its original balance unless it is desired to either increase or decrease the amount in the fund.

Income statement — A report showing the net income or net loss of an enterprise for a specified period of time and how it was calculated; also referred to as operating statement or profit and loss statement.

Independent contractor — A person who agrees to perform a service for a fee and who is not subject to the control of those served.

Input — Information about a business transaction in a form acceptable for use in automated data processing equipment.

Input device — Any acceptable means for presenting information about a business transaction to a computer.

Integrated data processing — The processing of business transactions by the use of office machines with card punches or tape writers attached.

Internal storage device — Devices for storing accounting information within a computer.

Journal — A record, frequently in book form, in which the first formal double-entry record of a transaction is made; also referred to as a book of original entry.

Journalizing — The act of recording transactions in a journal.

Keypunch — A machine used to punch information holes into punched cards from source documents.

Ledger — A group of related accounts for a specific enterprise; sometimes called the general ledger.

Liabilities — Debts owed by an enterprise to its creditors.

Long-lived assets — Assets such as land, buildings, and equipment which have a useful life that is comparatively long.

Long-term liabilities — Obligations such as mortgages payable that will not be due for a relatively long time.

Magnetic ink character recognition (MICR) — The use of magnetic ink symbol numbers in the processing of bank checks.

Matching principle — The principle that revenues earned and expenses incurred during a period should be matched against each other.

Mortgage payable — A debt or obligation secured by a mortgage which provides for the surrender of certain property if the debt is not paid at maturity.

Net income — The amount by which revenue earned exceeds the expenses necessary to earn the revenue.

Net loss — The amount by which expenses necessary to earn revenue exceed the revenue earned.

Net worth — The amount by which the assets of the enterprise exceed its liabilities; also referred to as owner's equity, capital, or proprietorship.

Notes payable — Formal written promises to pay creditors or lenders specified sums of money at some future time.

Notes receivable — Formal written promises by debtors to pay specified sums of money at some future time.

Operating statement — A report showing the net income or net loss of an enterprise for a specified period of time and how it was calculated; also referred to as an income statement or profit and loss statement.

Output — Business information from a data processing system in a form acceptable for human use.

Output device — Any acceptable means for converting coded machine information into English.

Outstanding checks — Checks issued during the period covered by the bank statement but which have not been presented to the bank for payment.

Overdraft — A check or checks issued against a bank in excess of the amount on deposit.

Owner's equity — The amount by which the assets of the enterprise exceed its liabilities; also referred to as capital, proprietorship, or net worth.

Passbook — A book given to depositors by banks in which bank tellers enter the date and amount of each deposit.

Payee — The person or enterprise to whom a bank is ordered to pay a specified sum of money.

Payroll register — A record of the entire payroll listing each employee's name, number of allowances, gross earnings, deductions, net pay, and check number.

Periodic summary — The process of adjusting the accounts at the end of an accounting period and of preparing an income statement and a balance sheet.

Petty cash fund — A small cash fund established for paying small items.

Post-closing trial balance — A trial balance prepared at the end of the accounting period containing only the balance sheet accounts after the revenue and expense accounts have been closed.

Postdated check — A check dated later than the date of issue.

Posting — The process of transferring information entered in the journal to the ledger.

Posting reference — A cross-reference between the journal and the ledger.

Profit — The amount by which revenue earned exceeds the expenses necessary to earn the revenue.

Profit and loss statement — A report showing the net income or net loss of an enterprise for a specified period of time and how it was calculated; also referred to as an operating statement or income statement.

Program — A detailed list of steps to be followed in completing the computerized accounting cycle.

Proprietorship — The amount by which the assets of the enterprise exceed its liabilities; also referred to as capital, owner's equity, or net worth.

Reconciliation of bank statement — A determination of the reason for differences between the balance on the bank statement and the balance on the depositor's books.

Report form of balance sheet — A balance sheet in which the assets are presented at the top and the liabilities and owner's equity elements are presented below.

Restrictive indorsement — An indorsement that specifies the disposition of the check; as, for example, the words "For deposit" written near the signature of the holder of the check.

Revenue — An increase in the owner's equity in an enterprise resulting from transactions of any kind except the investment of assets in the enterprise by its owner.

Salary — Compensation for managerial or administrative services.

Savings accounts — Interest-bearing deposits which are expected to remain in the bank for a period of time.

Self-employment income — The net income of a professional practice or business conducted by an individual or a partner's distributive share of the net income of a partnership.

Service charge — A charge made by a bank for the handling of checks and other items.

Signature card — A card signed by a depositor to give the bank a sample of his or her signature.

Sorter — A machine that automatically groups all punched cards of a similar kind and arranges them in some order.

Source document — The immediate record prepared either by hand or by machine which is always the key record in a manual or computer-based accounting system.

Special withholding allowance — An allowance granted to a single taxpayer with only one job and to a married taxpayer with only one job whose spouse is not employed.

Statement of financial condition — A statement which shows the assets, liabilities, and owner's equity of a business or professional practice at a specified date; also referred to as balance sheet.

Statement of financial position — A statement which shows the assets, liabilities, and owner's equity of a business or professional practice at a specified date; also referred to as balance sheet.

State unemployment tax — A tax assessed by the state usually only on employers for use in paying benefits to persons temporarily unemployed.

Storage — Location of information awaiting further use in computer-based accounting; often referred to as "memory."

Storage device — Any means of storing accounting information in between the steps of the computerized accounting cycle.

Summary account — An account to which the balances of the revenue and expense accounts are transferred when closing them at the end of each accounting period; a clearing account, also referred to as expense and revenue summary, income summary, profit and loss summary. The balance of the summary account represents the net income or net loss for the period.

Tabulator — An automatic printing machine that lists, totals, and prints information previously punched onto cards.

Taxes payable — Obligations of an enterprise to pay sums of money based on established rates to various governmental units.

Temporary owner's equity accounts — Revenue and expense accounts.

Time sharing — The joint use of a computer by several enterprises.

Transactions — The events or conditions taking place in an enterprise which must be recorded in terms of money or value.

Transposition — An error caused by the interchanging of digits in an amount.

Trial balance — A list of all the accounts showing the title and balance of each account.

Verifier — A machine that looks exactly like a keypunch and is used to find punching errors.

Wage and tax statements — Statements prepared in quadruplicate for each employee from whom income taxes have been withheld.

Wages — Compensation for either skilled or unskilled labor.

Withholding allowances — Deductions that reduce the amount of tax that is withheld from an employee's earnings.

Work sheet — A columnar device that assists the accountant in preparing the financial statements, in making needed adjustments in the accounts, and in closing the revenue and expense accounts.

Write-it-once principle — The basic idea in systems which prepare several records at once, such as a payroll check, an earnings record, and a payroll register.

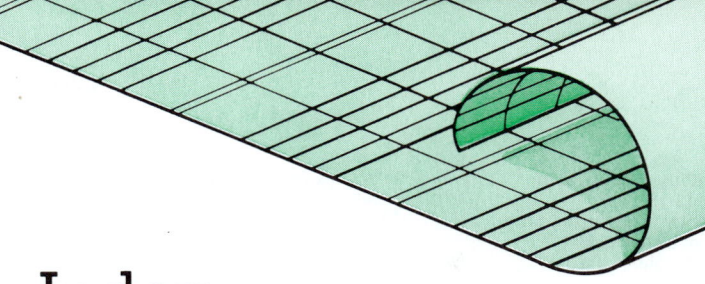

Index

A

Account, 11; books of, 111, 133; cash, 46; checking, 53; clearing, 169; contra, 109; defined, 12; expense and revenue summary, 174; in balance, 19; patient's, *illustrated*, 136; punched-card statement of, A-11; savings, 67; summary, 17
Accountant, certified public, 2; public, 2; registered, 2
Account form, balance-column, 112, *illustrated*, 126; standard, *illustrated*, 12; "T," *illustrated*, 13
Account form of balance sheet, 166, *illustrated*, 42-43, 166-167
Accounting, cash basis of, for attorneys, 108, for physicians and dentists, 131; defined, 3; for cash, 45; for wages and wage deductions, 89; nature of, 1; payroll, 69
Accounting board, defined, A-19; *illustrated*, A-20; systems using, A-19
Accounting cycle, defined, 180
Accounting elements, 4
Accounting equation, 5; effect of transactions on, 7; *illustrated*, 5; relationship of accounts to, *illustrated*, 20
Accounting period, adjusting and closing accounts at end of, 171
Accounting procedure, 22-44
Accounting systems, analysis of, A-2; computer-based, A-1; design of, A-3; implementation of, A-3; review of, A-2; structure of, A-1
Accounts, adjusting and closing at end of accounting period, 171; chart of, 25, 26, 109, 131; footing, 38; temporary owner's equity, 17; use of asset, liability, and owner's equity, 14; use of revenue and expense, 18
Accounts payable, defined, 4
Accounts receivable, defined, 4
Accumulator, A-17
Additional withholding allowances, 73
Adjusted trial balance, columns of work sheet, 161
Adjusting accounts at end of accounting period, 171
Adjusting entries, 171; Donald L. Cameron, Attorney, *illustrated*, 172; journalizing, *illustrated*, 172; posting, 173

Adjustments, columns of work sheet, 160
Advances on behalf of clients, 110
Allowance, additional withholding, 73; special withholding, 73, 74; withholding, 72
American Institute of Certified Public Accountants, 2
Application for social security and tax account number (Form SS-5), *illustrated*, 72
Arithmetic and logic, defined, A-8; in automated accounting, A-17
Asset, book value of, 109, 168; business, 5; current, defined, 167; defined, 4; long-lived, defined, 168; nonbusiness, 5; use of accounts, 14
Auditing, defined, 2
Automated accounting, arithmetic and logic, A-17; control, A-14; output, A-17; storage, A-14; use by professional persons, A-18
Automated data processing, arithmetic and logic, A-8; basic phases of, A-7; control, A-7; input, A-7; output, A-8; storage, A-8
Automated payroll systems, 81
Automatic posting, A-16
Automatic teller machines, 56
Automation companies, A-18; defined, 82; payroll accounting, 82
Auxiliary records, 113, 134; defined, 52

B

Balance, credit, 19; debit, 19
Balance-column account form, 112; *illustrated*, 126
Balance sheet, 9, 42, 45; account form, 166, *illustrated*, 10, 42-43, 166-167; classification of data in, 167; columns of work sheet, 162; defined, 10, 165; Donald L. Cameron, Attorney, *illustrated*, 166-167; Eason Employment Agency, *illustrated*, 42-43; form of, 166; importance of, 165; report form, 166
Bank, checking account, 53; ledger account with, 66; recording transactions, 62; records kept by a, 62; savings account, 67
Banking procedure, 53

Bank statement, 63; *illustrated*, 64; reconciliation, 63, 65, *illustrated*, 66
Blank indorsement, defined, 54
Bookkeeper, 4
Bookkeeping, defined, 3; double-entry, 11
Book of original entry, 23
Books of account, 111, 133
Book value, defined, 109, 168
Business accounting, defined, 3; nature of, 1
Business enterprise, 107

C

Calendar year, 16
Capital, 5
Cash, accounting for, 45; combined, journal, 111, 133; defined, 45; petty, 45; proving, 47
Cash account, 46
Cash basis of accounting, for attorneys, 108; for physicians and dentists, 131
Cash disbursements, 47; recording, 47; records of, 45
Cash receipts, 46; defined, 45; recording, 47; records of, 45
Cash short and over, 47
Certified Public Accountant (CPA), 2
Charge, 13; service, 66
Chart of accounts, 25, 109, 131; defined, 26; Donald L. Cameron, Attorney, *illustrated*, 109; Eason Employment Agency, *illustrated*, 26; Engle and Brenner, Physicians and Surgeons, *illustrated*, 132
Checkbook, 59
Checking account, 45, 53; bank statement, 63, *illustrated*, 64; checkbook, 59; credit advice, *illustrated*, 63; debit advice, *illustrated*, 57; deposit ticket, 54, *illustrated*, 55; mail deposits, 58; night deposits, 58; opening a, 54; outstanding checks, 64; overdraft, 57; service charges, 66; signature card, 54; withdrawals, 59
Checks, blank indorsement, 54; clearing, through Federal Reserve System, A-13; defined, 53; dishonored, defined, 57; drawee, 53; drawer, 53; electronic processing of, 61; encoding symbol numbers on, A-13; *illustrated*, 61; indorsement, 54; magnetic

I-1

ink symbol numbers, *illustrated*, A-12; negotiable, 54; outstanding, 64; payee, 53; post-dated, defined, 58; processing in individual banks, A-14; restrictive indorsement, 54, *illustrated*, 56; writing, 60
Check stub, 59; *illustrated*, 61
Checkwriter, 60
Clearing account, 169
Closing accounts at end of accounting period, 171
Closing entries, Donald L. Cameron, Attorney, *illustrated*, 175; journalizing, 175, *illustrated*, 175; posting, 176, *illustrated*, 176-179
Closing procedure, 174
Collection docket, 115; *illustrated*, 115
Collection fees revenue, 110
Combined cash journal, 111, 133; Donald L. Cameron, Attorney, *illustrated*, 122-125; Engle & Brenner, Physicians and Surgeons, *illustrated*, 144-147
Compensation, types of, 70
Compound entry, defined, 52
Computer-based accounting system, defined, A-1; language of, A-1
Computer system, diagram of basic, A-7
Constructively received revenue, 108
Contra accounts, 109
Control, defined, A-7; in automated accounting, A-14
Credit advice, *illustrated*, 63
Creditors, defined, 1
Credits, 13
Current assets, defined, 167
Current liabilities, defined, 168
Customer remittance stubs, posting, A-11; sorting, A-11
Cycle, accounting, defined, 180

D

Daily service record, 134; *illustrated*, 135
Data, defined, A-2
Data processing, basic phases of automated, A-7; defined, A-2; electronic (EDP), A-2; integrated (IDP), A-2
Debit, 13
Debit advice, *illustrated*, 57
Deductions, accounting for wage, 89; from total earnings, 69, 71
Deduction stub, machine prepared, *illustrated*, 86; manually prepared, *illustrated*, 79
Dependent, 72
Deposit activity analysis, 66
Deposits, mail, 58; night, 58
Deposit ticket, defined, 54; *illustrated*, 55; magnetic ink character recognition numbers on, 54-55
Depreciation expense, 108
Disbursements, cash, 47; petty cash, 49; recording cash, 47
Dishonored check, defined, 57
Docket, collection, 115; *illustrated*, 115; office, 113, *illustrated*, 114
Documents, source, 23, A-1

Double-entry bookkeeping, 11; *illustrated*, 13-15
Double-entry mechanism, 11
Drawee, of a check, 53
Drawer, of a check, 53

E

Earnings, 69; deductions from total, 71; determination of total, 70; report of, 164
Earnings record, employee's, 78, 116; machine prepared, *illustrated*, 84-85; manually prepared, *illustrated*, 80-81
Electronic data processing (EDP), defined, A-2; of checks, 61, A-13, A-14
Employee, defined, 70
Employee's earnings record, 78, 116; machine prepared, *illustrated*, 84-85; manually prepared, *illustrated*, 80-81
Employee's FICA tax withheld, 74
Employee's income tax, payable, 89; withheld, 72
Employee's Withholding Allowance Certificate (Form W-4), *illustrated*, 73
Employer, FICA tax, 91; FUTA tax, 92; identification number, 88; payroll taxes, 91
Employer-employee relationships, 69
Employer's Quarterly Federal Tax Return (Form 941), 95
Encoder, A-13
Encoding symbol numbers on bank checks, A-13
End-of-period work sheet, defined, 157
Enterprise, business, 107; personal service, 107; professional, 107
Entries, adjusting, 171; compound, 52; journalizing adjusting, 172; journalizing closing, 175; posting adjusting, 173; posting closing, 176
Equation, accounting, 5; effect of transactions on accounting, 7
Equity, owner's, 4, 168
Expense, 15; defined, 16; depreciation, 108; medical library, 133; payroll, 89; payroll taxes, 91
Expense accounts, use of, 18
Expense and revenue summary, 110, 174
External storage devices, A-14

F

Fair Labor Standards Act, 71
Federal Insurance Contributions Act (FICA), 75, 91
Federal Reserve System, clearing encoded bank checks through, A-13
Federal Tax Deposit Form, Form 501, *illustrated*, 96; Form 508, 97
Federal Unemployment Tax Act (FUTA), 91, 92
Federal Wage and Hour Law, 71
Fee, defined, 70
FICA tax, employees' withheld, 74; employer's, 91

FICA tax payable, 89, 92
Field, A-10
Filing returns, 95
Financial condition, statement of, 10, 165
Financial position, statement of, 10, 165
Financial statements, 9, 40, 45, 163; balance sheet, 9, 42, 45, 165; income statement, 9, 41, 45, 163
Fiscal year, defined, 16
Fixed liabilities, 168
Flowchart, A-4; defined, A-4; *illustrated*, A-5; symbols, *illustrated*, A-4
Footing accounts, 38; defined, 19
Form, (501), *illustrated*, 96; (508), 97; (940), 97; (941), 95; (SS-5), *illustrated*, 72; (W-2), 87, *illustrated*, 88; (W-4), *illustrated*, 73
Fund, petty cash, 48
FUTA tax, employer's, 92
FUTA tax payable, 93

G

General journal, 45
General ledger, 33, 45, 112, 134; Donald L. Cameron, Attorney, *illustrated*, 126-130, 176-179 (partial); Engle & Brenner, Physicians and Surgeons, *illustrated*, 149-155

H

Hardware, A-1
Health insurance benefits for the aged (HIP), 74
High-speed printer, A-11; output device, A-18

I

Identification number, employer, 88
Imprest method of handling a petty cash fund, 49
Income, net, 6, 9, 16; self-employment, defined, 181
Income and expense statement, 163
Income and self-employment taxes, 181
Income statement, 9, 41, 45; columns of work sheet, 161; defined, 9, 163; Donald L. Cameron, Attorney, *illustrated*, 165; Eason Employment Agency, *illustrated*, 41; form of, 164; *illustrated*, 10; importance of, 164
Income summary account, 174
Income tax, employees payable, 89; employees' withheld, 72; wage-bracket method of determining, 74; withholding table, *illustrated*, 75
Independent contractor, defined, 70
Indorsement, blank, defined, 54; restrictive, defined, 54, *illustrated*, 56
Input, defined, A-7
Input device, defined, A-7; magnetic ink symbol numbers, A-12; magnetic tape, A-12; OCR readers, A-14; punched card, A-9

Index

I-3

Integrated data processing (IDP), defined, A-2
Internal Revenue Service, 74, 95
Internal storage, devices, A-15; limitations of, A-17

Magnetic tape as an input device, A-12
Matching principle, 108
Medical library expense account, 133
Merit-rating system, 94
Mortgage, 168; payable, 168

J

Journal, 23; combined cash, 111, 133; combined cash, for Donald L. Cameron, Attorney, *illustrated*, 122-125; combined cash, for Engle & Brenner, Physicians and Surgeons, *illustrated*, 144-147; defined, 22; general, 45; proving, 32; two-column, 23, *illustrated*, 24; two-column, for Eason Employment Agency, *illustrated*, 31-32
Journal entries, externally stored, A-15
Journalizing, 25, 45; adjusting entries, *illustrated*, 172; closing entries, *illustrated*, 175; defined, 22; employer's payroll taxes, 94; *illustrated*, 27; payroll transactions, 90; petty cash disbursements, 53; transactions, 22

K

Keypunch, *illustrated*, A-10

L

Language of computer-based systems, A-1
Lawyer's docket, collection, 115, *illustrated*, 115; office, 113, *illustrated*, 114
Ledger, 23; Donald L. Cameron, Attorney, *illustrated*, 126-130, 176-179 (partial); Eason Employment Agency, *illustrated*, 35-37; Engle & Brenner, Physicians and Surgeons, *illustrated*, 149-155; general, 33, 45, 112, 134; internally stored, A-15; patients, 134; posting to the, 33
Ledger account, with bank, 66
Legal fees revenue, 110
Liabilities, current, defined, 168; defined, 4; fixed, 168; long-term, defined, 168
Liability accounts, use of, 14
Life insurance premiums payable, 89
Long-lived assets, defined, 168
Long-term liabilities, defined, 168
Loss, net, 9, 16

M

Magnetic ink character recognition (MICR), A-12; numbers, 54, *illustrated*, 61
Magnetic ink symbol numbers, as input devices, A-12; encoding on checks, A-13; on bank check, *illustrated*, A-12

N

Narrative of transactions, Donald L. Cameron, Attorney, 116; Eason Employment Agency, 27; Engle & Brenner, Physicians and Surgeons, 137; Minia Sarros' petty cash disbursements, 50
Net income, 6, 9; defined, 16
Net loss, 9; defined, 16
Net profit, 9
Net worth, 5
Night deposits, 58
Notes, payable, defined, 4; receivable, defined, 4

O

Office docket, 113, *illustrated*, 114
Old-age, survivors, and disability insurance (OASDI), 74
Operating statement, 9, 164
Optical character recognition (OCR), equipment, A-6; readers as input devices, A-14
Output, automated accounting, A-17; defined, A-8
Output device, defined, A-8; high-speed printer as, A-18; tabulator as, A-17
Outstanding checks, 64
Overdraft, defined, 57
Owner's equity, 168; defined, 4; temporary accounts, 17; use of accounts, 14

P

Passbook, 56
Patient's account, *illustrated*, 136
Patients ledger, 134
Paycheck and deduction stub, machine prepared, *illustrated*, 86; manually prepared, *illustrated*, 78-79
Payee, of a check, 53
Payroll, accounting, 69; automated systems, 81; deductions, 71; earnings, 69-71; employer-operated systems, 83; expense, 89; journalizing transactions, 90
Payroll records, 76; employee's earnings record, 78, *illustrated*, 80-81, 84-85; payroll register, 77, *illustrated*, 76-77, 82-83
Payroll register, 77; machine prepared, *illustrated*, 82-83; manually prepared, *illustrated*, 76-77
Payroll taxes, employees' FICA tax withheld, 74; employees' income tax withheld, 72; employer, 91; employer's FICA tax, 91-92; employer's FUTA tax, 92-93; expense, 91; filing returns and paying, 95; journalizing employer's, 94; state unemployment tax, 93-94; Wage and Tax Statement (Form W-2), 87, *illustrated*, 88
Periodic summary, 157
Personal service enterprise, 107; accounting for attorneys, 107; accounting for physicians and dentists, 131; business, 107; cash basis of accounting for a, 108; professional, 107
Petty cash disbursements record, 49, 113, 134; Minia Sarros, *illustrated*, 50-51; proving the, 52
Petty cash disbursements statement, 52; Donald L. Cameron, Attorney, *illustrated*, 124; Engle & Brenner, Physicians and Surgeons, *illustrated*, 148
Petty cash fund, 48; defined, 48; imprest method of handling a, 49; operating a, 48
Petty cash transactions, narrative for Minia Sarros, 50
Petty cash voucher, *illustrated*, 49
Post-closing trial balance, 179; Donald L. Cameron, Attorney, *illustrated*, 180
Postdated checks, defined, 58
Posting, 24, 45; adjusting entries, *illustrated*, 173; automatic, A-16; closing entries, *illustrated*, 176-179; customer remittance stubs, A-11; defined, 33; *illustrated*, 34
Printer, high-speed, A-11; output device, A-18
Professional enterprise, 107
Professional fees, 132
Profit, net, 9
Profit and loss account, 174
Profit and loss statement, 9, 163
Profit and loss summary account, 174
Program, defined, A-8
Programmer, defined, A-8
Programming, defined, A-8
Proprietorship, 5
Proving, cash, 47; journal, 32; petty cash disbursements record, 52; work sheet, 162
Public accountants, 2; certified, 2
Punched card, *illustrated*, A-9; input device, A-9; planning the use of, A-9; printing information on, A-11; punching information into, A-10; statement of account, A-11, *illustrated*, A-11; verifying information on, A-10

Q

Quarterly Federal Tax Return, employer's (Form 941), 95

R

Receipts, cash, 45, 46; recording cash, 47
Reconciliation of bank statement, 63, 65, *illustrated*, 66

Recording, bank transactions, 62; cash receipts and disbursements, 47
Record keeper, 4
Records, auxiliary, 52, 113, 134; cash receipts and disbursements, 45; daily service, 134, *illustrated*, 135; employee's earnings, 78, 116; kept by a bank, 62; payroll, 76; petty cash disbursements, 49, 113, 134
Registered accountants, 2
Remittance stubs, posting customer, A-11; sorting customer, A-11
Report form of balance sheet, 166
Report of earnings, 164
Restrictive indorsement, defined, 54; *illustrated*, 56
Returns, filing and paying payroll taxes, 95
Revenue, 15; collection fees, 110; constructively received, 108; defined, 16; legal fees, 110; use of accounts, 18
Revenue and expense statement, 163
Review, accounting systems, A-2

S

Salary, defined, 70
Savings account, 67
Self-employment, income, defined, 181; taxes, 181
Service charges, 66
Signature card, defined, 54
Social Security Administration, 88
Social security and tax account number, 72; application for, *illustrated*, 72
Software, A-5
Sorter, A-11
Sorting customer remittance stubs, A-11
Source documents, 23, A-1
Special withholding allowance, 73, 74
Standard form of account, *illustrated*, 12
Statement, bank, 63, *illustrated*, 64; financial, 9, 40, 45, 163; income, 9, 41, 45, 163; income and expense, 163; operating, 9, 164; profit and loss, 9, 163; revenue and expense, 163; wage and tax, 87
Statement of account, punched card, A-11, *illustrated*, A-11
Statement of financial condition, 10, 165
Statement of financial position, 10, 165

Statement of petty cash disbursements, Donald L. Cameron, Attorney, 124; Engle & Brenner, Physicians and Surgeons, 148; *illustrated*, 52
State unemployment tax, 91, 93; payable, 94
Storage, automated accounting, A-14; defined, A-8; limitations of internal, A-17
Storage device, defined, A-14; external, A-14, A-15; internal, A-15
Summary, periodic, 157
Summary account, 17
Systems, accounting board, A-19; analysis, A-2; automated payroll, 81; computer-based accounting, A-1; design, A-3; implementation, A-3; review, A-2
Systems manual, A-3

T

"T" account form, *illustrated*, 13
Tabulator, A-11; output device, A-17
Tax, employees' FICA withheld, 74; employees' income withheld, 72; employer's FICA, 91; employer's FUTA, 92; state unemployment, 93; state withholding, 76; wage-bracket method of determining, 74
Tax account number, social security and, 72; application for, *illustrated*, 72
Taxes, income and self-employment, 181; journalizing employer's payroll, 94; payable, 4; paying payroll and filing returns, 95; payroll expense, 91; payroll imposed on employer, 91
Temporary owner's equity accounts, defined, 17
Ticket, deposit, 54
Time sharing, defined, 83
Transactions, defined, 6; dual effect of, 11; effect on accounting equation, 7; journalizing, 22; journalizing payroll, 90; narrative for Donald L. Cameron, Attorney, 116; narrative for Eason Employment Agency, 27; narrative for Engle & Brenner, Physicians and Surgeons, 137; narrative of petty cash, 50; recording bank, 62
Transposition error, 65
Trial balance, 19, 33, 38, 45; adjusted, columns of work sheet, 161; columns of work sheet, 158; defined, 19; Donald L. Cameron, Attorney, *illustrated*, 130; Eason Employment Agency, *illustrated*, 39; Engle & Brenner, Physicians and Surgeons, *illustrated*, 156; *illustrated*, 21; post-closing, 179; post-closing, Donald L. Cameron, Attorney, *illustrated*, 180; preparing, 39

U

Unemployment tax, state, 93; state, payable, 94

V

Value, book, 109, 168
Verifier, A-10
Voucher, petty cash, *illustrated*, 49

W

Wage and hour law, federal, 71
Wage and Tax Statement (Form W-2), 87; *illustrated*, 88
Wage-bracket method, 74
Wage deductions, accounting for, 89
Wages, accounting for, 89; defined, 70
Withdrawals, 59
Withholding, employees' FICA tax, 74; employees' income tax, 72; wage-bracket method, 74
Withholding allowance, 72; additional, 73; special, 73, 74
Withholding allowance certificate (Form W-4), *illustrated*, 73
Withholding table, *illustrated*, 75
Work sheet, adjusted trial balance columns, 161; adjustments columns, 160; balance sheet columns, 162; completing, 162; Donald L. Cameron, Attorney, *illustrated*, 159; end-of-period, defined, 157; income statement columns, 161; proving, 162; ten-column, *illustrated*, 159; trial balance columns 158
Write-it-once principle, 82, A-6; as a labor-saving device, A-6

Y

Year, calendar, 16; fiscal, defined, 16